REDISCOVERING GENUINE ISLAM

The Case For A Quran-Only Understanding

A Guide To What Makes a True Monotheist

[A substantially rewritten, compact version of the earlier acclaimed work *Exploring Islam in a New Light: A View from the Quranic Perspective*, Brainbow Press, 2010]

ABDUR RAB

Copyright © 2014 Abdur Rab

All rights reserved.

ISBN-13: ISBN-13: 978-1495287176

ISBN-10: 1495287173

Let there arise from amongst you a community who invite to all that is good, enjoin what is right, and forbid what is wrong. It is they who are successful. – *The Quran*, 3:104

Praise for the Author's Earlier Work
"Exploring Islam In A New Light: A View From The Quranic Perspective"

"This is a surprising, inspiring, and ultimately, refreshing book. It is simultaneously a solid introduction to Islam, an ecstatic spiritual journey, and an analytical call for reform. Abdur Rab is not only a reliable and authoritative voice on modern Islam but he is an original and thrilling thinker. This is one book that is definitely well-worth the time investment and indeed it should be read widely by Muslims and non-Muslims alike."
–Dr. Khaled Abou El Fadl, Chair of Islamic Studies, Alfi Distinguished Professor of Islamic Law, UCLA School of Law.

"At a time when misconceptions about Islam are on the rise, even among Muslims, Abdur Rab has provided a compelling argument for returning to the Qur'an for a deeper, more complete, more original understanding of the meaning and message of Islam. The result is a book that posits not a NEW interpretation of Islam, but a more authentic one."
–Reza Aslan, Professor of Creative Writing, University of California, Riverside; author of No god but God: The Origins, Evolution, and Future of Islam.

"Abdur Rab offers a comprehensive vision of Islam using the Quran as his sole religious textual source. He intentionally avoids the Hadith literature, which he believes, and argues, has done much damage to the message of the Quran. His work provides many very thought-provoking insights and should be a significant contribution to the 'Quran only' movement in modern Islam."
–Jeffrey Lang, Ph.D., Professor of Mathematics, University of Kansas; author of Losing My Religion: A Call for Help.

Praise for the Author's Earlier Work

"Another valuable addition to a list of books that question the sectarian teachings [...] A scholarly contribution to the message of [the] Quran alone or rational monotheism movement." [Part of his review of the book]
–Edip Yuksel, Author; Professor of Philosophy, Pima Community College; an ardent advocate of Islamic Reform; co-founder of Muslims for Peace, Justice and Progress (MPJP).

"Dr. Rab has [...] produced a thoughtful, wonderful book that is constructively revolutionary." [Part of his review of the book]
–Khaleel Mohammed, Ph.D. (McGill), Professor and Undergraduate Advisor, Department of Religious Studies, San Diego State University.

"[This] book brings Islam nearer to modernity, more particularly challenging [...] aspects of practiced Islam so far thought unchallengeable. In that respect [the author's] contribution can be called revolutionary."
–Dr. Rezaul Haq Khandker (late), a former senior official of UNDP, New York, USA.

Acknowledgments

I am intellectually indebted to the labor of love of many minds. My greatest inspiration and guiding light has been my teacher Shah Aksaruddin Ahmad who was instrumental in bringing about a paradigm shift in my religious approach. This book basically draws on his ideas and those of his student Panaullah Ahmad. I have also benefited substantially from selected works of many modern Islamic scholars.

    I am grateful to Dr. Riffat Hassan, Professor of Humanities, University of Louisville, Kentucky, who wrote a foreword for the earlier work. I also wish to thank Dr. Khaled Abou El Fadl, Chair of Islamic Studies, Alfi Distinguished Professor of Islamic Law, UCLA School of Law, Dr. Reza Aslan, Professor of Creative Writing, University of California at Riverside, and author of *No god but God: The Origins, Evolution, and Future of Islam*, Dr. Jaffrey Lang, Professor of Mathematics, University of Kansas, and author of *Losing My Religion: A Call for Help*, Edip Yuksel, Professor of Philosophy, Pima Community College and co-translator of *The Quran: A Reformist Translation* and author, *Manifesto for Islamic Reform*, Dr. Khaleel Mohammed, Professor of Religious Studies, San Diego State University, and late Dr. Rezaul Haq Khandker, former Senior Official of UNDP, for providing strong endorsements and reviews for the earlier work. Late Dr. Rezaul Huq Khandker helped me immensely with constructive comments for the original manuscript. I also received praise and comments from many other readers and friends. (For reviews from all readers, please check out this link: http://explorequran.org/reviews.html.) My thanks are due also to the British Muslim convert Sam Gerrans for voluntarily editing the work.

Preface to This Edition

This substantially rewritten, compact edition with a new title is based on the earlier work *Exploring Islam in a New Light: A View from the Quranic Perspective*, published by Brainbow Press in 2010 (The original edition was titled Exploring Islam in a New Light: An Understanding from the Quranic Perspective, published by IUniverse in 2008). This edition embraces some new features. Chapter 2 of the earlier work, which included some general discussion on the rationale for religion and its relation to science, has been dropped. Two chapters on what makes righteousness have been integrated into one chapter with possible summarization. A previous section on tolerance in an earlier chapter on righteousness has been rewritten and expanded into a separate new chapter, embodying some new notes on pluralism and human rights. Most of the remaining chapters have been rewritten to lend more compactness and readability to the content along with possible updating. The first of the two chapters discussing the reliability of the Hadith has been updated and enriched, incorporating new information, especially from the latest research on the subject done by Professor Aisha Musa. In a nutshell, though the scale of revision done gives this edition the appearance of a new book, the substantive themes covered, for the most part, remain essentially the same.

Introduction

Islam has been much misperceived from day one of its inception. In today's world, Islam is often not only much misperceived but also much disparaged, dreaded, and even despised. The reasons for such misperception have not yet received much or adequate attention. Is there something terribly wrong with the generally understood Islam, or do we need a different understanding? This work is an attempt to offer an answer to this critically important question. It provides an analytical framework and a blueprint for a meaningful, extensive reform of the perceived, traditionally practiced Islam. It scrutinizes numerous misconceptions that have crept into the practiced faith, and calls for its essential, overdue reform. It promotes human freedom, human rights, human initiative and enterprise, an exploitation-free free-market economy, gender equality, traditional family values, and the abolition of modern-day slavery and slavery-like practices. The ideas and interpretations presented in the book are a response to the challenges of modern time, and resonate with much of the modern thought on various social and economic issues.

Islam has a huge image problem in the West. The Islam that the West often thinks of, especially in the post-9/11 world, is a fanatic, violent, and misogynistic faith. Islam is being held in ridicule and Muslims are being looked down upon. The recent wave of terrorist attacks and sectarian violence and atrocities, mostly attributed to Muslims, has probably no parallel in modern history. Muslims today are suffering from an identity crisis. The single most critical question Muslims face today is this: Does the faith they know and follow today really represent the true Islam that came with the Quran? They need to ask this question and do some serious introspection and soul searching since the Prophet of Islam would lament to God on the Day of Judgment that his own

Introduction

people have treated the Quran as a forsaken thing (Quran, 25:30). The heaped up misguidance that has come from the so-called secondary sources of Islam and from sectarian clerics in the last about one and a half millennia has made them deviate a great deal from the true intent of the Quran's message.

Never before has the need for a different understanding of Islam been so demanding as in today's post-9/11 world, where it is "radical Islam" or "Islamic fundamentalism" with which much of today's religious fanaticism, violence, strife, and terrorism is associated. Modern Islamic scholars emphasize that Islam essentially means peace, tolerance, and compassion. Yet, misperception or confusion about what constitutes genuine Islam persists and abounds. This book finds that a major source of such misperception is the Hadith literature that surfaced more than two centuries after the death of the Prophet Muhammad (Peace be upon him). Most Muslim scholars who portray Islam in a good light do so by tapping its best traditions. The issue, however, is not really about choosing between good and bad traditions; the issue is really about whether we can still afford to continue with traditions that often misguide us and continue to seriously misrepresent and undermine Islam. This book is an attempt to offer a well-argued case for rejecting the Hadith as an authoritative and reliable source of religious guidance and law in Islam.

A second source of misperception of Islam's message lies with the problems of interpreting the very message of the Quran. Arguably, the interpretation of the Quran's message is likely to, and does, vary from person to person. Yet, some of the obvious misperceptions result from interpretations that have been influenced by what are alleged to be Prophetic traditions, or because the meanings are taken out of context, or because the worldview of the Quran is missed. The book addresses several of such specific cases.

The book is intended to serve as a comprehensive and in-depth description of Islam in light of the Quran alone. It shows that Islam, seen from the perspective of the Quran alone, is a tolerant, humane, and progressive religion that meets the social and economic challenges of modern time. It is a religion of peaceful interreligious co-existence, justice, equality, compassion, and service to humanity – far too removed from a fanatic, militant, misogynistic, and cruel image in which it is most often portrayed in the West.

The book begins with a preliminary introduction to the Quran itself. This covers factors that suggest its Divine origin, its broad concerns, its continuation of the essential features of the same basic message from the Abrahamic religions, the nature of its text and its universal and dynamic character, its rational orientation, its comprehensiveness, and its lucid, straightforward, and self-explanatory power as an authoritative source of religious guidance and law in Islam. The question of how best to interpret its message is also addressed. True to its claim, the Quran provides detailed religious guidance to all humankind and has left nothing unmentioned that is worth considering in terms of religious significance.

The book's central focus is the moral, humane, and spiritual message of the Quran. It describes Islam in a way that makes spirituality an essential, integral part of religion. One important verse of the Quran sums up the purpose for which it has been revealed – the purpose is to purify or civilize humankind and teach it knowledge (62:2). The purification and knowledge the Quran refers to essentially point to the need for our spiritual uplift. The book cites and discusses some fundamental building blocks of human beings' spiritual progress or evolution such as ego, love, will, and knowledge. Love is a major propelling factor. The more intensely one develops one's devotion and love, the more one acquires Godly virtues and spiritual evolution. The Quran says that God endows righteous people with love (19:96), and it speaks highly of those who have gained knowledge (2:267, 58:11), and urges the Prophet to seek it (20:114). The book also calls for understanding Heaven and Hell in a new light. It suggests that human beings start experiencing the bliss of Heaven or the pinch of Hell right in this very life, depending on their conduct. It is by our own deeds that we can transform this dull, dreary, and troubled world into a Heaven.

The book suggests that a key thing to note is that religion cannot be defined rigidly in ritualistic terms. The outward appearance of what one does with religious practices can be utterly deceptive. Being religious is much more than just practicing of some rituals. Religious practices need to be coupled with consistent work in day-to-day life. Religious rituals such as prayer and fasting are aids to our broader goal of attaining spiritual development; they are not ends in themselves. The book provides broader and deeper meanings of the ritualistic tenets of the Quran such as prayer (*salat*), fasting (*siam*), pilgrimage (*hajj*), and charity (*zakat, sadaqa*) than are conventionally understood. The book identifies problems with the current religious practices of Muslims and suggests appropriate reforms. Muslims generally take the nominal observance of these rituals as end in itself and often overlook the real essence or true spirit of such practices.

The book also shows that while the Quran places great emphasis on humanitarian and welfare spending for the poor and disadvantaged people and for worthy social causes and broadly defines the depth and scope of such spending, such spending is very narrowly defined in the current Islamic discourses and practices. The conception of spending in God's way needs to be understood in a much broader sense in light of the Quran and the functions of a modern state. Such spending needs to embrace in a significant way the government taxation and expenditure system. It needs to guarantee an adequate safety net for the poor and disadvantaged segments of society as well as provide for other welfare needs of society. The purpose of such a system should be to alleviate poverty, help people become self-reliant, and bring about other social and economic developments.

In the backdrop of a situation where there is a resurgence of bigotry, intolerance, violence, and terrorism among Muslims, the book highlights anew the pivotal importance of the Quran-based Islamic ideas on religious tolerance and pluralism and human rights. And it outlines what makes us fully righteous or Muslim. It covers what makes our beliefs and attitudes right and what makes our actions right. The process requires us to be careful about all of our actions of the mind and the body. The Quran wants us to be right, just, and kind to all. The true image of Islam countenances neither intolerance nor violence nor harsh punishments. The Quran condemns violence and terrorist acts in the strongest possible terms. The rigid application of the so-called *shariah* (traditional Islamic) law is also not justified in the light of the Quran.

The book also discusses the issues of marriage, divorce, and the status of women, and the treatment of slaves in a modern light. It calls for fair and equitable treatment of women. The Quran depicts the relationship between husband and wife as one of mutual love, compassion, understanding, and complementarity. The book calls attention to the lousy way divorce often takes place in Muslim societies, whereas the Quran calls for going in a very gradual way. The Quran does not really sanction the despicable practice of requiring a divorced wife to marry another person in order to be eligible for remarrying her former husband after taking divorce from the second husband. The book suggests that the Quran wants us to root out all slavery and slavery-like practices from society.

This work outlines a dignified way of ridding the world of poverty and deprivation and describes how the economy should be efficiently run under the moral guidelines of the Quran. It

Introduction

xiii

shows that Islam promotes economic egalitarianism, while encouraging human freedom, initiative, and enterprise. It views Islam as embracing an exploitation-free, free-market, competitive capitalist economy with socialistic overtones to ensure proper and adequate care of the poor and disadvantaged segments of society. It shows that the Quranic message encourages an equitable distribution of productive resources, especially land, if these are found to be starkly unequal in a society. Another implication of its message is that none should fully enjoy his or her own fruits of labor but should share them with his or her fellow beings through an appropriate distribution system. It suggests that such a distribution system should encompass public welfare and development expenditures. It also suggests that interest used in modern finance is different from *riba* forbidden in the Quran. While the latter is clearly unethical, the former has come to play a vitally important role in the modern economy. The implication is that what the Quran disapproves of is interest charged only to people or entities that deserve humanitarian consideration. The book shows that Islamic banks have not really gotten rid of interest except only marginally.

Two chapters of the book are devoted to a critical evaluation of the Hadith that is widely revered as a second source of religious guidance and law in Islam. The book shows that its authority, authenticity, and reliability as a source of religious guidance and law have been challenged right from the time when such reports started circulating. During his lifetime, the Prophet himself prohibited the writing and transmission of the Hadith and ordered erasing of existing recorded Hadith. His four close companions who became caliphs after him also upheld this position. In early Islam, before and during and after Al Shaffi's (d. 204 AH/820 CE) time when Hadith was being collected, the groups called Ahl al-Kalam and Mutazilites were strongly opposed to the Hadith. However, with state support and patronization during the Umayyad and Abbasid regimes the Hadith critics were marginalized and Hadith compilation and acceptance became widespread. There was some Hadith criticism during the 14th century. But opposition to the Hadith re-emerged on a significant scale in the late nineteenth century in India and Egypt and continues worldwide to date. Two stark facts that undercut the reliability of the Hadith, especially the ones that have found wide acceptance among Muslims, are a huge time gap of their compilation after the Prophet's death and the compilation of only a miniscule fraction of a vast pool of available reports.

The book finds that the Hadith is in fact a source of great distortion of the true meaning of Islam. It details and demonstrates how the Hadith has perpetuated the harsh, extremist version of Islam, and created the fanaticism, violence, strife, and inequality and misogyny seen so often in western portrayals of Islam. The authority, authenticity, and reliability of the Hadith are critically examined in terms of theological (Quranic) sanction or authority, historicity, and objective criteria such as consistency with the Quran, reason, and scientific truth. The book shows that the criteria used to authenticate this literature are inherently flawed and awfully inadequate. The analysis in this book shows that the ideas that seriously distort religious conceptions and practices, insult and at the same time idolize the Prophet of Islam, demonize and weaken women's position in society, encourage fanaticism and fatalism, block progress and modernization, encourage archaic, barbaric, or harsh punishments, encourage intolerance, violence and terror, and extol the virtues of aggressive *jihad* ("holy war") against other communities — all come from the Hadith.

Finally, the book touches on the rise of religious fanaticism among "Muslims" and the directions for true Islamic revival. As pointed out by some modern writers, a disconcerting development has been the rise of a special ultra-conservative ideology known as Wahhabism. The appearance of much of the terrorism today can be traced to this special ideology, which is being taught in typically traditional *madrasahs* (Muslim religious schools), where no modern education is imparted. The true revival of Islam can come when these *madrasahs* are thoroughly remodeled on the pattern of modern schools, keeping religious education as an additional subject. The true revival of Islam can come only when Muslims return to, and understand, their only Holy Book, the Quran and heed its clarion call:

> 38:29 We have revealed unto thee a Book [that is] blessed that they may ponder its verses, and that those with understanding may take heed.

True?

Contents

Acknowledgments VI
Preface to this Edition VII
Introduction VIII

Chapters
- I. The Latest Book of God: How Does It Read? 1
- II. The Central Message of the Quran: The Road to Spiritual Progress 25
- III. Spiritual Evolution and Conceptions of Heaven and Hell 50
- IV. The Real Meaning of Prayer in the Quranic Light 67
- V. The Scope of Socioeconomic Welfare Spending in the Quranic Light 92
- VI. The Place of Tolerance, Pluralism, and Human Rights in Islam 107
- VII. What Makes Us Righteous? 125
- VIII. Marriage, Divorce, the Status of Women, and the Treatment of Slaves 149
- IX. Implications of the Quran's Message for the Economic System 178
- X. The Hadith is Unreliable: Earlier Hadith Criticism and Theological and Historical Tests of Hadith Authority and Authenticity 197

Annex to Chapter X: Criteria for Hadith Evaluation 238
- XI. The Hadith is Unreliable: The Objective Test 241
- XII. Epilogue: The Rise of Religious Fanaticism and The Direction For True Islamic Revival 259

Works Cited 273
Notes 281

I. The Latest Book of God: How Does It Read?

> Now hath come unto you from God Light and a profound Book whereby God guideth whosoever seeketh His good pleasure unto paths of peace and bringeth them out of darkness into light by His leave and guideth them onto a straight path. – *The Quran*, 5: 15-16

The Quran declares itself to be comprehensive Divine guidance for humankind (16:89; 39:27; 12:111; 10:37; 6:114). The questions why and how it came to Muhammad (pbuh[1]) and why in the seventh century Arabia still remain a mystery. Orphaned at a young age[2], Muhammad grew up to enjoy great respect from his community for his excellent judgment, trustworthiness, and character. The Divine guidance needed to come through a person like him, in the words of one commentator, "to repel the maximum of evil with what was the best."[3] Another noted contemporary Muslim scholar states: "Muhammad had to be humanity's greatest genius, for history has known many unusually gifted minds but none that transcended their time and place as he must have."[4]

As God's trustworthy emissary for delivering His message to humankind, Muhammad took adequate measures for its preservation, preaching, and dissemination. During his lifetime, as the Quran itself mentions, he had the revelations written by scribes (25:5, 80:11-16) on parchments and other writing materials of the time. They were also preserved orally, as some of his devoted followers memorized them (80:11-12). After his death, his trustworthy companions had them compiled in book form. The Quran thus appears to be the only known Divine Book that has remained unaltered and unadulterated in its original text.

However, both Muslims and non-Muslims do not pay much

attention to its message. The Quran itself states that the Prophet Muhammad himself would lament to God on the Day of Judgment that his community has treated the Quran as a neglected thing (25:30). Non-Arab Muslims are generally taught to just recite the Quran, without much understanding. They are taught to memorize some short *surahs* (chapters) from the Quran to recite in their prayers. As a consequence, most Muslims remain ignorant of the teachings of the Quran. Through ignorance, non-Muslims and, worse still, Muslims harbor many misconceptions about Islam.

Considerations that seem to lend support to the Quran's Divine origin include the following:

- The then socio-cultural development of the Arabian Peninsula and Muhammad's own lack of any literary background;
- The personal conviction of knowledgeable people;
- The accuracy of scientific observations in the Quran;
- The phenomenon of "religious experience" as a credible basis of revelation; and
- The veracity and coherence of the Quran.

About the first of these considerations, Jeffrey Lang remarks: "if Muhammad were the Scripture's [the Quran's] author, then he is undoubtedly the supreme human anomaly, and if he is not, then the true author somehow entirely escaped the view of history."[5] Muhammad was not illiterate, as the Muslim tradition alleges. He certainly could read, as a merchant. But, as the Quran itself declares, he was not a man of letters – he neither read nor wrote any book before (29:48). Lang aptly points out: "The whole style of the Quran, its stress on reason, its logical coherence, its ingenious employment of ambiguity and symbolism, its beauty and conciseness, suggests an author whose insight and wisdom come from far beyond the primitive confines of the then backward and

The Latest Book of God: How Does It Read? 3

isolated Arabian Peninsula."[6]

The Quran claims that those who are endowed with knowledge recognize its Divine origin (29:49; 34:6; 32:15; 13:36; 5:83; 17:107-108).

> 29:49 Nay, these are clear revelations in the hearts of those who have been endowed with knowledge.

Furthermore, some commentators marvel at the accuracy of scientific observations that look surprisingly modern, but held in a Book that came in the seventh century.

However, these arguments may not suffice to convince the skeptics. A more basic question lying at the heart of religion is whether there is any real basis in divine inspiration as a source of religious guidance. The condition known as "religious experience"[7] – which is indeed a high stage of spiritual attainment – can enable one to receive divine revelation. Such experience *if so facto* also proves God's existence. This is a special kind of human experience that comes only to a few, who have earned some special or extra-ordinary human abilities. The Quran illustrates this point as follows:

> 6:124 And when a sign cometh unto them, they say, 'We will not believe until we are given that which God's messengers are given.' God knoweth best with whom to place His message.

Religious experience, which is the basis of divine revelation, has been brushed aside by scientists "as psychic, mystical, or supernatural", but as Muhammad Iqbal has aptly observed, this description "does not detract from its value as experience; [...] religious experience has been too enduring and dominant in the history of mankind to be rejected as mere illusion."[8]

About internal coherence of the Quranic text, the Quran itself claims:

> 4:82   Will they not then ponder the Quran? Had it been from other than God, they would have found therein much inconsistency.

This claim may be open to criticism, in part, because of the reader's inadequate comprehension of its message or, in part, due to misinterpretation or mistranslation of relevant texts. Critics suggest, for example, that some verses in the Quran that speak of God preordaining things or speak about His Will or Knowledge, which point to predestination, are inconsistent with other verses that speak of free choice available to man. We will address such claims as we proceed.

Though this could be viewed as circular reasoning, the assurance the Quran itself gives us about its protection from any possible corruption and change deserves mention as part of the Quran.

> 15:9   Surely We reveal the Reminder (the Quran), and *We will assuredly guard it* (from corruption).
>
> 8:27   And read that which hath been revealed unto thee (Muhammad) of the Book of thy Lord. *None can change His Words.*

Western researchers confirm the assertion that the Quran is perfectly preserved in its original text. The French physician Maurice Buccaille, while comparing the Quran with the Old and New Testaments, states:

Thanks to its undisputed authenticity, the text of the Quran holds a unique place among the books of Revelation, shared neither by the Old nor the New Testament. [There were] alterations undergone by [both] the Old Testament and the Gospels before they were handed down to us in the form we know today. The same is not true for the Quran for the simple reason that it was written down at the time of the Prophet.[9]

To recapitulate, factors such as unparalleled profundity and literary brilliance of its text, unimaginable in a backward socio-cultural backdrop of the then Arabian Peninsula and Muhammad's known lack of literary background, its coherence, its accurate scientific observations, and its unchanged text since its compilation adequately assure the Quran's divine status. I do not think that we need a mathematical wonder as a further proof to establish this status. It is worth mentioning, however, that recent discovery by noted Egyptian-American scholar Rashad Khalifa, further explored by his close associate Turkish-American scholar Edip Yuksel, both great champions of the Quran-only movement in modern Islam, suggests some interesting mathematical features of the structure of the Quran using the number "Nineteen" mentioned in verse 74:30. According to them, there is something unique and extra-ordinary about the literary construction of the Quran. While I find some of their findings quite valid, I have difficulty accepting their full thesis, since a major part of their otherwise fascinating discovery is predicated on the premise that the last two verses of Surah 9 (9:128, 129) do not belong to the Quran, but are man-made insertions.[10] While I greatly respect and admire Edip Yuksel for his bold, imaginative leadership in the current Quran-only movement, in my personal correspondence with him, I have expressed my reservation about this finding saying that the omission of two verses of the Quran would remain an issue[11], and that the number "Nineteen" might be better interpreted to denote the degrees or stages of progress in knowledge and power one needs to acquire to decisively conquer Hell fire mentioned in adjoining verses.[12]

Not all of divine revelation has reached humankind through compiled books. Earlier revealed books mentioned in the Quran are the Psalms, the Torah, and the Gospels. Other known divine oriental books, all of which proclaim the message of One God, include the Vedas (the Rig, the Atharva, the Sama and the Yajur), the Bhaghavad Gita, and the Zend Avesta. The Tripitaka, the book of Buddhism, emphasizes the need for and importance of striving for truth and enlightenment on the part of every human being who is a true seeker of truth.

The Broad Concerns of the Quran

Unlike science, which has made tremendous progress in enhancing human knowledge and enriching human life, the religion professed by the Quran provides extensive moral and ethical guidelines to bring about overall moral and spiritual uplifting of humankind at large. Such a remit goes far beyond the role that modern science has been able to play, or even to recognize as essential for humankind.

The Quranic guidance is comprehensive in its scope. It covers every aspect of individual and social life that is of any religious or spiritual significance. Being the last of all revealed books, the Quran takes account of all human errors in the past, and recounts the salient histories of God's prophets providing invaluable lessons for humankind. An excerpt from John L. Esposito aptly describes the scope of the Quranic concerns:

> The Quran envisions a society based on the unity and equality of believers, a society in which moral and social justice will counterbalance oppression of the weak and economic exploitation. [...] The scope of Quranic concerns reflects the

The Latest Book of God: How Does It Read?

comprehensiveness of Islam. It includes rules concerning modesty, marriage, divorce, inheritance, feuding, intoxicants, gambling, diet, theft, murder, fornication and adultery. The socioeconomic reforms of the Quran are among its most striking features. Exploitation of the poor, weak, widows, women, orphans (4:2; 4:12), and slaves is vividly condemned. [...] False contracts, bribery, abuse of women, hoarding of wealth to the exclusion of its subordination to higher ends, and usury are denounced. The Quran demands that Muslims pursue a path of social justice, rooted in the recognition that the earth belongs ultimately to God and that human beings are its caretakers. While wealth is seen as good, a sign of hard work and God's pleasure, its pursuit and accumulation are limited by God's law. Its rewards are subject to social responsibility toward other members of the community, in particular to the poor and needy.[13]

In sum, as Fazlur Rahman aptly puts it, the Quran's major concerns are the moral conduct of man and the establishment of an order of socioeconomic justice and essential human egalitarianism. This is underpinned by the guiding ideas of God and the Last Judgment, as outlined in the Quran – ideas that "exist for religiomoral experience and cannot be just intellectual postulates to be 'believed in'."[14]

Religion of the Quran is a Confirmation of Earlier Religions

The Quran emphasizes the point that it introduces no new religion:

> 41:43 *Naught is said unto thee (Muhammad) except what was said unto the messengers before thee.*

The Quran mentions that it confirms all earlier Books

(5:48). It points out Islam's Abrahamic roots and declares that that it is Abraham who gave us the name "Muslims" (22:78). It corrects the human errors that have crept into the scriptures of Judaism and Christianity (5:15). "Islam" means "peace" as well as "submission to God." Correspondingly, a Muslim is one who is for peace, and who surrenders to God, and follows His guidance. All earlier prophets and their followers were Muslims just like Abraham, who, the Quran states, was neither a Jew nor a Christian, but one who submitted to God (3:67).

> 42:13 He (God) established for you the same religion as that which He established for Noah, that which We have sent as inspiration through Abraham, Moses, and Jesus, namely that you should remain steadfast in religion and make no divisions within it.

To the People of the Book in particular, i.e., to Jews and Christians, to whom the Torah and the Gospels were sent, the Quran specifically proclaims:

> 5:15 O People of the Book: Now hath Our Messenger come unto you revealing unto you much of what ye have concealed of the Book, and passing over much. *Now hath come unto you from God Light and a Profound Book.*
>
> 27:76 Verily this Quran explaineth to the Children of Israel most of that, in which they differ.

The latest revelation, while confirming the earlier ones, points out at the same time the corruptions made in the word of God at various points in history. Particularly worth noting are the human distortions seen in the presentation of Elijah and Jesus as

The Latest Book of God: How Does It Read?

the Son of God in Judaism and Christianity respectively, and the introduction of the idea of a trinity in Christianity. The Quran strongly denounces the ideas of sonship (2:116; 19:35; 6:100-101) and the trinity (5:73, 116). Its most important message is that there is no god but One God who neither begets, nor is begotten (112:1-3); who has no daughters or consorts (6:100-101; 72:3), nor any partners (6:22-24).

> 3:79-80 It is not for any human being unto whom God hath given the Book, wisdom and the Prophethood that he should afterwards say unto mankind: Be ye worshippers of me instead of God. But rather (he would say): Be ye worshippers of the Lord.

Polytheism, idolatry, and association of anyone or anything with God (*shirk*) are the worst forms of unbelief in Islam (31:13; 4:48), a great deviation from the strict monotheism that Islam has restored one final time.

Nature of the Quranic Text

The consideration that the Prophet Muhammad did not bring anything new to humankind as emphasized at (41:43) points to another related characteristic that the religious principles or values that he brought could not also be transient in character, for in that case religion would have little significance for humankind. These are values that are of enduring or eternal benefit to humankind. God's words are essentially Principles or Laws in the metaphysical world, which are comparable with the Laws of Nature in the physical realm and are unchangeable:

> 10:64 No change there is in the Words of God; that is indeed the supreme triumph.

God's signs or messages are evident throughout creation, history, and nature. His Laws emanate from Him, i.e., are subject to Him; and He is also subject to His own Laws. God compensates us for our deeds in ways that always remain the same and He never does the least injustice to anyone (46:19). Divine revelation thus transcends time and space. Von Grunebaum has aptly expressed the unchanging character of divine revelation:

> Originality is not a religious value. Religious truth is experienced, and is 'rediscovered' because of its content; it has 'existed' unchanged since time began. The Prophet, in his own view and in the view of the Community, is not an originator of teachings but an awakener and a warner, and where necessary a creator of a form of life and community fitted to his newly acquired understanding of God, since this understanding can only be made concrete in the execution of commands and prohibitions. Understood thus, Muhammad was a creative religious spirit and an emissary of God.[15]

Some consider this unchanging character of the divine message static and an obstacle for progress. However, this is a superficial view. The divine message is both unchanging and flexible. The immutability of God's Law cannot preclude it from being flexible or elastic at the same time since it needs to allow for all possibilities and complications, which may arise. Indeed the principles that the Quran lays down are immutable, but they accommodate flexibility to deal with varying contexts and circumstances. The Quran asks us to judge between people with justice (4:58 and other verses). This is a general principle we all need to follow. But its practical application to particular cases may vary with the specific contexts and other specifics of such cases for which the Quran does not give any specific guidelines. At the same time where it provides specific guidelines, as in the case of the law of requital, the Quran enunciates a fundamental principle, for example in avenging – without committing excesses – wrongs done to us by others (2:178, 194), and at the same time urges us to forgive others' faults (5:45), wherever appropriate. The Quranic prescriptions for dispensing criminal justice are flexible between two extremes: the highest possible exemplary punishments and straightaway forgiveness depending on circumstances. The Quran forbids some foods, but allows them in moderate amounts in unavoidable circumstances (2:172-173; 6:145).

The principles enunciated in the Quran are compatible with changing contexts and circumstances. But such principles need to be applied judiciously in particular circumstances. That is also the reason why God sometimes introduces better advice replacing an earlier message in order to better suit changing circumstances, but the amendments do not affect the central themes or principles, however.

> 2:106 Whatever Sign (*ayat*) We abrogate or cause to be forgotten, We bring in (in its place) a better one or the like of it. Knowest thou not that God hath power over all things?

Unfortunately, however, this verse has caused confusion and a wrong impression among Muslims who toe the traditionalists' line that some verses were abrogated or replaced by later ones.[16] This is a serious misconception, since the Quran strongly warns us against its partial acceptance or rejection (2:85).

Also note, as the Egyptian writer late Nasr Abu Zayd appropriately comments, the Quranic revelation is "a cultural and social phenomenon [...] [T]o faithfully and completely comprehend Islam's universal message, one must understand the seventh-century cultural and linguistic environment of Prophet Muhammad, the Arab-speaking human being to whom God revealed the Quran. [...] The Quran is divine as revelation and human as interpretation."[17] The orthodox Islamic view, Abu Zayd claims, is "stultifying; it reduces a divine, eternal, and dynamic text to a fixed human interpretation with no more life and meaning than a trinket, a talisman, or an ornament."[18] This modern view of the nature of the revealed text is related to the long-running theological debate about whether the Quran is the eternal, uncreated, and exact word of God (the position of the traditionalists), or is a created, or humanly understood version of divine revelation or inspiration (the rationalists' and modern dominant position).[19] The Quran itself bears witness to the fact that many of its verses are metaphorical or allegorical in nature (3:7) and amenable to multiple interpretations. Its verses should not be always understood in a strictly literal sense.

Not always literal

The Quran's Rational Orientation

Admittedly, "the essence of religion is faith," Iqbal says.[20] But faith, as he notes, goes with ideas, which should have a rational foundation.[21] The Quran's scientific orientation is evident in its numerous passages as well as in the essence of its overall message. Especially significant is its appeal to humankind to reflect on the creation of the universe, their surrounding environment, and the alteration of the day and night:

> 3:190-1 Verily in the creation of the heavens and the earth, and in the succession of the night and the day, are signs for men of understanding.

> 29:20 Say: Travel through the earth, and see how God hath brought forth all creation.

The Quran also urges man to take lessons from the vicissitudes in human fortunes and from historical events. "The Quran opens our eyes to the great fact of change, through the appreciation and control of which alone it is possible to build a durable civilization."[22] Change points to causal relation. The principles that the Quran presents constitute a science. It makes man conscious of how he can change both his lot and the lot of his society, and how he can make all round progress: temporal and non-temporal, worldly and spiritual. "And in this process of progressive change", as Iqbal puts it, "God becomes a co-worker with him, provided man takes the initiative."[23] The Quran states:

13:11   Verily God changeth not the condition of men until they change their own selves (*nafs*). (See also 8:53)

The Quran, Jeffrey Lang rightly observes, encourages a rational approach to faith, as evidenced by the tenor of arguments offered in many of its verses, e.g., in the many verses that say that people should apply their *aql* or reason and where Abraham had arguments with disbelievers, which cornered the disbelievers.[24] The Quran points out that it is only one's work that determines one's fate and reward (2:286; 20:15; 28:84; 53:31, 39; 42:30; 6:132; 46:19; 17:19; 5:35; etc.). As Ahmad aptly remarks, God never really rewards or punishes anybody. It is actually the creature that does this work to fulfil or correct its own deed or misdeed.[25]

Is it then an echo of what scientists say: God does not intervene? In a way, yes, and it is at this juncture that science and religion meet. But while science sees no divine presence in human affairs, religion shows how the All-Pervading and Responsive God acts even though we may interpret this divine action in different ways. "Response, no doubt, is the test of the presence of a conscious self", says Iqbal.[26] The Quran shows how man can receive God's mercy and help in his work and life. Believers experience such divine mercy and help in their multifarious situations and activities. Those who pray to God with heart-felt sincerity and devotion can receive His kind response (2:186; 40:60; 27:62).

A question may arise: if it is work alone that determines one's fate, then what meaning is there to the Quranic message that God is Forgiving and Most Merciful? The way God forgives is worth pondering:

> 16:119 Then, verily thy Lord – to those *who do evil in ignorance, repent afterward and do right* (mend their conduct) – to them thy Lord is Forgiving, Most Merciful. (See also 6:54)
>
> 3:135 And Who forgiveth save God only those who, when they commit sins or wrong themselves, remember God and implore forgiveness for their sins, and *who do not knowingly repeat their sins*?

It is evident from these verses that God does not forgive in the way most think. God does not forgive one without one's adequate repentance, which is also a punishment. Thus, none escapes the punishment of evil deeds. Three preconditions that make a man or a woman eligible for getting God's forgiveness are: first, that he/she does not commit the wrongdoing knowingly; second, that he/she mends his/her ways; and third, that he/she does not repeat the wrongdoing. God does not favor anybody, or bestow any mercy on any unless he deserves it.

If work determines one's fate, it then also follows that there should be no such thing as predestination by God or fatalism, i.e., the belief that all events are preordained by God. There has been a lot of confusion and misunderstanding among both Muslims and non-Muslims about the question of predestination by God, surrounding the Quranic word *taqdir*, which literally means "measure," or "proportion," or "destiny." The following Quranic verse, among some, has been misunderstood by many:

> 25:2 He (God) hath created everything in due measure (proportion or destiny).

This verse is related to other verses that describe God's will and knowledge, which have also given rise to confusion that is of the same nature as that with predestination. The idea that has often been mistakenly advanced is essentially that God knows in advance all events, He predetermines all events, and He wills all events and, therefore, all events take place in accordance with what God knew, planned, and willed. But if this idea is true, the Quranic verse "*laisa lil insani illa ma saa'a* – Man has only that for which he makes effort" (53:39; 20:15) cannot have any meaning. For, if God decides beforehand what man will do, He cannot legitimately make him accountable for anything he does and the whole system of rewarding for good work and punishing for bad work completely breaks down, there remaining no role for religion to play for man. God has endowed man with free will and freedom of action; He has given him freedom to choose between good and evil (18:29; 76:3).

The only sensible meaning that can be attached to the verse 25:2 concerning God's assignment of measure to everything and other related verses relating to His knowledge and will is that man has to work with his own given situation and his given possessions including his own qualities, which may have been influenced by his own previous actions or by actions of others, including his predecessors, and in an environment or situation which is external to him. Thus man works with certain favorable or unfavorable conditions or constraints, which so to say, are given for him or, if you will, which are already willed or predetermined by God. Man needs to accept such factors as given and work within that context. He cannot be held accountable for such givens.

Note also that God's foreknowledge of events does not necessarily imply that He predetermines them. For example, a man planning to kill another person, or to steal something, at a particular time is known to God, but it cannot be said that this planning and the actual events of killing or stealing when they take place are predetermined by Him. He certainly has not preordained someone to be a killer or a thief. Simply put, divine knowledge is irrelevant to the claim that God predestines our choices and state in the afterlife.[27] Also, as Iqbal forcefully and beautifully points out, God's fore-knowledge is that of open possibilities of future events, not of events as such as a fixed order of things – a notion that admits of freely exercised creativity on the part of humankind as participants in the divine course of events. "The future certainly pre-exists in the organic whole of God's creative life, but it pre-exists as an open possibility, not as a fixed order of events with definite outlines," he notes.[28]

However, even as things happen according to the natural laws of causation, which are after all God's laws, when such things were determined beforehand and are given for the present, we may term such events as God-willed or God-given. So it is also true to assert that our fate is predetermined in part, and that our free choice or room for action is not fully free after all. We often bind ourselves by our own actions or actions of others. So this is a fully logical thing.[29]

Thus, what the Quran professes for man is based on a rational foundation.[30] What ostensibly appear to be miraculous activities of prophets and saints, or God-sent boons or scourges that are described in the Quran are rationally explicable and can be explained by men of insight and knowledge. The

The Latest Book of God: How Does It Read?

Quran itself suggests that, as Jeffrey Lang aptly puts it, faith is undermined when reason is ignored or poorly applied.[31] The Quran thus characterizes people who reject faith as those who are devoid of *aql* or reason (2:171; 5:58, etc.), and encourages men to apply their reason to see the truth of the revealed word (2:44, 76, etc.). Citing Quranic verses, Lang further remarks: Those who benefit the most from the Quran are 'persons of insight,' 'firmly rooted in knowledge,' 'use their reason,' and 'stand on clear evidence and proof'. While those who oppose revelation are 'deluded,' 'in manifest error,' 'ignorant,' 'foolish,' 'have no understanding,' 'only follow surmise and conjecture,' and blindly adhere to tradition.[32] The Quran also repeatedly asks us to think and ponder. Thus as Lang further notes: The message is plain enough: to gain truer faith, we need to free ourselves from inherited notions and examine our beliefs rationally.[33]

The Quranic Message Is Comprehensive, Lucid, and Self-Explained

In many places, the Quran states that its message is easy to learn, straightforward with no ambiguity, detailed, and self-explanatory (44:58; 54:17, 22, 32, 40; 39:27-28; 12:111; 6:114). One can gauge how detailed its messages are by simply looking at some of the minute details of its admonitions relating to such matters as how we should conduct ourselves in what many might think to be even ordinary or petty matters of etiquette or behaviour. For example, the Quran teaches us to be duly polite to others in conversation and arguments; to salute or to return salutation; to be polite to superiors, and to speak to them in a voice not higher than their voice, and not walk ahead of them; to enter a house not without the due permission of its occupants; to seek permission to enter rooms of couples at specified private times; not to ridicule, or make faces at others; not to back-bite; to record loans or other transactions in order to avoid possible future misunderstandings; and other do's and not-do's, which benefit us enormously in our day-to-day affairs, and add to our overall spiritual development. In addition, the bigger issues are not lost sight of. What else one needs for guidance in life? It is hard to imagine why one should not regard the Quran as a complete guidance for humankind. No wonder then that God should emphatically declare:

> 16:89   We reveal unto thee the Book as an explanation of everything, and a Guidance, a Mercy, and Good News to Muslims.

The Quran is self-explanatory. No human explanation is necessary to understand it, not even from the Prophet Muhammad. He was urged just to recite the Quran, not to explain it, and leave the explanation to God Himself (75:18-19). Muslims in general mistakenly consider that the Hadith literature complements and explains the Quran, and is an essential aid to understanding it. We will, however, see later that the Hadith, instead of clarifying things, rather confuses them.[34]

It should also be noted that while none should find it difficult to understand most of what the Quran contains, there are also verses in it that are allegorical, which are not easily understood by all. Only knowledgeable, i.e., spiritually advanced, people understand them. Those who do not understand such verses do not have to be too concerned about their meanings. The Quran mentions about these verses and states that some people who do not understand such verses create confusion among people with them:

> 3:7   He (God) it is Who hath revealed unto thee (Muhammad) the Book wherein are clear revelations – they are the fundamental part of the Book – and others

(that are) allegorical. But those in whose hearts is doubt pursue that which is allegorical, seeking dissension and seeking to interpret it. None knoweth its true interpretation except God and those who are of sound knowledge.

As many Quran scholars point out, the Quranic verses convey two types of meaning: one *zahir* or apparent (or literal) and another *batin* or hidden (or deep or esoteric). The Quran thus is an inexhaustible source of knowledge to those who truly seek knowledge.

How Should We Best Interpret the Quran?

Modernist Muslim scholars have developed methods by which we can appropriately interpret Quranic texts, which constitute Quranic hermeneutics, whereby Muslims can interpret Quranic texts coherently and meaningfully. Many modernist, reform-minded scholars like Fazlur Rahman point out that the texts of the Quran are often not seen in their proper contexts. As time and society's conditions change, the meanings that need to be drawn from particular texts also need to change, because the Quran is not something static.

The Quran is often treated in a piecemeal and ad hoc manner, losing sight of its worldviews and relevance to changing contexts. For instance, Islam is portrayed by many as a militant creed and as a threat to the West. But this is a misperception based on piecemeal, out-of-context texts from the Quran (and the Hadith, which, after all, gives a distorted view of Islam). Even Muslim extremist splinter groups such as al-Qaeda, the Taliban, and their allies, take piecemeal passages from the Quran, losing sight of its worldviews and the proper contexts in particular cases, to advance their aggressive *jihadist* agenda against non-Muslims. However, as will be shown in Chapter VI, if the full proper context of such Quranic texts is taken into account, the overall peaceful message of the Quran cannot be lost. Another example is the mistaken patriarchal notion of Islam, deduced from some passages of the Quran, which, as will be explored in Chapter VIII, is due to a failure to see the changing context in which such passages need to be reinterpreted. Some more relevant examples are well illustrated by late Professor Fazlur Rahman:

> The basic elan of the Qu'ran – the stress on socioeconomic justice and essential human egalitarianism – is quite clear from its very early passages. [...] To insist on a *literal* implementation of the rules of the Qur'an, shutting one's eyes to the social change that has occurred and that is palpably occurring before our eyes, is tantamount to deliberately defeating its moral-social purposes and objectives. It is just as though, in view of the Qur'anic emphasis on freeing slaves, one were to insist on preserving the institution of slavery so that one could "earn merit in the sight of God" by freeing slaves. Surely the whole tenor of the teaching of the Qur'an is that there should be no slavery at all. The sort of reasoning that would retain slavery is, of course, seldom employed by any intelligent and morally sensitive Muslim. But there is an argument used by the vast majority of Muslims, and indeed primarily by the majority of Muslim religious leaders, that is very similar in nature. It is that, since it is a "pillar" of Islam to pay zakat levy, a tax the Qur'an had imposed primarily on the rich for the welfare of the poor, *some people must remain poor in order for the rich to earn merit in the sight of God.* There is, of course, no society on earth in which there are no needy people, and in Islam the state, through its zakat system, has to fulfill their needs; but an argument like this one seeks to give a decisive blow to the orientation of the Qur'an ... Or, again, to say that, no matter how much women develop intellectually,

their evidence must on principle carry less value than that of a man is an outrageous affront to the Qur'an's purposes of social evolution – and so on.[35]

Human interpretation of the Quran has changed from person to person and over time, due to the essentially dynamic nature of the Quranic text as well as the human element involved in interpretation. As pointed out by modern reformist thinkers like Muhammad Iqbal, individual interpretations of the Quranic message by early scholars, which gave four [or five] different schools of law, cannot claim any finality.[36] He notes that the principles that are immutable should be distinguished from those regulations that are the product of human interpretations and are thus subject to change.[37] There has been a surge in new thinking in recent years about how to interpret the Quran or Islam, which emphasizes the value of *ijtihad* (new interpretation and thinking) in understanding Islam in order to effectively come to grips with the challenges and realities of modern time.

The great miracle of the Quran, as the nineteenth-century Muslim thinker-reformer of India Sir Sayyid Ahmad Khan aptly observes, is its universality. "Each generation continues to find the Quran relevant despite the constant increase in human knowledge. Too heavy a reliance on Hadith for the interpretation of the Quran puts at risk this eternal and universal quality. Hadith-based tafsir [commentary] tends to limit the meaning of the Quran to a particular historical situation, thus obscuring its universality."[38]

This characteristic of universality highlights the point that the Quran is amenable to reaching non-Arabic speaking people through appropriate translations into different languages. It also means that there is a need for such efforts to be pursued in competent quarters. The Quran categorically states that it was revealed in Arabic for a reason:

> 42:7 And thus We have inspired unto the thee the Quran in Arabic, in order that you mayst warn the mother-city (Mecca) and those around it and warn of a Day of Assembling whereof there is no doubt. (See also 14:4)

Ironically, however, while the Jewish and Christian scriptures were translated into Greek and Latin at an early date and disseminated in vernacular languages, the Arabic Quran was not translated into other languages in Muslim countries until modern times.[39] After the Bible, the Quran is probably the most translated book of religion in the world. It should be noted, however, that for readers who do not know Arabic, it is advisable for them to consult several of the available translations, as translations are found to differ in regard to various verses of the Quran. In cases where such differences are found – such differences are found only in sporadic cases of verses and are not too substantive in most cases – the reader should reflect on the meaning of the verse(s) concerned and make his own judgment about its (their) proper meaning. "The Quran stands on its own, requiring the application of a dedicated and enlightened mind for its understanding."[40] God Himself has made the Quran so clear, easy and self-explanatory that the reader should be able to get its full message himself without the help of any commentaries.

A Final Note

The Quran is a book to learn, understand, ponder, and apply in day-to-day life, not to blindly recite. It came in Arabic precisely and specifically to teach the Arabs (43:3; 38:29). But it is also a message for the whole universe (38:87, 68:52, 81:27-28). Ironically, however, many of those who do not understand the Arabic Quran, recite it in Arabic without trying to understand its meaning. Muslim religious teachers teach young students to memorize the first Quran chapter (*Surah* Fatiha) and other short chapters of the ending part of the Quran in order for them to recite in prayer, but without much understanding. And there are even the whole Quran memorizers (*hafizes*) in some non-Arab countries, who do not care much about its meaning. Religious teachers put a lot of emphasis on the pronunciation of the Arabic text of the Quran. All this they do by wrongly thinking that the recitation of the Holy Quran *per se* is a virtue (*thawab*), an idea that is borrowed from the Hadith. It is ironic that, in Bangladesh for example, the Quran is recited in Muslim families by hired *qaries* (Quran reciters) over the bodies of their dear and near ones who have just passed away. This is a practice, which is hard to comprehend. The dead cannot hear it, nor do those who are around the dead body. Neither the Quran reciters (*qaries*) nor those who hear them understand anything of the Quranic message in the foreign language. Such a practice is against the very message and spirit of the Quran, which specifically urges us to listen to its message (i.e., with understanding) when it is recited so that we may receive God's guidance and mercy (7:204). The Quran repeatedly urges us to understand and reflect on its message (38:29 and 10:24).

Another point to note is that the Quran is, in a special sense, a healing for believers. By inspiring them to shun all misdeeds, do good deeds, and purify their body and mind, it does work as a healing influence for their diseases, physical or mental, or as a preventive antidote for them (10:57; 17:82). This does not mean that every Tom, Dick, and Harry can cure diseases by uttering some Quranic verses like a mantra. If this were true, all and sundry would be able to cure diseases by simply uttering some Quranic words. Since all cannot perform this feat, it means that the power of healing is not in the verses themselves but in the persons themselves. Only certain people, who can acquire some extra-ordinary power through meditation, *dhikr* (remembrance) of

God, or *jappa* (repeated chanting of some name), or because of endowment with special inborn gift, can exhibit such healing power by uttering Quranic verses, or through other means.

Conclusion

The Quran is indeed a wonderful book, unrivalled by any in the world. Confirming and upholding earlier divine messages and excelling in eloquence, profundity, coherence, and scientific orientation, it embodies the latest genuine, comprehensive guidance to humankind in Arabic. Its main purpose, to quote Iqbal again, is to awaken in man the higher consciousness of his manifold relations with God and the universe.[41]

Religion as practiced today by most Muslims has little of what the Quran has to offer. It is time we all rediscover the Quran anew and sincerely strive to know what genuine Islam is about.

II. The Central Message of the Quran: The Road to Spiritual Progress

The command belongeth to God alone; He hath commanded that ye serve none but Him. That is the right religion, but most men know not. – *The Quran,* 12:40

Muslims appear [...] to have almost killed the spiritual message of Islam and the powerful spiritual potential of Islam's rituals by putting so much stress on rules, regulations, punishments, formalities, and politics to the near exclusion of the spiritual and ethical dimension, which is the predominant message of the Qur'an. – Jeffrey Lang, *op. cit.*, 2004, p. 470

What makes the Quran's core message spiritual? Spiritual gurus such as Eckhart Tolle and Deepak Chopra think that spirituality is different from, and outside of, the structures of institutionalized religions or belief systems with fixed ideas. They recognize at the same time that there are pockets of spirituality in religions also. Most Muslims prefer to steer clear of spiritual-like practices such as those of Sufis. Sufi Muslims have often been the target of persecution and torture from ultra-conservative Salafi and Wahhabi Muslims.

However, when we come across verses in the Quran such as those that say, for example, that the Quran's inherent purpose is to purify or civilize humankind and make it wise (62:2), or that it is not the eyes that are blind, but it is the hearts, which are within the bosoms, that are blind (22:46), or that turning to the East or the West is not righteousness (2:177), or that it is not the flesh or blood of sacrificed animals that reaches God (22:37), or that they think that they are deceiving God and believers; nay, they are deceiving none but themselves, but they do not realize (2:9), we cannot but conclude that the Quran's central message for us is spiritual. We need to care about the inner meanings, the kernel and essence of things, not the outward and superficial structures and forms. We need to ask about the deeper, more fundamental, questions: Why are we here, what is the meaning and significance of our life's existence, how can we make our life worth living, how can we make it more enriched and blissful? And so on. We need to concentrate on things that make for our real progress on earth in terms of piety, knowledge, creativity, benevolence, and real contentment and happiness. The effort for such progress critically consists in one's turning to God and devoting wholeheartedly to His service or worship.

How Should We Conceive God and How We Turn to Him?

This brings us to considering the perennial question of Who God is or how we should conceive Him. The very quest to know God is part of our spiritual pursuit. Such a quest led Abraham, Moses, Muhammad and many others to receive Divine inspiration (*wahy*). The Quran speaks of God's face, hands, and throne, but only in a symbolic sense. As Mutazilites, the rationalist school in Islam, have rightly observed, God cannot be conceived in physical perimeters or in anthropomorphic terms. This way we limit God's vision. The Quran also states, "No human vision comprehends Him [God], but He comprehends all vision. He is Subtle, Well-aware." (6:103) Another verse says that He is the First and the Last, the Manifest and the Invisible, the Knower of everything, […] and the Omnipresent and the Omniscient (57:3-4). He is the most abiding Essence, Energy, or Light (*Nur*) of the universe, as the Quran calls it – a Light that fire never touched (24:35) and a Light that blinds others and makes Him invisible.

From the above verses, two ideas that appear to emerge prominently about God are: First, God is Energy or Light (*Nur*) that is spread throughout the universe and second, that He is the only Energy that is ever lasting or eternal. Because He is Ever-Lasting,

He is Indestructible, Overpowering, or Supreme. The Scriptures present Him also as the Creative Power behind the universe. But this creation idea should be taken in a figurative sense, as in the case of other texts that speak of God doing various things such as those that say that He gives life and death (2:258), or that He feeds us (6:14), or that He sends winds, clouds and rain, and thereby brings forth fruits of all kinds (7:57). We know that these things happen when the forces or laws of Nature and human and other agents of God are in action in the universe. The creation idea thus needs to be understood in a way that it is compatible with the idea of evolution that is also clearly set out in the Quran – for example, the idea of the creation of the universe and all that is therein in six *ayyums* or stages (32:4). As I have argued in a recent article, we need to conceive God in a way that is different from the idea of a Creator.[1]

> [W]e [should] conceive Him as Immanent in the universe – manifest in the laws of nature and the actions of human and other agents. The Quran reveals this idea, if we read into its relevant texts carefully. The Quran likes us to reflect on the causes that brought the universe and other things into existence and the laws that cause the alternation of the day and the night (3:190-191, 29:20). Recounting the routing of Goliath's army by David's one, the Quran states that if "He" does not repel some men by others, this earth would remain corrupt (2:251). Another verse reads, "You did not slay them, God slew them; and when you threw, it's not you who threw, but God threw..." (8:17). [...] All this illustrates how God acts through [Nature and] human agents. God acts through [...] other living beings as well.[2]

This conception of God should never be confused with pantheism. Although God is everywhere and in everything or every being, nothing or no being can claim to be God Who represents Perfection and is Unique – Naught is as the likeness of God (Quran, 42:11, 112:4). The point that God is the Light of the universe also refutes pantheism.

This conception of God as being Immanent in the universe is compatible with both evolution and **human free will**.[3] As process theology puts it, "God has a will in everything, but not everything that occurs is God's will." As the philosopher and process theologian Alfred North Whitehead aptly remarks, "God is responsible for ordering the world, not through direct action, but by providing the various potentialities, which the physical universe is then free to actualize. In this way, God does not compromise the essential openness and indeterminism of the universe, but is nevertheless in a position to encourage a trend toward good."[4]

God's existence cannot be proved, but can only be experienced by an internal spiritual journey, as by prophets, saints, and mystics. It's left for others to follow their footsteps and embark on this journey. That is quintessentially the essence of the message of every religion.

Turning to God and serving Him alone means forsaking the path of evil and going along the straight and righteous path (*sirat-al-mustaqim* – 1:6), which is really the path of God (11:56). It means that we do nothing but what is right, good, just, and kind, appropriate, and productive, and all that God stands for. Numerous verses of the Quran point to such attributes or qualities of God. God is True (4:87, 122) and He represents Truth (18:44; 24:25). God is Just (39:75; 40:20), and also Beneficent, Merciful, or Kind (1:1, 3; 2:163; etc.). His are the most beautiful names (*asma-ul-husna*) or attributes (59:24). God represents the Highest Ideal. He is unique, unrivalled, and unsurpassable.

2:163   And your God is one God; there is no god save Him, the Beneficent, the Merciful. (Also see 42:11; 112:1-4)

This oneness or uniqueness (*tawhid*) of God symbolizes the perfection of virtues and signifies that He is our ultimate goal – our first priority, and the only one to be most revered and served, and that all other things must be subordinate to Him, or to His cause. It also means that we should endeavor to acquire such virtues. As we grow in various virtues of God such as mercy, compassion, forgiveness, "love, truth, justice, kindness, and so on, [...] the greater our ability becomes to receive and experience God's attributes of perfection."[5]

We benefit by following God's path because His is the highest and unsurpassable ideal, and because His path is flawless, most bountiful, and blissful. He hears everything, sees everything, and knows, and has record of all events. Nothing can be hidden from Him. He is Most Wise, and the source of all knowledge. He has power over all things, and is the source of all power. He is the source of all bounty. We can gain in sight, hearing, knowledge, and power if we seek His help. The final judgment belongs to Him alone. "He encompasses everything, enters everything, and as He is bigger than, or transcends, everything, He is not visible anywhere although He pervades everywhere."[6]

God responds to our prayers. This divine response, sometimes manifested in religious experience leading one to receive divine message or revelation, is ample proof that God exists. Being the Highest Ideal in all qualities, He is Most Deserving of all praise. That makes Him most worthy of our service, emulation, or worship.

How Should We Interpret Divine Will and Our Own Will and Responsibility?

Many misjudge God about His will from such verses in the Quran that say that He gives sustenance to whoever He pleases

(2:212; 3:27); that He guides whomever He wills (2:213, 217); that He purifies whomever He pleases (4:49; 24:21); and honors whomever He pleases and humiliates whomever He pleases (3:26). From such verses and others, a reader may infer that nothing is really possible without God's will, help, or grace. In a vital sense this conclusion is quite correct, but only if we have a proper perception of the conception of God. The truth is that God does not will or predestine in the generally understood sense, which negates free human will, and the relevance of his effort. God says that He will test who is best in conduct (11:7; 67:2). He cannot have a legitimate basis for testing us, if He wills or predestines our fate.

> 36:47 When it is said unto them: Spend of that with which God hath provided you, those who disbelieve say to those who believe: Shall we feed those whom God, if He willed, could have fed? Ye are naught else than in clear error.

In this verse God rebukes those who skirt their duty to help the poor and the helpless on the plea that if God willed He could have fed them (See also related verses 107:1-7; 90:12-16). This clearly suggests that God does not make one rich or poor of his own volition, and that it is the duty of the rich to feed the poor. He never does any wrong or injustice to men; it is men who do it to themselves (3:117). Additional statements in the Quran reinforce the point that God does not will or act in the popular sense. God says that if He willed He could have guided all of us (6:149), that if He willed He could have made humankind one nation (5:48), and that if He willed all would have believed (10:99). The import of all these verses is that God does not directly determine our affairs. He has given us free will (18:29; 76:3). It is up to us alone to shape our destiny by deciding where to go and what to do. God turns us whichever way we choose to turn (4:115). He does not help anyone unless he or she deserves it by his or her own individual effort, or by a sustained combined effort of heredity and/or environment. A good example of the fruit of a sustained combined effort of heredity is the Prophet Jesus who was a prophet from the day he was born (19:29-34), while the Prophet Muhammad was predominantly the result of his individual effort.

The Quran points out that God helps only those who help themselves. At the same time God is also Ever Forgiving and Most Merciful. His Mercy lies in the fact that man can recover from any sliding back through wrongdoing if he is truly repentant about his wrongdoing, and in the fact that with good work he can erase the effect of bad work, and make onward march toward spiritual evolution. "Man is prone to [making] mistakes but the real man is he, whose failures turn into pillars of success."[7] God forgives the sins of those who turn to Him truly repentant, and who do not persist in their sins (3:135. Last-minute repentances are not acceptable, however, from one who continues doing evil until death and says:

> 4:17-18 I surely repent now. Nor (is it acceptable) from those who die as ingrates (or rejecters of faith). It is they for whom We have a terrible punishment in store.

Addressing the Prophet Muhammad, the Quran further states:

> 9:80 Ask forgiveness for them (O Muhammad), or ask not forgiveness for them – even though thou ask forgiveness for them seventy times, God will not forgive them. That is because they disbelieve in God and His Messenger, and God guideth not wrongdoing people.

Jeffrey Lang notes that it is the doer himself "who benefits or loses the most from a good or evil act. [...] The harm that evildoers experience as a result of persistent wrongdoing is intrinsic. Evil deeds hamper growth in virtue and erode spirituality, so that those who stubbornly reject righteousness do violence to their [own] being and experience spiritual decay. [...] One of the great risks taken by the unrepentant sinner is bringing damage to his moral and spiritual center, or what the Qur'an refers to as the 'heart'. [...] The Qur'an asserts that the hearts of these persons become dark, veiled, rusted, and hence impenetrable to guidance, while the hearts of the virtuous become soft, sensitive, and receptive to God's guiding light. The more we persist in wrongdoing, the more desensitized we become to the evil of it. [...] It is the evil that human beings acquire that covers their hearts like rust (83:14). It is because the deniers follow their own low desires or lusts that their hearts are sealed (47:14-16). God does not make people deny [H]is signs; rather their hearts grow hard by their own wickedness (2:74)."[8]

Ahmad adds: "Only a prayer or wish not to commit a wrong again is not sufficient amends. One must efface past mistakes by encountering bitter facts of life in course of living. [...] Repentance therefore is no effortless task or is not merely an expression of remorse said in a closet or before the Confessional or upon the hands of one's Peer, Guru or religious teacher. The possible hypocrisy in it is to be annihilated."[9] Indeed, penance or suffering on one's part is a necessary corrective process to remove one's dross and move toward purification.

When one deserves to be helped, God helps. There is no basis in the belief that all happens according to a predestined plan, which implies that man is preordained to act in certain ways, and is powerless to do anything about the course of events. God does not act irrationally. "He has not certainly predestined a man to be a thief or a good man. [...] man only comes to naught by worshiping predestination in the act of foolish acceptance of the so-called inevitable."[10] At the same time events can, of course, be predetermined based on underlying predetermining factors - a matter of causation. There are references in the Quran to certain past events, e.g., calamities that struck wrongdoing people during the times of certain prophets, which were willed and pre-announced by God. But it would be wrong to think that God predestined these events without any reason. These events were instances of a natural reaction to certain immoral behavior patterns of people, and thus logically predetermined. Where things are predetermined, God knows them in advance, and so God willed them in a way. It is on the basis of such predetermining factors that those who walk in the way of God can also correctly predict future events. Scientists who discover natural laws behind events can also foretell many things (e.g., the movements and relative location of planetary bodies on a future date).

God is subject to His own immutable laws – the Laws of Nature. There is full logic in His system of creation. The Quran states:

> 67:3-4 Thou (Muhammad) canst see no flaw in the creation of the Most Gracious. So turn thy vision again; seest thou any flaw? Then turn thy vision again and yet again; thy vision will return unto thee dazzled and fatigued.

Whatever God does is a creation. So if there is no flaw in His creation, that *if so facto* implies that He does not, and cannot engage in any irrational or whimsical action. So He cannot predestine or seal the fate of any man or woman. However, part of the fate or destiny of a person may be already predetermined because of the work that has already gone forth – that has been done by the person concerned, or by his/her parents and ancestors (hereditary factors) and/or due to what society has already done. Such predetermined aspects of destiny of a man due to hereditary or other factors may act adversely as a constraint on one's own development, but one can often overcome such adverse factors with sufficient determined endeavor. With things that are given and unalterable, human beings have to work with certain limitations. But this is not to suggest that God predestines everything. The doctrine of predestination is inconsistent with the rationality that the Quran so powerfully espouses, and also "with assertions in the Qu'ran concerning God's justice, mercy, compassion and transcendence."[11] Though with God-given factors, so to say, man is not as free as he might think, and though there is some element of destiny that influences his fate, this should not obscure or belittle the importance or value that attaches to human endeavor.

Man is largely the architect of his own destiny. The history of human endeavor so far amply proves the point that virtually nothing is beyond man's reach and control. Man can now predict, and in some cases even control natural events. Indeed the Quran affirms that God has subjected the universe to the service of humankind:

> 31:20   See ye not that God hath subjected unto you whatever is in the heavens and the earth, and hath made His bounties available unto you in abundance, seen and unseen? ...(See also 16:12-14; 45:13)

God has endowed man with faculties and qualities, which if developed properly, can work really wonders. Should man ever succeed in reviving or resurrecting a dead man, it should not bring religion into disrepute, since the true vision of religion does not mean that man should not acquire God's creative powers. Man now applies, sometimes successfully, the CPR (cardiopulmonary resuscitation) technique as an emergency procedure to revive patients whose hearts have suddenly stopped beating for some reason (e.g., cardiac arrest). At the present time scientists have already succeeded in cloning animals, and in cloning a human embryo for therapeutic purposes, and it is believed that cloning a human baby is within reach in the near future. However, scientists should wonder whether cloning a human baby is worth the effort morally and ethically, and whether it will serve any noble human purpose.[12]

By becoming God's servants, emulators, or representatives, we act as His agents – we act in conformity to His nature or way of creation, i.e., His law, method, or ideal. This is real service to, or worship of, God. This way alone we live in God's way, and this way we evolve spiritually. This is true religion:

> 30:30 So set thy purpose truly (O Muhammad) for religion as a man by nature upright, the nature (made) of God, in which He hath created man. There is no change in the way God createth. That is the right religion, but most men know not.

If the way God creates or acts is true religion, and if there is no change in this way, then true religion must be one that comes from the divine source, and must reflect the Way God acts, which is immutable and valid for all time and space. God wants us to act in His Way. Thus prophets have brought to humankind essentially the same religion from the same divine source, and they could not introduce anything of their own that could be labeled as their way or *sunnah*, as they were obligated to follow and profess only God's Way or *Sunnah*.

Knowing God by His Attributes

To know God, We may conceive Him by His various attributes. He has manifold attributes, and has many corresponding beautiful names.

> 7:180 God's are the most beautiful names; so call upon Him by them. And leave the company of those who distort His names.

We need to reflect on the various names or attributes of God since these names provide the clues to the great variety of ways in which we can develop our own personality and march ahead spiritually. For example, God is Loving, Beneficent, Kind, and Forgiving. Thus we need to develop our character in such a way that we become loving, beneficent, kind, and forgiving in our conduct. He is Truthful and Just. He does not cause the slightest injury to any of His servants. He is appreciative of whatever good one does and rewards one accordingly. We also need to develop these qualities. God is All-Seer, All-Hearer, and Most Wise. We also need to develop our seeing or perceiving and hearing capabilities, and we need to enhance our knowledge and wisdom. Striving to reflect God's attributes or qualities in one's life is the greatest *salat* or prayer one can perform. Elevating us in such qualities will be our true spiritual pursuit and development.

Another good example of God's attributes is that He is independent and free of want. We also need to try to be independent as far as possible. This means that we should not be parasites or beggars. A begging action or mentality degrades one's soul. We can attain nearness to God when we shun such mentality, try to become self-reliant and are independent of others' help. We will then be free of want or become rich, and enjoy a life of abundance. True Muslims cannot remain poor if they really follow God's way. At the same time, this does not mean that we do not come to others' help when others really need our help. God is most kind and helpful to those who need and seek such help. So we need to do the same to others who are in need of help. Serving

God really means serving His creation in the same way and spirit as God serves it. God is helper to those who need and seek help. He is Reliever of our misery and Protector from all kinds of danger. However, while trying to help the helpless in God's way, we should be conscious of the need for helping others in a way that we would like for ourselves should we need help. Since we would like to be self-reliant, our help that reaches others should also be aimed at making them self-reliant. That should be the hallmark or whole purpose of help or assistance. Help or assistance should be for a temporary or transitional phase. Otherwise, help or assistance will make one a permanent beggar, which is like making one a slave to others. That would be against the spirit of religion.

There are many other attributes of God. The Quran mentions numerous attributes of God. One needs to reflect on these names to try to understand God in His true personality and qualities (*jat* and *sefat*), and to mold one's character accordingly. It helps one to envision God in very many ways, and be conscious of such attributes or qualities. When we emulate all such qualities of God, we become His real worshippers. He and His angels bestow their blessings and mercy on His faithful and devoted servants who glorify Him, which essentially means coveting and emulating His qualities (33:41-43).

Knowing God's Way basically means knowing His Laws. One essentially knows God and achieves nearness to Him through knowing His Laws, which are the Universal Laws. By knowing such Laws, one gains the knowledge of the secrets of all creation, events, or actions, which are logical chains of causation. Indeed, it is this knowledge that is most valuable to humankind to enrich their life.

No Room for Polytheism or Idolatry

In the conception of God as outlined above there is no

room for either polytheism or idolatry. It is one God Who is the source of all knowledge, guidance, power, and all good, and the perfection of all qualities. It is all good that we need to strive for. Thus the central message of Islam is *la ilaha illallah* - There is no god but God (2:163). To be truly religious, we need to tenaciously reflect this fundamental faith in all of our behavior and actions. The most significant implication of this belief is that we accept all that God represents or stands for – truth, reason, justice, knowledge, guidance, power, and all that is good, beneficial, noble, and beautiful. We thus need to worship only Him.

This is not to say that we should not respect, and follow our fellow men that are more respectable and knowledgeable than us. In fact, following those who walk in the way of God implies the same thing as following God Himself. And not respecting those who are more respectable and knowledgeable than us really amounts to disrespecting God Himself. That is precisely the reason why God has urged us to follow the prophets, and those who have authority or justification to be followed (4:59), and to show due respect to the Prophet:

> 33:56 Verily God and His angels bless (or support) the Prophet. O ye who believe! Ye also bless (or support) him, and greet him with due respect.

We need to appreciate the qualities of, show due respect to, and bless and support, superior persons. Such appreciation, blessing, or support has a special spiritual significance. By extending such appreciation and support, we in the process enlist their blessing or support in return. Our remembering the Prophet, and expressing our appreciation and reverence to him by salutation has significance only if we become in the process conscious of his great qualities, and if we develop our love toward him in order to enlist his love and blessings for us. Muslims generally use the *milad* institution to verbally shower praise and blessings on the Prophet. However, such an institution has been reduced to a largely barren one, as it has failed to contribute to any spiritual uplifting of the participants. There is little discussion of the qualities and teachings of the Prophet, and of the guidance he has brought us through the Quran.

Note also that respect for a person should not degenerate into worshiping him. No one deserves God's status, as all are God's servants, and prophets are also His worshippers. Worshiping prophets is like worshiping idols, and such worship idolizes them. Worshiping any living being other than God limits the vision of God Who is Infinite. So the Quran emphatically warns us against worshiping anyone other than God (3:79-80). At the same time, the Quran makes it also amply clear that we can respect and follow others only when, and to the extent, they follow God. We have been urged to follow the Prophet precisely because he followed only God (6:50; 46:9). It follows that if we follow the Quran, which incorporates all divine revelations to the Prophet, we follow his *sunnah* (way) as well.[13]

True religion, the basic postulate of which is that God must be Supreme and All Transcending, thus necessarily rules out multiple gods. The Quran gives the reason why we should eschew the idea of multiple gods:

> 21:22 If there were therein (in the heavens and the earth) other gods beside God, verily there would have been chaos in both. (See also 17:42-43)

For the same and even more compelling reasons, there is also no place for idolatry in Islam. Idolatry represents in essence the act of being bogged down with something powerless to do anything or effect any change.

> 17:56   Say (O Muhammad): Cry unto those whom ye assume (to be gods) beside Him, yet they have no power to rid you of misfortune, or to change. (See also 46:5)

While certain diversity in religious practices can be compatible with the true spirit of religion, differences in faiths underscore the need for distinction between what is the intent of true religion and what is apocryphal, peripheral, or wrong. Clearly, idolatry and polytheism are aberrations from the true religion based on monotheism.

The Way Forward to Spiritual Enlightenment

The attributes of goodness are godly qualities. Unless man strives to attain such qualities in his life, his life becomes devoid of meaning and he becomes a candidate for moral and spiritual degradation. For, man who wishes to become truly religious needs to strive for real progress, and should never be satisfied with his current state of progress, for progress is infinite.

The essential message of religion is spiritual. As Ahmad puts it, man needs to develop in such a way that he is able to receive and grasp the divine message or revelation, "either from the Divine Book [...] or from the universe or Nature, which is the other form of the very same Book"[14]. Ahmad further notes:

> [T]he word (of God) reigns everywhere. But blessed is he who chooses to catch it. Want of effort or half-hearted effort can never reach it. The mind of one who makes little or no effort gropes in the dark, as the word does not reach him.[15]

One needs to have transcendental knowledge to avoid pitfalls and shocks of life and evolve progressively. In his quest for spiritual development, man needs to take his cue from his own change as well as from the change that is constantly taking place around him. Man needs to take lessons from the change of day and night, and all the creation that is in the universe.

> 10:6 Verily in the variation of the night and the day, and all that God hath created in the heavens and the earth, there are signs for those who are righteous.

Ahmad aptly observes:

Men who have been able to read the sign, catch the idea, feel the urge or hear the word to get nearer and nearer the principle or code of action till it has been discovered have kept the torch of progress burning.[16]

The Quran affirms the fact that man is changing:

84:19 Ye shall certainly march from state to state.

What religion does is to teach man to reflect on this change and to consciously direct his own change into a progressive one to evolve spiritually. He needs to be conscious of whether he is changing in the right or wrong direction and whether he is changing with the desired speed. The process of evolution, which man undergoes deliberately or unconsciously, is expressed in the following verse:

> 84:6 O humankind! Verily thou art ever toiling on toward thy Lord, a hard striving until thou shalt meet with Him.

Man needs to make conscious efforts to make a change in the right direction, and with desired intensity of effort. He needs to work hard to achieve desired progress. The kind of hard work that man needs to do to achieve desired spiritual evolution is illustrated well by what the Prophet Muhammad himself was urged by God to do, and what he actually did.

> 94:5-8 Verily with hardship goeth ease; with hardship surely goeth ease. So whenever thou (O Muhammad) art relieved, strive hard, turning exclusively to thy Lord.
>
> 73:1-8 O thou (Muhammad) wrapped up in garments! Rise during the night, save a little. A half thereof or a little less. Or a little more, and read the Quran in measure. Surely We will send thee a weighty message. Surely the rising by night is at a time when the impression is keener, and the speech is more certain. Indeed thou art preoccupied with other matters during daytime. So remember thy Lord and devote thyself to Him with a complete devotion. (See also 73:20)

These messages confirm that even the Prophet Muhammad, who received Divine revelation of the Quran after a lot of hard work and meditation, was urged by God to continue striving hard to stay in the path of, and attain further, spiritual progress. The Quran mentions that by dint of his hard work he could attain ascension (*miraj*) whereby he performed a night journey from Masjidul Haram to Masjidul Aqsa (17:1). This journey was of a spiritual kind, not in physical sense that most Muslims understood.

Those who can make sufficient progress on the spiritual path can develop a sixth sense whereby they can hear things that are not audible by the ordinary ear and see things that are not visible by the ordinary eye. They can see with eyes that lie within their hearts.

> 22:46 Have they not traveled in the land and have they hearts

wherewith to understand and ears wherewith to hear? For *indeed it is not the eyes that are blind, but it is the hearts, which are within the bosoms, that are blind.*

At another place, the Quran mentions that historical events carry a good reminder or message for him who has a heart and who lends ear and is a witness (50:36-37). Ahmad describes such people who are able to apply their sixth sense as:

> [...] the keepers of the conscience of the whole universe. They bring themselves as also others out of darkness into the light. Such persons are clairvoyant. They are the protectors of the standard or are landmarks of progress upon progress. [...] [E]xcept very few clairvoyant persons, none else numbering millions who are the rest of the inhabitants of the earth see or hear the happenings behind the Screen of Death. They form the Highest Civil List of the Walis or the Keepers of God's secrets [2:257; 7:196; 10:62; 58:22]. They are the successful persons from whom sprang the Prophets.[17]

Recent developments in psychology and parapsychology provide some valuable insights on psychic, mystical, or religious experiences. Philosopher, mathematician, and psychologist Michael Scriven calls to task those who maintain that all psychic claims (about, say, extra-sensory perception or ESP, telepathy, clairvoyance, precognition, etc.) must be either fraud or error, since such an attitude implies that current scientific models will never be superseded.[18] Stanislav Grof, an innovative psychotherapist who has attempted to integrate divergent schools of Freud, Jung and Reich with insights from the leading edge of contemporary physics and biology, contends that in extraordinary circumstances the human mind is capable of accessing information from anywhere in time and space.[19] Psychic mediums can contact spirits from across the Wall of Death and channel information from them.

The Quran refers to bees receiving divine inspiration (*wahy*) about the places where to build their hives (16:68). Indeed reaching the stage where we can receive divine inspiration or revelation is a coveted spiritual goal in order for us to be able to lead our lives in a flawless, productive, and progressive manner. And that way one acquires some of the Godly qualities and becomes a true servant or representative of God and a source of real happiness and abundance not only for himself or herself but also for others. That God's righteous servants (should be righteous enough) receive divine communication is affirmed in the Quran in following reassuring words:

> 41:30-32 The angels descend on those who confirm "Our Lord is God", and lead a righteous life (saying): Fear not nor grieve, but receive the good news of the Heaven that ye are promised. We are your protecting friends in the life of this world and in the Hereafter. There ye will have all that your souls desire, and there ye will have all that ye ask for – a welcome gift from the Forgiving, the Merciful.

Note that for making such a spiritual journey, one does not need to forsake the world, forsake one's family, and go to a jungle. However, one needs to earmark some time at day and/or at night to contemplate, pray, and meditate in seclusion or in a congregation, keeping away from the din and bustle of daily life.

Prayer (*salat*), meditation, or remembrance of God (*dhikr*) that is basically prayer – the best according to the Quran (29:45), fasting (*siam*), charity (*zakat* or *sadaqa*), and pilgrimage (*hajj*) are some religious rituals or institutions, which are prescribed for us in the Quran, along with essential, consistent, and complementary righteous deeds, to make progress on the spiritual front. The topics of *salat* (including *dhikr*) and *zakat* are discussed respectively in Chapters 4 and 5.

In a wider sense, the other two institutions, fasting and pilgrimage to the Holy Kabah in Mecca, are essentially parts of the prayer of the believing Muslims. During the fasting and the pilgrimage, Muslims have been urged by God to be especially devoted to God so that they get further golden chances to receive spiritual enlightenment. Here we make some brief references to these religious institutions.

Fasting has been prescribed to help believers guard against evil and become upright:

2:183   O ye who believe! Fasting is prescribed for you as it was prescribed for those before you, that *ye may become upright*.

The basic purpose of fasting is thus to help man attain uprightness (*taqwa*) and piety. It provides one a golden opportunity to devote himself fully to prayer and meditation, as he or she has to not only refrain from eating and drinking, but also to abstain from any sexual activity during the day-long fasting, and the latter activity also during the period of one's retreat for worship in the mosque (See 2:187). Fasting should help one learn sexual restraint, which is an essential ingredient for spiritual progress. Fasting has been prescribed for a full month during the Ramadan. However, if one is unable to fast because of sickness, or if one is on a journey, he or she can fast the equal number of days later, or if this still is not possible he or she needs to feed one poor person. If one does good deeds of his own accord, it is better for him and it is still better if one fasts (2:185).

We have been urged also to perform pilgrimage in the well known sacred lunar months, which are known to be Zil Hijja,

Muharram, Safar, and Rabi al-Awwal, or failing that to send an offering that is easy to obtain (2:196-200). Here also the emphasis for the pilgrims is for attaining righteousness and piety, as the Quran has urged complete abstinence, no misconduct, and no angry conversation during the period of the pilgrimage, and complete devotion to God:

> 2:196-7 Perform the Pilgrimage and the visit (to Mecca) for God. And if ye are prevented, (send) gifts that are easy to obtain. And shave not your heads until the gifts have reached their destination. And whoever among you is sick or has an ailment of the head, (for him) a ransom of fasting, or almsgiving, or sacrificing of an offering. And if ye are safe, whoever wisheth to continue with the visit and the Pilgrimage (should provide) such offerings as are easy to obtain. And who cannot find (such offerings), then a fast of three days while on the pilgrimage, and of seven days when ye have returned; that is ten in all. That is for him whose folk are not present in the Sacred Mosque. Be careful (of your duty) to God, and know that God is stern in punishing. The pilgrimage is (in) the well known months, and (for) whoever wisheth to perform the Pilgrimage therein, there (should be) no lewdness, no misconduct nor quarrelling during the Pilgrimage. And whatever good ye do God knoweth it. So make provisions for yourselves, but the best provision is to attain righteousness. Therefore, be careful (of your duty) unto Me, O human beings of understanding.

Fasting and pilgrimage are additional religious rites for worshippers to perform so that they can purify themselves and make spiritual progress. If, however, these institutions do not help them make some headway in fulfilling these objectives, such institutions degenerate into mere rituals devoid of any real meaning. Among Muslims, there are many who perform fasting and pilgrimage, but at heart they have not become Muslims in the proper sense of the term because they have not refrained from doing the heinous things they used to do previously.

Muslims regard the *kalima* (belief in one God), prayer, fasting during the month of Ramadan, and the pilgrimage as four of five obligatory duties. The fifth obligatory duty is considered to be *zakat* or charity to the poor and deserving. However, it should be emphasized that whatever is mentioned in the Quran as worth doing or following by us should be regarded as *fard* (or obligatory). Indeed the whole Quran has been made *fard* for us. Whatever God exhorts us to do, whatever He forbids us to do, and whatever He designates as acts of righteousness for us, are all binding on us:

> 28:85 Verily He (God) Who hath made the Quran binding (*fard*) on thee (O Muhammad) will bring thee back to the destination.

It is misleading to limit the main obligatory religious duties only to five things and omit altogether so many other things of right conduct or righteousness, which have been mentioned and emphasized in the Quran. One cannot be a good Muslim without strictly observing such prescriptions of righteousness.[20]

Also and importantly, prayer and other rituals, as described above, should be considered means to an end, not ends by themselves. They are important aids for a believer to attain piety, self-purification, and spiritual development. However, the performance of rituals can be deceptive as an indicator of real religiosity if they are not observed with the right earnestness and devotion and if they are not accompanied by good deeds at the same time. It is ironic that the *ulama* (traditional learned men in Muslim religion) lay a lot of emphasis on the nominal performance of the rituals rather than on their observance in spirit and they make these rituals difficult for the believers by introducing unnecessary rules, regulations, punishments, and complications in terms of attaching levels of compulsiveness to various rituals such as *fard* (obligatory), *wajib* (semi-obligatory), *sunnah* (in line with what the Prophet is alleged to have done), *nafl* (optional), etc. They present the rituals in such a way as if these are the things God wants from us as a matter of duty to Him and as the principal means of attaining God's pleasure and mercy to go to Heaven. Failure to perform such rituals is depicted as something that earns wrath and punishment from God. But this conception is at odds with the statement of God that He does not need anything from us (35:15; 51:56-58; 47:38). What we need to realize is that we should not observe the rituals as a matter of obligation to God, but should do them for our own sake — for our own benefit. Being led by a feeling of obligation to God does not lead the worshipper very far in his spiritual pursuit. Thus spontaneity on one's part in observing the rituals is of the essence of the real worship of God. "True submission [to God] is predicated upon the principle of personal freedom. [...] Is there any merit in imposed religion or forced prayers?"[21] Indeed, it does not help the worshipper much if he feels compelled to observe the rituals under some duress, explicit or implicit community pressure, or just because the *ulama* so insist.

A misperception entertained among Muslims is that performing *hajj* is so important — if one can financially afford it in one's lifetime — that one must travel to Mecca from far-flung corners of the globe to perform it at any cost, even though there may be more pressing demands to be met at home for such causes as caring for the family and parents, poor relatives, and other poor and needy people. A careful study of the Quran does suggest that we should prioritize what we should do keeping in view our limited time and resources. God rebukes the worshippers who neglect the necessary caring of orphans and poor and needy people (107:1-6). Also, the *ulama*, influenced by the Hadith, assign so much virtue to the performance of *hajj* that many old, sick people undertake arduous travel and ritual requirements to perform *hajj* thinking that it will wash away their life's sins, while the spirit or lesson to be taken from *hajj* is meant for younger people so as to lead a better, righteous life. And the *hajj* institution has been corrupted by certain things such as the kissing of a black stone in the Kabah – an idolatrous practice counter to the spirit of the Quran, and the throwing of pebbles at a pillar at another place, symbolizing an imaginary Satan, while the real Satan is with us, when we entertain evil thoughts from ourselves or wrong whispering suggestions from others (112:4-6). Some Muslim scholars also point out that the *hajj* institution, where millions of Muslims merge together from all over the world, provides a good forum where Muslims' problems and Islamic ideas could and should be discussed for promoting world peace, justice, and progress in general, and amity, solidarity, peace, justice, and progress for the Muslim *ummah* in particular. However, this potentially beneficial feature of the *hajj* institution is currently conspicuous by its absence.

III. Spiritual Evolution and Conceptions of Heaven and Hell

And vie (ye) one with another for forgiveness from your Lord, and for a Paradise as wide as the heavens and the earth, prepared for the righteous. – The Quran, 3:133

Spiritual Evolution: The Basic Propellers

How one can move forward on the religious or spiritual path is a question that warrants further scrutiny. We can conceive of just a few building blocks, or propelling factors, the development of which can help one move forward on the spiritual path. This idea, essentially a Quranic one, is borrowed from my religious teacher Shah Aksaruddin Ahmad.[1] According to him, an advance that we make on the spiritual front is the result of our having developed four primary and fundamental factors, faculties, or qualities:

EGO (entity or energy that can perceive, judge, and will);
LOVE (feeling of need or likeness);
WILL (desire or prayer); and
KNOWLEDGE.

It could be said that Ego, when developed to express itself in some way, translates into feeling a need, or likeness, or Love (for something or somebody). With likeness or Love, a Will to do something is developed. Will needs to be combined with knowledge to do something, as the knowledge of what to do and how to do is essential to proceed. "Then when Ego, Love, Will, and Knowledge are of equal dimensions, concentration or potency, they conjointly lead to action or creation."[2] It may be noticed that the process of accomplishment into creation or action also involves the employment of two additional factors, which are:

> Planning and
> Command or Execution

These six factors, or as one might also label them as stages, can be conceived as the basic factors that underlie all creative process. The Quran states:

> 32:4   God it is Who created the heavens and the earth and all that is between them in six "*ayums*" (days or stages).

The significance of this idea of action, or creation, or evolution should be evident in the context of spiritual development. We will concentrate our discussion on the four basic factors or faculties. A harmonious development of these basic faculties is of the essence of the process of progressive religious or spiritual development. A lack of balance and a deficiency in the development in any of these faculties will result in stalling, hampering, or even reversing of the process of spiritual development. One example of an unbalanced development is excessive development of the Love faculty without sufficient concomitant development of, say, Knowledge might risk one becoming insane. On the other hand, insufficient development of the Love faculty often lies at the root of insufficient spiritual development. Sufficient development of Will enables one to realize what one wants to do or get done. Differences in the behavior patterns of different people should be largely explicable in terms of the differences in the combination and development of these four basic faculties.

Another point to note about these four factors is that none

of them can exist or manifest itself without the other three being embodied in each of them in some way. In other words, these faculties cannot exist separately and independently of each other, although each one of them can be felt separately when it is expressed in a pronounced manner. Each of the four faculties affects the other three. Hence lack of development of any of these faculties is bound to hold back one's spiritual development.

Ego embodies in itself the actor's living entity, self-consciousness, ability, power, and self-confidence to act. Iqbal defines "ego" as "directive energy" that manifests "itself in the act of perceiving, judging, and willing" and "is formed and disciplined by its own experience." He refers to it as an independent human soul (*ruh*) that flows from the command (*amr*) of the Ultimate Ego, i.e., God (17:85).[3] Each man or woman has a distinct individuality. That is why each man is accountable for his own actions, not for another's actions:

> 17:15 Whoever goeth aright goeth aright for his own self or soul (*nafs*); and whoever goeth astray goeth astray only to his own harm. No bearer of a burden beareth the burden of another. (See also 29:6, 6:164)

Ego here is not meant to imply egotism, which is an exaggerated view of one's own self or of one's own importance. Such an attitude is unacceptable and deplored in religion, as it retards one's spiritual development. In fact one needs to feel very humble before those who have a greater level of spiritual attainment and wisdom, and much more so before his or her All–Transcending and Supreme Lord. The aim of one should then be to proceed toward a stage where he can merge his own Ego with the Ultimate Ego, which is God's Ego. Whatever he does then is perfectly in tune with the Divine Ego or Will (see: 53:3; 18:79-82).

Now to act, one must feel the need for action. Thus the

second essential ingredient is need, or likeness, or Love. The more intensely one feels the need, or loves a thing, to do, the more effort one would employ to achieve his or her goal. Love or devotion is a key component of one's spiritual advancement. It is Love that underlies all creative activity. God manifests Himself through His rule of mercy or Love throughout the universe (6:12). He is full of Love. He loves those who are righteous (2:195; 3:76, 134, 148; 5:13, 93; 9:4, 7), who purify themselves (2:222; 9:108), who are just (5:42; 49:9; 60:8), and those who fight in His cause (61:4), and who are patient and perseverant (3:146). He loves those who sincerely turn to Him for guidance, seeking forgiveness and mercy of God (11:90).

Those who have firm faith in God are staunch in their Love for God (2:165). Those who wish to earn the pleasure of the Prophet and hence of God, need to love the Prophet and God as they love their near and dear ones. If we love God, we need to follow the Prophet as well (3:31). As will be explained later, to follow the Prophet is essentially to follow his message, which is nothing else than the Quran.

> 42:23 This is of the good news God giveth unto his servants who believe and do good deeds. Say (O Muhammad): I ask of you no reward for it but the Love (like that) of near kinsfolk. And whoever earns any good, We add further good for him. Verily God is Forgiving, Grateful.

Indeed noble actions are inspired by Love rather than by any selfish motive. With such actions we can do the maximum good for all. Love prevails eventually. The path of human progress is toward Love, and those who love God will ultimately prevail over those who reject Him, i.e., over those who abandon the path of progress toward good or godliness.

> 5:54 O ye who believe! If any from among you turneth back from his religion (should know that in his place), will God raise a people whom God loveth as they love Him.

Noble or righteous deeds on one's part in turn enhance one's Love:

> 19:96 Verily the Beneficent (God) endoweth with Love those who believe and do righteous deeds.

To do righteous deeds, what we need to do is try to emulate God and acquire His qualities, which also implies that in the process of such endeavor we also develop our Love. The flipside of this is that the more sinful we are and the more we persist in sinfulness, the more hardened and rusty our hearts become. Those who are endowed with Love, which is an embodiment of Divine Love, are very blessed indeed, for such persons are not very many on earth. They are forerunners of spiritual progress for themselves as well as for others in society. God loves them (3:31), and God and angels bless and support them (33:41-43).

One who is on a spiritual training knows how difficult it is to develop the faculty of Love. A true aspirant should endeavor to increase his love for God by good thoughts and deeds. He needs to live strictly in conformity with moral principles, which is conducive and critical to spiritual development. Thoughts and acts of indecency give rise to a feeling of rancor or enmity, and blunt the nobler human qualities. Those who become dwellers of Heaven get rid of their feeling of rancor or jealousy in their hearts among themselves (15:47). True Love is free of any touch of lewdness.

> 4:27 And God wisheth to turn to you in mercy, but those

> who follow their low desires (or lusts) wish you to deviate a great deal. (See also 7:28; 79:40-41; 25:43-44)
>
> 5:5 And so (lawful unto you) are the chaste from among believing women and chaste from among those who have been given the Book before you, when you have given them their marriage dowries; and seek chastity, not lewdness, nor taking them as paramours.

Adam and Eve found themselves ousted from their heavenly state of Love and happiness, and there arose enmity between them, when they transgressed their limits and became conscious of their nudity (7:19-24; 20:117-124). The Quran exhorted the Prophet Muhammad not to pay attention to that with which human beings enjoy worldly life:

> 20:131 And strain not thy eyes toward that with which We cause parties of them to enjoy the splendor of this worldly life, that We may test them thereby. The provision of thy Lord is better and more enduring.

Thus those who sincerely desire to go forward in the way of God, i.e. the spiritual path, need to keep their desire for carnal pleasure in check. As Ahmad puts it, they need to "cure" their sex, which means that they need to attain the state when their sexual urge is fully contained:

> The Prophet [...] had also to cure the sex in him as also his wives for God is neither male nor female and Muhammad is nothing but His last Prophet to illustrate this view of life in the most beautiful way.[4]

Hunger and thirst under check lead to moral living; when let they end in carnal lust, and sensuousness turns into sensuality which is nothing but conscious nudity.[5]

Thus failure on one's part to keep carnal lust in check is a major stumbling block to developing one's pure Love, which in turn is a major driving force for spiritual progress. To strive on one's part to restrain any evil propensity is an integral part of one's striving or struggle (*jihad*) for attaining righteousness or piety.

The Prophet Muhammad was exceedingly kind and loving to the believers, as the Quran confirms:

9:128 There hath come unto you a Messenger from among yourselves, grievous unto whom is any misery that befalleth you, full of concern for you, to the believers compassionate and merciful.

In view of the beneficial Divine message he has brought us, he has indeed been a mercy to the whole universe:

21:107 And We have sent thee (Muhammad) not but as a mercy for the whole universe.

Love for anything symbolizes appreciation for that thing, or attraction to that thing, and concentration of one's attention upon that thing. That evokes a natural reaction from that thing, which translates itself in the form of a desire on the part of that thing to reveal itself to the person who appreciates it. Observing Nature and appreciating its splendor and beauty has thus a good meaning to the Nature observer. Such observation is a source of insight and power to the observer. Abraham reached his goal of reaching God through observing Nature (6:75-79). And thus it is not for nothing that God has urged man to observe Nature in the Quran (3:190-191; 2:164; 31:29).

We may be relatively brief on the two remaining faculties: Will and Knowledge. If one likes to have something, his likeness or Love for that thing needs necessarily to be accompanied by his Will to have that thing. The degree of Love dictates, or translates into, the degree of Will one needs to employ. Will translates into effort, mental or physical. One cannot make progress simply by a pious wish. One needs to strive hard in the way of God to achieve success. It is lack of effort or half-hearted effort that holds us back in the path of progress. The Quran urges us to strive in the way of God. The importance of Will is evident from the adage "Where there's a Will, there's a way." The Will leads to the way. The way signifies the knowledge of how to proceed. Will or determination to improve one's condition, to march forward on the path of progress, has indeed been a linchpin in the progress of human civilization. Will or desire is really prayer. We pray to seek something. Whether we formally pray or not, we may mentally keenly desire something, and try to get that thing by practical means. That is also prayer. However, the will should not degenerate into greed – hankering after others' property, or exploitation of others' sweat, or desire for any kind of transgression of limits. That kind of Will or desire is degrading to human soul and impedes spiritual progress. The Quran has condemned and forbidden such behavior (2:188; 17:34; 2:190, 5:87).

Knowledge represents both an input and an output. For seeking Knowledge we need Knowledge as one of the basic inputs. When one exerts one's Ego, employs one's Love and exercises one's Will, one can do all this only when one has knowledge of how to proceed. So Knowledge enters the equation simultaneously with the other three faculties. Differences in the level of Knowledge among people are important distinguishing marks for them. It is Knowledge, with which man has been endowed, that characterizes humankind's superiority over all other living beings. Knowledge of how to proceed in spiritual pursuit is without doubt the key to progress (58:11). God exhorts humankind to travel through the earth to gain knowledge about how creation is originated (29:20). And those who have been able to acquire Knowledge or wisdom have indeed received a great good:

> 2:267 He (God) giveth wisdom unto whom He pleaseth, and he unto whom wisdom hath been given hath indeed received a great good. But none takes admonition except men of understanding (or intelligence).

The Prophet Muhammad was urged by God to pray for an increase of his Knowledge (20:114). Also, God lifts to higher ranks those who have knowledge:

> 58:11 God will exalt those to high ranks who believe among you, and those who have gained Knowledge.

Indeed God requires us to acquire Knowledge to pursue our goals, and not rush into things whereof we have no Knowledge or verification:

> 17:36 And, (O Man), pursue not that of which thou hast no Knowledge, for surely the hearing, the sight and the heart, each of these shall be questioned about that.

It is lack of Knowledge, imperfect Knowledge, or guesswork on one's part that leads one to confuse things, and err. Knowledge is thus a *sine qua non* of proceeding properly with any action. Man needs to have clear, flawless knowledge to live in a flawless way. That is why it is so important for man to strive to attain divine Knowledge, which is flawless and inexhaustible.

Note also that Knowledge comes only to those who earnestly seek it. It does not come to those who think that they already know enough. As Ahmad puts it:

> [The] portals of the gate of knowledge open only to the hard knocks of those whose quest after knowledge does never quench.[6]

It is a great pity that Islam, which has proclaimed such messages of Love, Will, Knowledge, etc., has reached so poorly its self-proclaimed followers. It is Muslims today who appear to lack such qualities the most. Most of them are steeped in moral, cultural, and spiritual degradation, ignorance, poverty, inter-communal intolerance and violence, and sectarian strife and killing. Muslims pay little attention to the valuable lessons of their Book of Wisdom, the Quran.

The Conceptions of Heaven and Hell

Those who walk in the way of God – do right deeds and attain spiritual enlightenment – attain great or real success. They become dwellers of Heaven, or the heavenly state. On the other hand, those who reject faith – do misdeeds – live in Hell, or the hellish state. We need to have some idea about Heaven and Hell in light of the Quran. But at the outset it is important to underscore the point that it is neither the fear of Hell nor the lure of Heaven that should really drive one to do good deeds and strive for spiritual uplift. One should be temperamentally inclined to do good deeds regardless of the fruits of such actions. Prophets did not work expecting any rewards (6:90). Work in expectation of rewards for good work and in fear of punishment for misdeeds befits only those who are not mature, or intelligent enough. Those who are inherently good and intelligent do not need to be lured by Heaven, nor do they need to be intimidated by the fear of Hell.

God does, of course, point out the consequences of good or bad work, but that for our own enlightenment, not to lure or scare us. Selfish work, or work in expectation of some return, does not always promise to be ideal work, as it does not guarantee the best result. As Ahmad puts it:

> The ideal worker or creator is he or she who bestows his or her whole attention or being in the work undertaken to deny selfishness or participation in the result thereof. By so doing a creature emulates God the Creator.[7]

This is not to say that one should be oblivious of the consequences of one's work. Indeed, those who are inherently good are conscious of the fact that their ultimate fate will be good. They are conscious that what they do is good and is bound to have a good end result. Wise men know whereto they are destined. They harbor sure conviction, and they see signs in the earth as well as within their own selves (51:20-21). It needs also to be noted that those who are striving in the way of God should not be too much concerned about the immediate effects of their efforts. If their persistent efforts do not show any signs of progress, they should rethink their efforts, as there may be something wrong with, or something lacking in, their efforts, and they should accordingly try to make renewed efforts. Nobody should be obsessed with the absence or presence of any signs of progress that one experiences in his or her spiritual endeavor. Continuation of a meaningful effort is more important than the immediate result one succeeds or fails in perceiving. And in the process, when one succeeds in getting some real spiritual fruits, he should steadfastly stick to such achievements to make sure that there is no retreating.

In a vital sense God does not really create any Heaven or Hell for us; it is we who create them by our own deeds. And as the

Quran assures us, no one should despair of God's Spirit (*ruh*) that embodies His Mercy and Forgiveness (12:87). There should be no such thing as condemnation of anyone to a permanent hell. No sin is so great that it should condemn one to Hell forever. Many have erroneously translated some Quranic verses to suggest that the wrongdoers will live in Hell forever. Living in Hell for good does not advance the cause of evolution. It is by virtue of our corrective deeds, which is our own evolution, that we can transform Hell into Heaven. It is through our deeds that we can transform this troubled, dull and dreary earth into a Heaven, and create a still better afterlife (see: 16:30, 97). This is essentially the purpose of religion.

The conceptions of Heaven and Hell, as described in the Quran, are most often taken literally in physical terms, and are thus misconstrued. But their subtle or allegorical meaning is more significant. What is Heaven or, more appropriately, the heavenly state? Using the Quranic ideas, we can say that one characteristic of this state is that it is a state where man does not have to fear, regret, or grieve anything, and where there will be no remorse or sorrow for him:

> 46:13 Verily those who say: Our Lord is God, and remain steadfast (on the path of God), there shall be no fear for them, nor shall they grieve. (See also 43:68)
>
> 35:34 And they (the dwellers of the Garden) will say: Praise be to God Who hath removed from us (all) sorrow! Our Lord is indeed Ever Forgiving, Grateful.

If we reflect on these verses, we should not fail to perceive the deep implications of qualifying for a no-fear, no-grief, or no-sorrow state. This we can realize in our day-to-day activities. If we plan and decide some action properly, and execute that action properly – indeed it needs to be a good action – we find ourselves not regretting our action. This is how we create our own Heaven. But if we do plan an evil deed, and execute it, and even if we plan a good deed, but execute it half-heartedly, or improperly, we find ourselves regretting that action of ours. That is the Hell we create for ourselves, and we suffer accordingly. We start enjoying the bliss of Heaven, or suffering the pinch of Hell from the very time of our action, i.e., from this world, while we are still living. The long-term and afterlife effects may be of still greater importance.

> 16:97 Whoever doeth right, male or female, and (who) is a believer, verily We will grant him (or her) a life (in this world) that is good, and verily We will bestow on them a reward in keeping with the best of what they did.
>
> 16:30 And it is said unto those who are upright: What is it that your Lord hath revealed? They say: All that is good. There is good in this world for those who do good deeds; and the home of the Hereafter is even better. Excellent indeed will be the abode of those who are upright.

The *ulama* generally convey the impression that we should not be interested in this world, but only in the Hereafter. But such an assertion belies what the Quran states. The Quran clearly states that those who are righteous receive good results in both worlds. Another verse of the Quran confirms that the dwellers of Heaven enjoy the likes of fruits they enjoyed before (i.e., on earth) (2:25). Muslims should wonder why they should live a pitiable life in this world, when God promises that His righteous servants are made inheritors and rulers of the earth (21:105; 24:55; 7:128-129; 10:14). Of course, if we seek this world alone, we lose the good of the Hereafter; but those who sincerely seek the good of both worlds do get both (2:200-202).

Another important characteristic of the Heavenly State is

that it is a state where the dweller gets whatever he wa
the Quran states:

> 25:16 Therein (in Heaven) abiding, they (those who are righteous) will have all that they desire. It is a promise (which is) binding upon thy Lord. (Also see 42:22)

No fear or regret, and getting whatever one wants are the most important godly qualities or gifts that man can ever covet. For, man can find himself not fearing or regretting anything, only when there is no fault or flaw in the feelings and thoughts he has and actions that he does. Anc he can get anything he wants only when he attains a very high level of creative power or talent and perfection. These characteristics of the heavenly dwellers clearly point to the necessity for man to attain real spiritual progress to be able to display such heavenly qualities.

The Quran provides other descriptions of Heaven. It is a state where man does not have to taste death again after his first death (37:58-60; 44:56), but lives forever in a perpetual state of bliss. It is a place or state where there is no boredom or weariness (35:35), where there is peace and security (6:127; 15:46), where there is abundance of fruits (food and drink) (56:32), where there is no futile conversation and no lying 78:35), where there is purity and no foul play (56:25), where there is peace and salutations of peace (19:62; 56:26), where there is no feeling of rancor, but only brotherhood (7:43; 15:47), where there is grace and beauty (55:70), and pure companionship and love (56:36-37), where it is neither too cold nor too hot for the dweller (76:13), and where there is the light of those who are admitted there, and where they pray for perfection of the light, which is nothing but striving for perpetual progress (66:8).

These and more characteristics of Heaven described in the Quran speak of things, which a human being always cherishes.

These are the things, which we need to have in this very world so that the world can be transformed into a heaven. Heaven is a state from which no one wants to go backward (18:108). That implies that the heavenly state represents a maximum vantage point for human evolution, which is implied also by the verse where the dwellers of Heaven pray to God to perfect their light (66:8).

If we have an idea of Heaven, it is not difficult to know what Hell is. It must be the place or state where all the good things that the dwellers of Heaven have or enjoy are conspicuous by their absence. The other name of Hell is Fire (2:24; 3:131; 4:56; 6:27; 25:11; 40:71-2).

> 10:54 If each soul that doth wrong had all that is in the earth, it would seek to offer it for ransom; and they will feel remorse within them, when they see the punishment. And it would be judged between them fairly and they would not be wronged.

These verses reflect the suffering that one needs to undergo to atone for one's misdeeds. The sinner would be prepared to part with everything of his possession – even if he possessed all that is in the earth – to atone for his misdeeds. The greater the degree of misdeeds, the greater is the scale of suffering. This is the necessary evolutionary or corrective process of purification for one who makes mistakes, or commits misdeeds.

Evidently, Hell is a state that is most resented by all, who really wants to escape such a fate. If a man is wise, he will not knowingly jump into such a frying pan. It is so important for all to know how to evolve spiritually to avoid pitfalls in order for him no to regret his actions later. Indeed, we should think in terms of turning this dull and dreary earth into a garden of bliss.

This earth is a safe place to live for good and pious people:

Spiritual Evolution and Conceptions of Heaven and Hell

> 29:31-2 And when Our messengers (angels) came to Abraham with the good news (of a son to him), they said: "We are indeed going to destroy the people of that township, for its people are wrongdoers." He said: "But Lut is there." They said: "We know well who is there; we will certainly save him and his family except his wife; she is of those who lag behind"

The angels then advised Lut and members of his family to leave the township before it was destroyed. God does not send a punishment to a habitation as long as there are good people there or while they seek forgiveness (8:32-33). It is incumbent upon God to save the righteous believers (10:103).

This earth or its designated regions are continually purified and changed into a New Earth by replacement of bad people with good people:

> 10:13-4 We did destroy generations before you when they did wrong. ... Then we made you successors in the earth after them, that We might see how ye behave.
>
> 47:38 And if ye turn away (from the right path), He will replace you by some other folk who would not be the likes of you.

Because of the good work being done by good people and because of their good wishes or prayers, as time rolls on, we should be moving forward to seeing better and better days ahead, though this progress may be punctuated by periodic lapses. Ultimately over the long run, the good and the true prevail over the bad and the false, and the earth gets rid of the bad and false or meaner elements (see: 5:56; 8:7-8; 9:48; 20:68-70; 26:45-48;

21:18; 58:19-22).

Civilization thus marches forward, not backward, over the long run. One need not predict doom, destruction, or dire consequences for the fate of this world. Such predictions ignore the clear indications God has given us in the Quran. *Qiyamat* (resurrection) should not be interpreted as destruction of the earth. It must be understood in a different light. The time of *qiyamat* is one when the dead will rise from their death or slumber (36:51-52), when to every soul will become clear what it earned in the past (81:14), when the curtain will be lifted from them, and they will be able to see clearly (50:22), and when the guilty people will fully realize and accept their guilt (6:130). This should augur well for the time that follows.

IV. The Real Meaning of Prayer in the Quranic Light

O ye who believe! Remain conscious of God, seek a way unto Him, and strive in His way that ye may succeed. – *The Quran*, 5:35

When my servants ask thee concerning Me, then surely I am nigh (unto them); I answer the prayer (*dua*) of every suppliant when he crieth unto Me. – *ibid*, 2:186

My view on *salat* (or *salah*), generally understood as prayer, has evolved over time. I do not accept it as a mandatory five-time ritual in a rigidly defined form, as in traditional Sunni Islam. But at the same time I have no problem with that form either. It is only that I do not regard it as the only normative pattern one should follow. I think that that is precisely the reason the Quran does not explicitly specify a particular form like the one being followed by Muslims, which embodies some *rakahs* (a *rakah* combines the forms standing, bowing, and prostrating in a sequence, with also sitting after two or four *rakahs*). A particular form without a heart of humility and devotion accompanying it and appropriate for supplication before God is of no real value. The Quran declares remembrance of God as the best (29:45). It tells us to do this remembering either standing, sitting, or even reclining, or lying down on one's sides (3:191; 4:103).

The Quran mentions that all living beings including birds glorify God and perform *salat* (24:41). But their *salat*, that we do not observe, is not the type of ritual prayer traditionalist Muslims understand and perform. Also, the Quran's reference to standing, bowing, and prostrating should be understood in a broader sense of submitting to God's Will or Laws, just as it refers to all living beings prostrating before God (13:15). This suggests that *salat* need not be understood strictly in the traditional sense of ritual prayer.

In a broad sense, prayer is nothing but desire or aspiration, or will or determination, or commitment on one's part to be something, to have something, or to get something done. Whether one formally prays or not in a particular form to a higher power, everyone really prays in some way.

The discussion in the preceding chapter centered on the question of how we can evolve ourselves, which essentially involves quest or prayer for spiritual evolution. The desire on one's part to upgrade oneself is instinctive human nature. The poet Alexander Pope famously writes, "Hope springs eternal in human breast." Every creature has such instinctive yearning, which is its prayer for evolution. To accelerate our spiritual evolution, we need to take recourse to sincere prayer. We often experience receiving external help in the process of our work. Some of this help may indeed strike us as surprising, and we may characterize such help as Divine help. But all help that we get is Divine help. Only those who recognize help as such are grateful to God (14:7; 27:19, 40).

The Quranic Conception of Salat

The existing practice of *salat* has certain inherent shortcomings that could be largely attributed to the influence that came from the Hadith (see below). To rid *salat* of its current deficiencies, we need to understand and formulate it exclusively on the basis of the Quran alone.

It is generally believed by Muslims that the Quran does not provide sufficient guidance on *salat*. Thinking or believing so amounts to contradicting the Quran itself (12:111; 16:89). The Quran provides detailed guidance about *wudu* (ablution), about bath or *tayammum* (wiping face and hands with earth) (5:6; 4:43) instead of the ablution, about the clean, decent dress we should wear for the *salat* (7:31), and about the *qiblah* (the direction of the

Kabah at Mecca) we should face (2:144-150). In addition, the Quran describes the inherent purpose and spirit of prayer and its nature and content. It also provides many examples of prayers of past prophets and believers.

Salat, which essentially includes *dua*, is a way of connecting to God, a platform for remembering Him (20:14; 3:191; 4:103), and a process of transforming oneself into a better being by helping one keep away from indecency and evil (29:45), which is essentially a process of self-purification – that of effacing one's bad or negative traits by developing good or positive ones (11:114). This is spiritual evolution whereby one acquires Godly qualities.

The Quranic conception of *salat* is implicit in its very first *surah*, the *fatiha*, of which the first four verses, including the first verse containing *basmalah* (In the name of God, the Most Gracious, the Most Merciful), are words of remembrance and glorification of God, and the remaining three verses constitute general prayer to God to lead the worshipper to the righteous path. In a nutshell then, *salat* on one's part is remembrance and glorification of God with sincere devotion and seeking of His help to walk aright and get success in real life.

Several elements that characterize *salat*, then, are: (1) remembering and glorification of God, (2) sincerity expressed in due personal humility and devotion, (3) seeking His help for various things, and (4) working consistently in accordance with what is sought. These points are worth some elaboration.

God urged the Prophet Moses to establish *salat* to remember God:

>20:14 Verily I am God; there is no god but I. Therefore, serve Me and *establish salat for My remembrance.*

Indeed, remembrance of God (*dhikr ul-Allah*) is

characterized as the best act in the Quran (29:45). God has advised the Prophet Muhammad and us to remember Him to find refuge from devilish thoughts and actions (7:200; 41:36; 23:97-98; 114:1-6) and to get blessings of God and His angels and to move from darkness into light (33:41-43). God and His angels bless those who remember and glorify Him much. And our hearts do find rest and satisfaction in God's remembrance (13:28).

And importantly, we remember and glorify God inherently to admire His qualities and at heart to seek such qualities. That way we seek our spiritual evolution. The whole universe remembers and glorifies God in some way or other (57:1; 17:44). We are urged by God to remember and glorify Him by conceiving Him by His numerous attributes or beautiful names. We may choose any of such names to call upon Him:

7:180   And God's are the most beautiful names; so call upon Him by (any of) them. (See also 17:110)

We may devoutly chant God's name or meditate, at the same time visualizing Him in His various attributes, and seeking His mercy and help to acquire such qualities, as in the box below.

> **An Example of Mental Glorification and Prayer While Chanting God's Name or Meditating**
>
> A prayer to God, while chanting His name or meditating, could be like this: "O my Lord, Most Kind, Merciful, and Loving! Touch me with Thy Mercy and manifest Thyself in me with all Thy qualities. Endow me with Love and Knowledge so that I can understand Thee and I can make others understand Thee! O my Lord, Ever Living! Make my life worth living – give me new life! O my Lord, All-Seeing! I am blind! Give me sight! O my Lord, All-Hearing! Bestow on me real hearing capacity! O my Lord, Most Wise! Increase my wisdom!"

God wants us to grow in purification and piety, and He wants to complete His Grace on us. To manifest His Mercy (*rahmat*) and Grace (*niamat*) in His creation is what God Himself considers His duty or rule (6:12), and accordingly the rule of His Mercy reigns everywhere.

> 5:6   God wisheth not to place any burden (or difficulty) on you. But He wisheth to purify you, and to perfect His *niamat* (grace) for you, that ye may be grateful.

Spiritual development helps one become clairvoyant, i.e., to see beyond the way one sees with one's normal eyes (22:46; 51:20-21) and clairaudient (the capacity to hear beyond the way one hears with normal ears). It is thus that prophets hear God's words and receive His revelations. We need to emulate prophets in like manner.

A crucial element of the vision of *salat* is sincere devotion – more than the love and devotion we show to our parents (2:200). *Salat* requires expression of a special attitude of mind – a mind not proud, but which is one of devotion and humility. People who are proud and arrogant lack such an attitude. Those who think that they know enough learn or gain nothing. Indeed, as the Quran reiterates, praying meaningfully is hard except for people who are sufficiently humble (2:45). Humility grows when one recognizes, and is fully conscious of, one's own deficiencies and past mistakes, and when one truly seeks to improve himself or herself. God asks us to call upon Him with awe, reverence, and hope (7:55, 56, 205).

Seeking Divine help is another key element, the very essence and *raison d'etre* of prayer. We are needy in some way or other, and directly or indirectly dependent on God Who is free of wants and independent of all His creations (2:263, 267; 4:131;

6:14, 133; 35:15; 47:38). He admonishes us to seek His help through perseverance and *salat* (2:45, 153).

> 2:153   O ye who believe! Seek help through perseverance and prayer (*salat*). Verily God is with the perseverant. (See also 2:45-46 and 3:26)

Perseverance or patience signifies that help does not always come automatically, instantaneously, or with ease. Help often comes after enormous effort and waiting and, at times, with vicissitudes of events in life, which one needs to endure with patience (2:155-157). The victory of Muslims over the persecuting and attacking disbelievers during the Prophet's lifetime is a good example to cite. The Prophet and the believers along with him prayed to God for such victory (2:286). The final or ultimate victory, however, did not come instantaneously. They had to undergo trying periods. Believers faced a lot of obstacles, torture, and persecution. Many had to migrate to other countries. At one point, the Prophet and his close associates also had to migrate to another land. There were several battles between the believers and the disbelievers. The great victory then finally came when the disbelievers were decisively overcome, and Islam took hold in the land.

Prayer is an avenue for seeking whatever good one likes or needs – livelihood, financial freedom, healing of one's diseases or of those of near and dear ones, success in one's work or mission, prosperity, peace, joy and happiness in life. You may seek answers to your questions. The Prophet Moses prayed to God for his mate (28:24). We need to seek God's help to lead our life flawlessly and to enrich it by receiving His manifold bounties (*niamat*). Among the things we should seek, increasing love and devotion for God and knowledge should count as the most important. Progress in this regard is more effective for one to move along the righteous path (*sirat al-mustaqim*).

Salat is not just a pious wish. One needs to work consistently with the spirit of what one seeks. Prayer necessarily implies that one has to refrain from all wrongdoing and engage in only decent, appropriate, and noble deeds in feelings, thoughts, and other actions. The test of sincerity of a prayer is in the actual deeds one does. The prayer of a person will be devoid of meaning if he or she is oblivious or neglectful of doing the right or appropriate things on any occasion. One glaring example of prayer that will go to waste is that of those who neglect their duties to help the indigent and needy; God curses such people (107:1-7). The Quran says: *Innas salata tanha a'nil fahshaai wal munkari wa la zikrul lahi akbar* – *salat* keeps one away from indecency and evil and *zikr* or remembrance of God is the best (29:45). It follows that if *salat* or *zikr* of God does not inspire and drive one to keep away from evil and do good and noble deeds and become fully righteous, that *salat* or *zikr* has little meaning and significance; that is no real *salat* or *zikr* or that *salat* or *zikr* remains incomplete.

That verbal praying without it by heart and without reflecting it in all of one's thoughts and actions does not make much sense is captured beautifully in the words of Shah Aksaruddin Ahmad as follows:

> Just saying verbally is not enough; just saying is not enough
> That for God is your *salat*,
> Your actions,
> Your life,
> And your death (6:162);
> Just saying is not enough.
> Seek in *salat* what you need,
> But act you must accordingly
> Going along the path that helps you get what you seek.[1]

The Quran repeatedly exhorts us to establish or keep up prayer in the verse "*akimus-salat*", which means "establish or keep up prayer", and not "read or recite prayer" (2:3, 43, 177; 4:162; 5: 12, 55; etc.). Establishing or keeping up prayer implies that we should keep praying for the things we want until our prayer has been fulfilled, and that along with the prayer we should also act in accordance with the spirit of that prayer, and not commit any wrongdoing. Muslim religious teachers generally interpret establishing prayer as observing the timings of the prayer. However, establishing the real intent of the prayer in all actions of the worshipper is really what matters, and is much more important than just establishing the timings of the prayer.

Another important thing to note in this context is that we need to pray for our own sake, not because God needs or wants it. God declares in the Quran that He is independent of all of His creations (35:15; 3:97; 2:267; 4:131; 6:14, 133).

> 29:6 And whoever striveth, striveth only for his own soul, for God is fully independent of anything in the universe. (See also 31:12)

The idea prevalent among Muslims that we have to perform prayer because God wants us to do so as a matter of duty imposed on us by Him is a misconception that needs to be dispensed with for good. By doing good things, we no doubt please God and may legitimately think so, but ultimately this contentment is going to be our own, as reflected in 29:6 above.

Salat is one's overall effort for self-purification and spiritual evolution. Purification does not come unless one washes away one's dross by repenting and atoning adequately for one's past mistakes. *Salat* is a place where one can at least partly, if not fully, wash away one's blemishes by expressing deep regret and repentance before God and by imploring His forgiveness and help in mending things. Human beings are prone to making mistakes. They need to regret committing mistakes, repent adequately for such mistakes, and mend their ways so that they can lead a flawless and blissful life afterward. God forgives the sins of only those who turn to Him truly repentant, and who do not persist in their sins (3:135; 16:119; 66:8).

Relentless striving or struggle (*jihad*) for good against evil and moral living help one successfully overcome evil and attain purification, which is the key to success.

> 87:14-5 He succeedeth who purifieth himself, and remembereth the name of his Lord, and prayeth. (See also 91:9-10)

The Quran emphasizes the importance of moral living. Strict adherence to righteous conduct of oneself – living strictly in conformity with moral principles – is critical to fostering the faculties such as ego, love, will, and knowledge, as discussed in the preceding chapter.

Such living, in turn, helps us acquire some of God's qualities. But such accomplishments do not make us gods; it only helps us comprehend Him in a better way, and unearth some of the mysteries of the creative process that is at work and spread throughout the universe, and thus to reap some of His *niamat* or boons for us. None should despair of God's mercy. The Quran assures us that none despairs of His spirit or mercy except disbelievers (12:87). A sinner has always a way out for him or her to come out of his dark days into God's mercy and light.

Our prayer remains incomplete unless and until we are able to receive God's response in some way - feel some divine impulse or receive divine revelation. As Ahmad puts it, "Prayer or desire is not therefore ideal until and unless we can decipher the real message either from the Divine Book, i.e., Revelation or from the universe or Nature which is the other form of the very same

Book.[2]

The prayer of a person necessarily implies that he or she should understand it and express it from his or her heart. That is why God has forbidden us to go near prayer when we are drunk:

> 4:43 O ye who believe! Go not near unto prayer when ye are drunk till ye know what ye say.

Also, it is important to note that, in *salat*, we need to be careful about what we say to God Whom only we address. Saying or reciting things that are irrelevant to prayer and glorification of God, or reciting things like a parrot without understanding, defeats the very purpose of prayer. The revelations are for our own guidance. There is virtue in reading and studying the Quran for our guidance. However, this does not warrant us to recite the Quran in *salat* thinking that that would also be a virtue.

Muslims are taught by the *ulama* to recite in *salat* short *surahs* or passages from the Quran and, sometimes, even the whole Quran. However, the most of such recitations such as those of *Surah Lahab* (111), *Surah Nasr* (110), *Surah Kafirun* (109), *Surah Kauthar* (108), *Surah Maun* (107), and *Surah Al-Fil* (105) run counter to the very spirit of prayer. Also, some *surahs* or passages, which begin with the command word "*qul*" (say), could be used in *salat* if these are words of prayer or glorification, as in *surahs ikhlas* (112), *falaq* (113), and *nas* (114), but omitting the word "*qul*." Reciting with the "*qul*" will foolishly miss the true intent of God's advice. Omitting this command word will be more sensible and dignified. God has urged us to ponder and reflect on His revelations and thus exercise our wits (38:29; 10:24). Likewise, when we recite in prayer other texts of the Quran that glorify God, we should omit the word "*qul*" wherever it occurs, e.g., in verse 3:26.

Salat is prayer of a personal, devotional, and spontaneous type, not bound by any rituals or formulas. No particular form or mode of prayer is worth considering as important by itself. Any of the forms that are mentioned in the Quran such as standing, bowing, prostrating, sitting, reclining, or any combination of them should be all right so long as prayer is done sincerely. With an empty heart or without sincerity or devotion in prayer, the forms are of no religious significance. This can be inferred from verses where the Quran states that turning to the East or the West is not righteousness (2:177) or that it is not flesh or blood of sacrificed animals that reaches God (22:37). "[B]id goodbye to all systems, come out of their rigid shells (Quran V-48 Maida) to remember God [...] for, is not remembrance of God the greatest achievement? (Quran XXIX-45 Ankabut) [...] The right religion is above its form whatever it might be."[3] Indeed, one may stand, bow, or prostrate before God numerous times without making any real headway whatsoever in terms of piety or spiritual development. God in fact looks at, and knows best, what is in one's hear or mind, not at the outward form or posture one takes (2:284, 225; 17:25).

Conventionally *salat* is defined and performed in the form of some *rakahs*, each *rakah* constituting a prayer cycle. Undoubtedly, it is a very good and beautiful form, which combines standing, bowing, prostrating, and, in the second and last *rakah*s, also sitting in a particular sequence. One does not need the reference of the Hadith to sanctify its use. It can be logically assumed that this practice has been followed, and it came down to us from generation to generation. Yet it would not be an appropriate approach to consider the *rakah* as an indispensable form or part of prayer. Hence attaching importance to the *rakah* is misplaced.

Also, can we discount the devotional practices or modes of worship or prayer that other communities resort to? God says:

22:67 For every community We have established its own devotional rites, which they are to perform. So let them not dispute with thee on the matter, but do thou invite to thy Lord. Most assuredly, thou art on the right path.

This brings us to the consideration of whether there are appropriate timings for *salat*. The Quran advises believers to perform prayer at specified timings:

11:114 And establish *salat* (prayer) at the two ends of the day (morning and evening), and some part of the night. ...

17:78 Establish *salat* at the declining of the sun (*le-dulukis shamsi*) until the dark of night, and (the reading of) the Quran in the morning. Verily (the reading of) the Quran in the morning is witnessed (most effective).

Some translators or interpreters have interpreted "*le-dulukis shamsi*" in the verse above at (17:78) to mean "setting of the sun" rather than "declining of the sun." If we grant that it means "declining of the sun," then the verses cited above together specify (1) morning, (2) afternoon including evening (since the declining of the sun until the dark of night also includes evening or dusk), and (3) some part of the night as the timings of *salat*. Thus according to the Quran, the specified timings really add up to three, rather than five, since the evening mentioned in the Quran can be considered as included in the afternoon extending up to the dark of night, and since *zuhr* (afternoon) and *asr* (late afternoon) are also included in the afternoon mentioned in the Quran. However, it has become customary to count the timings given in the Quran at (2) above (as in verse (17:78) as combining three timings such as *zuhr*, *asr* and *maghrib* (evening) rather than

The Real Meaning of Prayer in the Quranic Light

just one. Together with the morning and night, these timings add up to five. Note, however, that the Quranic verse (24:58), which mentions about private times of married couples, mentions about morning and night prayers, and it mentions about the time *zuhr* (noon or afternoon), when the couples take rest but does not mention about any prayer at that time. The verse at (17:78) clearly lays more emphasis on the establishing of *salat* during the afternoon, and on the studying of the Quran in the morning. A question may naturally arise, why *salat* timings are regarded as mandatory while the morning timing for studying the Quran mentioned in this verse is not so regarded. In other words, the timings given in the Quran should be considered as suggestive in nature for our benefit. Just as prayer should be a spontaneous activity on our part for our own sake, not imposed as a matter of obligation to God, observance of such timings should also be taken in that light.

The verse at (2:238) refers to midmost prayer, which is interpreted by many as the late afternoon (*asr*) prayer. However, interpreting this verse in this way will be inappropriate, and will rob the verse of its true message, which is that one should be mindful of the main or central theme of his or her prayer. Even if one interprets this verse as referring to the late afternoon prayer, this timing can be considered as included in the afternoon that is mentioned in the verse at (17:78).

Note, however, that the Hadith, from which the five-time *salat* appears to have been taken, is not credible enough (see below). And importantly, according to historical records, the requirement of five-time daily *salat* was not laid down during the Prophet's lifetime; what was enjoined was three-time *salat*.[4] Shiite Muslims observe the five prayers at three timings rather than five.[5] Admittedly, however, it is not of much significance to squabble over the number of times one should pray. Praying five times with the same amount of devotion is admittedly an act of greater devotion and piety than praying a lesser number of times. What is more important and worth emphasizing, however, is that a worshipper should be more concerned with maintaining the spirit of *salat* than with strictly observing its timings.

Also, the above timings of the Quran should be taken in the same light as the time of the night, less than half or more than half of the night, which God enjoined on the Prophet for prayer and meditation, and for studying the Quran (73:1-8). God enjoined this timing for the Prophet precisely because he was preoccupied with other things at daytime. Following this, the Prophet and his close associates devoted one third to two thirds of the night to prayer, and remembrance and glorification of God, and studies of the Quran (73:20). Separately, specific timings have been mentioned in the Quran for remembrance and glorification of God, which are the morning, afternoon, evening, and night (20:130; 30:17-18; 33:41-43; 52:48-49).

One can notice in the Quran that there is specific instruction for us to complete the period of *siam* (fasting), provided we are not sick or on a journey, and to fast other days afterward if we miss certain days to fast in the Ramadan for such reasons, or to feed poor people (2:185), while in the case of *salat* there is no such specific instruction to complete all the timings. There is a reason for this. One may devote a lot of time to *salat* in one or two sessions, which may obviate the need for keeping all the timings. Insisting that all the timings must be observed by us as a matter of course enjoined on us by God would serve no real spiritual purpose. The real spiritual purpose is served when one observes the timings spontaneously and inclines to God with real devotion.

The language in which we should pray is also a relevant consideration. Praying in a language, which the person who prays does not understand, cannot make any sense. Muslims who do not understand Arabic are also generally taught to pray in Arabic. As mentioned above, the Quran has forbidden us to go near prayer when we are intoxicated and we do not know what we pray (4:43). This Quranic verse clearly underscores the importance of one's understanding of what one says in the prayer. Unfortunately, however, it appears that the verse has been misinterpreted in different quarters to mean that the person should only recognize what he recites in the prayer, and whether or not he or she understands the language in which he or she recites the prayer does not really matter. However, this sort of reasoning is clearly unconvincing in light of the Quran. God is not kind to those who do not apply their sense.

The Quran likens those who are disbelievers to those who do not apply their sense:

2:171 The likeness of those who disbelieve is that of those who repeat naught but sounds of what they hear of shouts and cries, without understanding; deaf, dumb, blind, for they use not reason.

The language or utterances should be one's own. The idea that the language of *salat* has to be Arabic for all people is not a tenable proposition. One should pray in any language one fully understands and is comfortable with. It cannot be right to insist as the *ulama* do that God requires us to pray in only one language, Arabic, and that Arabic is God's or heavenly language. This assertion is clearly contradictory to the spirit of the Quran, which states that God never sent a messenger except with the language of his (own) folk, that he might make (the message) clear for them (14:4). Certainly earlier Prophets and their followers prayed in their own languages. The fact that Islam was revealed in the Arab world does not mean that all Muslims whether Arabs or non-Arabs must pray in Arabic. How does God know what we are communicating if we ourselves do not know what we are saying? Ahmad appropriately comments: Muslims "worship in their barren mosques with hearts empty of faith for want of proper understanding."⁶

Finally, our prayer becomes meaningful or effective only when God responds to our prayer in some way and when we can feel or perceive that response. The Quran proclaims that God responds to every devoted worshipper when he cries to Him (2:186 cited at the beginning of this chapter). Look at some more:

40:60 And your Lord saith: Call upon Me; I will respond. (Also see: 42:26; 27:62)

13:14 Unto Him (God) is true prayer. Those unto whom they pray beside God respond to them not at all.

We have numerous examples before us from the past prayers of distinguished men and women, and of the corresponding divine responses they received, and benefited from. Indeed every person with a strong faith in God experiences God's response in some way or other. What can one say or make of precognition one may experience, which is a kind of divine response? This is foreknowledge of future events, which one may receive through dreams, or some extra-sensory perception such as visions, revelations, or through some other ways. One is surprised when one has such an experience, and sees things happen exactly the way they could perceive beforehand. Such precognition is a definite response from the divine source, which the devotee may have earnestly sought, or which has been communicated to him because of his piety, even though he may not have thought about it at all in the immediate past. God-loving devotees often receive divine reminders of impending bad news or dangers through dreams or visions or other ways. They receive such extra-ordinary information so that they can take necessary precautionary measures. Or they may be informed in advance of good news, so that they can be reassured, especially if they are worried enough.

The Prophet Zachariah and the Prophet Abraham received good news of a son to them through messengers in response to their prayer. The Prophet Muhammad was reassured by God, and he received revelation from Him of the impending victory over the disbelievers, and he was advised to inform the believers accordingly (3:124-127; 61:13), God was so kind and responsive to him that he was repeatedly consoled by Him through revelations not to grieve over what the disbelievers did to him, and also assured of the more rewarding and blissful future that awaited him (16:127; 18:6; 27:70; 31:23; 35:8; 36:76; 93:3-7).

Though prayer is largely a matter of individual effort for one's own spiritual evolution, congregational prayer is also of considerable significance. In practice, Muslims prefer congregational prayer led by an *imam* (leader) to individual prayer, which they unnecessarily consider as *fard* (obligatory) prayer. Additional significance is derived if such prayer is led or conducted by spiritually capable and advanced people. The Prophet and his close associates used to pray, remember and glorify God together (73:20), and he used to lead the prayer even in the battlefield (4:102). Thus, congregational prayers, or acts of remembering and glorifying God which are led and conducted by capable spiritual teachers are often instrumental in inspiring those who are initiated, and who are beginners or novices in the process of spiritual pursuit and transformation. However, it should always be borne in mind that spiritual guides can only inspire others, and give them some knowledge and guidance; they cannot by themselves raise others in spiritual development unless they themselves put in their own efforts. The effort one individually puts in is always the real determinant of what one achieves.[7]

Problems with the Currently Practiced *Salat*

The foregoing analysis of *salat* in light of the Quran should

84   Rediscovering Genuine Islam

enable one to perceive that *salat* as prescribed by *shariah*, and conventionally conceived and practiced by Muslims suffers from a number of inherent deficiencies, and this mainly due to the influence of the Hadith. Some of the misconceptions or problems with the currently practiced *salat* are:

- Holding the notion that *salat* is a duty imposed on us by God, or something we owe to God, which we need to pay off;
- Laying emphasis on five-time observance of *salat* every day rather than on maintaining the spirit of the prayer;
- Sanctifying recitation of Quranic verses in *salat*, which are not relevant to the spirit of prayer or glorification of God;
- Attaching undue importance to the *rakah* system, and assigning virtue to the number of *rakah*s one performs;
- Introducing different categorizations of *salat* as *fard* (obligatory), *sunnah* (allegedly in conforming to what the Prophet did), *wajib* (near-obligatory) and *nafl* (optional);
- Conceiving and using only the Arabic language as the only usable medium of communication; and
- Projecting *salat* as a ritual that automatically washes away one's sins.

Most of these points have already been covered. As pointed out above, we need to perform *salat* for our own sake, not because God has told us to do this. To understand this conception in the correct perspective is very important since the difference in conception has made a big difference to the whole approach to religion and prayer. Most Muslims offer *salat* as a matter of course, but hardly pay any attention to what they pray, and to the requirement that the essence of what they pray must be reflected also in all of their thoughts and actions. They do not care whether they receive any divine response to their prayer. So if they pray their whole life without getting any response to their prayer, and if they have never found whether their prayer was ever effective in some way, they should ponder whether in effect they have really prayed! Poor faith in God does not make one eligible to receive God's mercy and response. Only strong faith in God expressed in <u>sincere prayer with full devotion to Him</u> can elicit such response.

    The weakness of the notion that *salat* has to be performed five times every day can be demonstrated by scrutinizing the relevant widely cited Hadith texts. One text says that one day the Prophet Muhammad ascended to the heavens and received divine direction for 50-time prayer. But while he was returning, he passed by the Prophet Moses who advised him to go back to his Lord and ask for a reduction in this number. He went back, then the number was reduced to one half. But again on Moses' advice, he returned to the Lord and came back with a further reduction by another half. This process continued until the number was reduced to five. (Narration by Abu Dhar, *Sahih Bukhari*, VOL. 1, BOOK 8, # 345). A second text says that the number of times of prayer was reduced on the first occasion to forty, on the second occasion to thirty, and then to twenty, and so on until it reached five (Narration by Malik bin Sasaa, *Sahih Bukhari*, VOL. 4, BOOK 54, # 429). The difference in the two Hadith texts but included in the same compilation by Bukhari is both striking and puzzling. The inconsistency in the two versions of the Hadith reveals weakness in their reliability in support of the five-time *salat* contention.

    This Hadith is not credible also for more substantive reasons. It demeans both God and the Prophet, and directly contradicts the Quran in more than one way. First, it misjudges how God acts. Is it conceivable that God should prescribe or reveal something, which He will need to change soon afterwards?

The Quran clearly gives the idea that God does everything with firmness, and His ways of treatment or *sunnah* never change (35:43); nor do His words (10:64; 30:30; 17:77; and 18:27).

Second, can we ever conceive that God can ever impose in the first place any burden on man that is beyond his capacity to bear? The Quran makes it clear that God never tasks any soul beyond its capacity (2:286; 6:152; 7:42; 65:7). Third, what reason is there to think that any Prophet should judge God's certain prescribed direction or advice as beyond man's capacity, when God says He never imposes any such burden on man? The Hadith also indirectly casts aspersion on the wisdom and judgment of the Prophet Muhammad shown considerably poorer to that of the Prophet Moses. Also, the story of the back and forth journey of the Prophet to and from God, or the divine sphere, appears suspect, not simply because it belies the conception of God as Omnipresent. The question also arises if this number of *salat* times was so important, why has this prescription not been included in the revelations of the Quran, when it states that it does not leave anything of concern to us untouched (12:111; 16:89).

The unnecessary insistence on observance of five-time *salat* as a matter of compulsion has resulted in the notion that if one misses the so-called *fard salat* at a given time, he or she can make it up by so-called *qada* (make-up) prayer. How so-called *qada* prayer can make up for the missed prayer is beyond one's comprehension. Such a conception sends the wrong message that *salat* of a certain prescribed form at a specified time is something that we owe to God, and it must be paid off some how. This is contrary to the Quranic message that God does not need anything from us. Attaching importance to the times of prayer rather than to the spirit of prayer and to its establishment in terms of one's *amal* or work consistent with that spirit must be considered as misplaced and misleading.

The Hadith has done a great damage to the conception of

salat by also suggesting that it should be performed using recitations from the Quran. The Quranic verse (73:4) is cited in support of the contention that the Quran also prescribes recitation of Quranic verses in *salat*. However, this verse is wrongly cited as neither this verse nor the associated preceding and succeeding ones explicitly mention *salat*. It will be more appropriate to interpret these verses along with the other related ones as emphasizing that we should devote ourselves to worship and prayer, along with reading or study of the Quran.

Another verse that is also sometimes cited to support recitation of the Quranic verses in *salat* is, "Recite that which hath been revealed unto thee of the Book, and establish *salat*" (29:45). However, this verse could not be interpreted as necessarily meaning that the recitation has to be done in the *salat*. The two are separate activities, and are better done separately. Recitation, reading, or study of the Quran is more appropriately done outside the prayer. Of course, as mentioned above, it is quite reasonable to think that the Prophet used some verses of the Quran in *salat*, which are in the nature of prayer or glorification of God, but when he used them he used as his own words. To assert that the Prophet used to recite any verses of the Quran regardless of their relevance to the spirit of *salat* was a wrong attribution to him. The Quran urges us to reflect on, and understand, His signs or revelations, and apply our sense (10:16, 24; 38:29; 45:13). The Prophet who followed nothing but the Quran (6:50; 46:9) must have applied his good sense while using verses from the Quran in *salat*. Worshippers should be under no illusion that reciting verses from the Quran in *salat* regardless of its relevance to the context of prayer is a virtue.

Another weakness of the prevailing *salat* conception is its emphasis on the *rakah* system with particular physical postures and movements and with their particular sequencing. As discussed earlier, the Quran speaks of standing, bowing, reclining, sitting, and/or prostration that can be used in *salat* or *dhikr*. Any of these forms or any of their combination should be considered as good for purposes of *salat* or *dhikr*, which is also prayer. It should be left to the worshipper whether he should use the *rakah* or any other form of his choosing, but it is certainly not right to assert as the *ulama* do that a *salat* cannot be performed without the *rakah*s. Muslims are also led to believe that the number of *rakah*s of prayer one does counts as a virtue in itself. This is a misconception, because it is the content of prayer or devotion of the worshipper that really reaches God, not the *rakah*s just as the flesh or blood of a sacrificed animal does not reach God (22:37).

Also, the existing conception embodies or introduces unnecessary complication by distinguishing between different kinds of *salat* (*fard*, *sunnah*, *wajib*, and *nafl*), and attaching different levels of virtues to certain recitations. Postulating that one has to perform certain *rakah*s at every time as *fard salat* is incomprehensible, as what is not mentioned in the Quran cannot be declared as *fard* or obligatory. *Salat* is *salat*. How one can gain anything by considering some *rakah*s as *fard*, some as *sunnah* (i.e., conforming to the Prophet's practice, or in some cases *wajib* or almost obligatory), and some as *mustahab* (preferred) or *nafl* (optional) is beyond comprehension. *Shariah* has created unnecessary complications for the worshipper also by introducing rules that certain factors cause annulment of ablution (*wudu*) or of prayer, or diminish their virtue (*makruh*). A true worshipper does not need such minutiae to pray effectively. The Quranic conception of prayer is simple and straightforward. One only needs to pray sincerely and devoutly; and God responds to such prayer.

There are also other ideas borrowed from the Hadith embedded in the existing *salat* conception, which send wrong messages to Muslims. Such messages relate to things such as that such and such *salat*, or such and such recitation, gives such and such virtue to the worshippers, including, in many cases, forgiveness of all past sins, regardless of whatever sins one has incurred. Such messages are clearly at odds with the spirit of the Quran, which emphasizes righteous deeds, effective repentance and atonement for past misdeeds, and no recurrence of misdeeds along with prayer.

In the *tashahud*, which is taken from the Hadith, and recited in the sitting position of the last *rakah* of *salat*, the text includes such wordings as "Peace be on you, O Prophet, and Allah's mercy and blessings be on you." This expression of blessings on the Prophet by directly addressing him is counter to the very idea of prayer that the worshipper should address only God.

Conclusion

In sum, there is not much prayer in the current practice of *salat* in accordance with God's advice "Seek help through perseverance and prayer" (2:153). It has been relegated largely to a mere ritual often devoid of any real seeking of help from God. By upholding the imaginary virtues of reciting from the Quran, by emphasizing physical postures and movements, and insisting on the use of one language by all worshippers, the prevailing conception has robbed *salat* of its true and essential intent expressed in the Quran.

This conception of *salat* in light of the Quran draws on the ideas of late Shah Aksaruddin Ahmad. This chapter is aptly concluded with some of his profound lyrical words on this topic.

(1)

Know by the Quran
How you should do your *salat*.
God's message in the Quran is:

"*Akimus salat.*"
"Establish *salat*"
Is what God the Pure has said.
What is the use doing it like doing a rite?
Salat is no child's play
Five times ever day and night.
Seek power and help; seek forgiveness of your sins
Humbly and devoutly.
Seek in *salat* what you need,
But act you must accordingly
Going along the path that helps you get what you seek.

(2)

Salat is to get one's peace,
Keeping away from indecency and evil.
Nigh is God
Who hears the call of the heart
Of one who implores Him humbly and devoutly.
He forgives one's sins,
And removing one's dross,
Purifies one's mind.
Sorrow and grief goes away;
No regret remains in one's heart.

Seeking power and help,
Do your *salat* without recitation.
God will wash away your mind.
You will get peace and happiness and all that you need
In this world and also in the Hereafter.
Instead of doing the *salat* of the Quran,
Why recite the *namaz* (Persian for *salat*)
Like doing one's rite?
Make no mistake, even by mistake.

(3)
Through *salat* burn all your sins
And all the dross of your heart.
Present in your front is your Lord,
Salat is the platform for imploring God.
Salat is giving away (one's heart and soul),
Forgetting one's self,
Salat is commitment
To serve God,
To seek the straight path,

The path of those
Who receive God's *niamat* (bounties),
To go along that path,
To get that *niamat*.
Salat is meeting with the Lord –
Miraj (ascension) in this world.
By remembering the *alhamdu* mantra (the *surah fatiha*),
Dances the heart,
Filled with love; and the soul is sacrificed![8]

V. The Scope of Socioeconomic Welfare Spending in the Quranic Light

> It is through spending, seeking no reward except God's countenance, that one grows in purification and receives contentment – *The Quran*, 92:18-20

> It is in sharing the most, not in gathering the most, that the most is received – Neale Donald Walsch

No topic seems to have received so much attention in the Quran as socioeconomic welfare spending, which the Quran labels as "spending in God's way." It is replete with verses that underscore the merit of such spending (92:18; 9:103; 107:1-7; 2:261; 30:39). God curses those worshippers who care not to help those who are in need (107:4-7). Through these and other verses (See also 90:12-116), the Quran places service to humanity at the top of the ladder of virtue, and equates serving humanity with serving God.

However, such spending has been identified in traditional Islam with a very narrowly defined concept of *zakat* (or *zakah*) – a term that really means purification. It's not clear whether this term is derived from a verse in the Quran that says that spending in God's way leads to an increase in one's *zakat* or purification (92:18). Note, however, that although the Quran mentions *zakat* many times along with *salat*, nowhere it specifically uses the term to explain its meaning or to detail how much one should spend and where it should go, as it does with general spending (*infaq*) in God's way and *sadaqa*, which means almsgiving.

The depth and breadth of what is detailed in the Quran as spending in God's way in fact go way beyond the narrow confines of the traditionally understood *zakat* system. The Quran's overall orientation is a stress on socioeconomic justice and egalitarianism, where the poor and disadvantaged segments in society are freed from poverty and deprivation and empowered to live healthy, productive lives. Some of the salient features such spending should embrace are as follows:

- The ultimate purpose of such spending should be to make the poor and disadvantaged people in society stand on their own feet – not to perpetuate a beggars' class in society, which is really a social nuisance, degrading to humanity.

- Such spending, according to the Quran, well exceeds the 2½ percent of assets (excluding one's homestead) generally understood by Muslims as the *zakat* amount. And it should come out of both earnings (income) and wealth.

- The scope of such spending covers not only welfare payments for the indigent and the needy and poor relatives but also those for other causes, lumped up as God's cause, which covers a whole host of things, as would be mentioned below.

- Finally, the state has an important role to play in such programs besides what individuals can and should do at their own levels on top of taxes they pay to the government to cover welfare needs at the state level.

Rationale for Spending in God's Way

Some of the reasons why those in society who can afford to engage in such spending should do so are as follows:

- Such spending forms an integral part of our service to humanity that could be viewed as equivalent to our very service to God;

- It is through such spending that we bring about greater

social and economic egalitarianism in society;

- Such spending is self-purifying, and it brings real contentment and happiness to the giver; and
- Such spending also makes economic sense.

The Quran emphatically declares, "Never shall ye attain piety until ye give out of what ye love (3:92). It characterizes such spending as the gateway to ascent:

90:12-16   What will convey unto thee what the Ascent is!
(It is) to set a slave free,
And to feed the hungry in a day of hunger,
An orphan near of kin,
Or a poor person in misery.

There is no merit in the amassing of wealth, as it has no value as a measure of virtuousness of a human being before God (34:37). The Quran warns that those who amass or hoard wealth and are stingy in humanitarian spending would eventually find that wealth too burdensome for them on the Day of Resurrection (3:180).

Islam promotes neither pure capitalism nor socialism. It promotes free-market competitive capitalism with socialistic overtones. The Quran sanctifies private property ownership (2:188; 4:2, 10, 29, 58; 17:34; 26:183) and respects individual freedom, enterprise, and businesses to mutual benefit (4:29). But the individual owners are only caretakers of their earned or inherited wealth. They are entitled to use such wealth subject to the understanding that everything really belongs to, or is for, God (2:284; 3:109) and should be used for only godly purposes, i.e., to serve only God (12:40). This fundamental philosophy underpins the safety-net system for the poor and needy people and spending for other welfare needs of society. The Quran urges such spending to rid society of poverty and deprivation and to guarantee overall social welfare.

There is also a deep philosophical reason for humanitarian spending on the part of the rich people in society. The Quran directs us to be fully alive to the need for ensuring distributive justice in society. It strongly urged the Prophet Muhammad, who was an orphan and a needy person, not to be oblivious of the needs of the orphans and the needy (93:6-10). The Quran envisions for us an egalitarian society. A society is neither egalitarian nor healthy for its all-round development when some people swim in wealth while others are ill fed, ill clad, and ill housed, and when they cannot provide for their food, shelter, health, and education even at a basic level. Spending on the helpless and disadvantaged groups in society helps overall moral and spiritual uplifting of all humankind, which is the only way we elevate all men and women, and help develop their latent potentials and bring about all round progress in society.

Man can hardly live alone in happiness without sharing his earnings and possessions with others in society. Spending for a benevolent cause, i.e., in God's way, is a way of purifying oneself (92:17-21). God-loving people spend for the poor, the orphans, and the captives out of love for, and pleasure of, God – which is essentially their own pleasure, and they seek or expect no reward or thanks in return (76:8-9; 92:20-21). *Zakat* means "purification" and is traditionally identified with charitable giving. But it could mean sharing a portion of one's blessings with others for free, i.e., *pro bono* – where the giving is without expectation of any return (76:8-9; 92:20-21). Blessings could be in any form such as friendship, professional skill, knowledge, manual work, beautiful voice, and real or monetary resources. However, both *zakat* and *sadaqa* could be interpreted to mean the same thing for all practical purposes – sharing of one's resources (or spending) –

material or non-material — for God's cause.

> 92:17-21 As for the righteous, he will be spared it (the blazing Fire), one who giveth from his riches for self-purification. He seeketh nothing in return, but seeketh (only) the pleasure of his Lord, the Most High. *It is he who verily will find contentment.*

It is only the wrong-headed people who dispute the case for spending for others:

> 36:47 When they are told: Spend of what God hath provided you, those who disbelieve say to those who believe: "Shall we feed those whom God could feed, if He so willed?" Ye are naught else than in clear error.

The economic rationale for such spending is no less compelling. A high concentration of income and wealth in fewer hands is counter-productive. Such a concentration adversely affects the development of human resources, and holds down effective demand, and holds back economic expansion. High inequality of income and wealth destroys social cohesion, peace, and harmony, and breeds bitter feelings on the part of the poor and deprived people, and creates scope for social crimes, immorality, and frustration. In a recent survey of studies on the relationship between poverty, growth, and inequality done by the World Bank, major conclusions drawn include the following:

- While economic growth itself is fundamental for poverty reduction, growth accompanied by progressive distributional change is better than growth alone.

- High initial inequality of income is a brake on poverty reduction.

- While poverty itself is also likely to be a barrier for poverty reduction, asset (wealth) inequality seems to predict lower future growth rates.[1]

These conclusions appear to be equally valid for both developing and developed economies. In a 2012 article, Jonathan Rauch challenges a long-standing consensus that "inequality is the price America pays for a dynamic, efficient economy," and concludes that growing inequality is seriously hurting the U.S. economy.[2]

The Scope of Spending in God's Way: the Broader Meaning

Spending in God's way means much more than is conventionally understood. A careful reading of the Quran does reveal that such spending should be from both income and wealth, that the amount we should spend should be a considerably higher proportion of our income and wealth than is currently being practiced, and that the purposes for which we should spend are much more varied than are usually thought.

The Quran urges us to spend out of our wealth and income or production (2:254; 6:141). Besides, we should use part of our income for our and our families' current consumption, and save and invest part of our income for our future consumption, but we should not keep it idle or hoard it. Hoarding is bad for an economy. It deprives others; it curbs effective demand in the economy and holds back economic expansion, and if the hoarding is done in goods, it creates artificial scarcities and high prices of the hoarded goods. The Quran strongly condemns hoarding (3): 180).

Though everything prescribed in the Quran is *fard* or obligatory for us, God specifically mentions *sadaqa* as *fard* for us and mentions where such spending should go:

9:60 The alms (*sadaqa*) are for the poor, the needy, and

those who administer them, and those whose hearts are to be reconciled (to truth), and to free the slaves and the debtors, and for the cause of God, and (for) the wayfarers; an obligatory duty (*fard*) imposed by God. God is Knower, Most Wise.

Such spending is for those who are needy, and for those who are deprived, or poor (70:25), for parents, near relatives, orphans, wayfarers, and for those who ask (2:177), and for other causes of God, including that for freeing of captives or slaves, and for necessary reconciliation or rehabilitation of new converts to religion (2:177, 215; 8:41; 9:60; 24:22). Spending is also for those who are in need of help, but being involved in the cause of God, are unable to move about in the land, and who do not beg importunately (2:273). Likewise, we need also to spend for other noble causes such as for relieving the burden of those who are heavily laden with debt (9:60) and for miscellaneous other noble purposes, which can be termed as causes of God. As for the spending for the new converts, the Quran speaks well of the God-loving believers during the Prophet's time, who were so generous to those who came to them for refuge that they gave preference to the refugees over themselves in helping them, even though they were poor (59:9).

God advises those of us who are affluent that we should not make such promises as not to help our relatives, poor people, and those who leave their homes for the cause of God; and we are urged to forgive them and ignore their faults (24:22). He loves those who spend not only when they are in affluence or ease, but also when they are in hardship (3:134). He admonishes us to give others what is good, and not what we regard as bad and do not want to receive for ourselves (2:267). God characterizes freeing of war captives or slaves, or marrying them as equal partners as very important righteous deeds. Spending for such purposes is likewise a great virtue in the sight of God (2:177; 9:60).

The current practice of *zakat* at a low proportion (2½ percent) of one's wealth (which includes the value of most of one's assets (with some exceptions such as the family house) appears inadequate in light of the Quran, especially for high-income people, as well as from the point of view of the demands of society for a multiplicity of beneficial works (for God's cause) on top of the provisions for the poor.

Concerning what to spend in God's way and how much, the Quran explicitly states:

2:267 O ye who believe! Spend of the good things, which ye have earned, and of what We bring forth from the earth for you, and seek not the bad to spend thereof when ye would not take it for yourselves unless ye close your eyes.

2:219 They ask thee concerning what they should spend. Say: That which is in excess (of your needs).

25:67 And they, when they spend (in charity), are neither extravagant nor stingy; they keep a just (balance) between these (two limits).

In these verses, the Quran asks us to spend out of what we earn and produce (i.e., from our income and production), out of what we like for ourselves, and from that which is in excess of our needs. Our needs can be understood as those for our own consumption, including needs that accommodate provisions for savings and investments for our needed future consumption. "Need" is a subjective term and hence can be interpreted variously. The same is true of the term "stinginess". In one of the above verses the Quran exhorts us not to be stingy in spending as well. When deciding about how much to spend in God's way, individuals concerned need to make their decisions according to what they feel or think about their own needs and what they consider as stingy. Thus the amount of spending in God's way should be in excess of our needs and a reasonable balance between extravagance and stinginess.

Two other verses of the Quran also shed more light on how much one should spend out of windfall income or wealth like the spoils of war and other gains:

8:1 They ask thee (O Muhammad) about the spoils of war. Say: The spoils of war are for God and the Messenger.

8:41 And know: Of anything ye gain, a fifth is for God and His Messenger, relatives, orphans, the needy, and the wayfarer, if ye do believe in God and in what We have revealed to Our servant.

The first of these verses relates to gains such as the war booties. Such gains wholly belong to "God and the Messenger," which means that such gains should be distributed entirely for God's cause – for meeting the needs of the poor and needy people and other welfare needs. The handling and distribution of these gains should be done and administered by the state or by state-sponsored appropriate public or private sector organizations (modern-day NGOs, for example). There may be other gains of the nature of what economists call "windfall gains", the handling and distribution of which warrant similar treatment. Some examples of such gains are instant treasure troves found by some people, and real estates, bank deposits, and other assets left by deceased people who have no near relatives with any legitimate claim to such assets. Lottery earnings also fall in the category of windfall gains, which deserve to be heavily taxed by the state for welfare needs. Note, however, that the Quran strongly discourages us to indulge in games of chance (2:219; 5:90–91).

Hence, in Muslim countries lotteries and gambling should not be allowed in the first place. However, if any citizens in these countries receive profits from lotteries overseas, such profits deserve to be highly taxed by the Muslim state.

The second verse (8:41) calls for spending or distribution of a fifth of other gains or income we earn for God's cause and for near relatives, orphans, needy, wayfarers, etc. That implies that there should be a twenty percent tax on normal or regular gains or income for both the state and other welfare activities. These verses warrant drawing the following summarized implications concerning how much we should spend in God's way:

- First, we should spend in excess of our needs, and choose an appropriate balance between extravagance and stinginess;

- Second, the excess over needs implies a more than proportionate ability to spend in relation to income and wealth of a person suggesting a need for progressive taxation for welfare needs;

- Third, windfall gains such as war booties and other gains of the essentially same nature should be spent entirely in God's cause, and their distribution should be left at the discretion of the public authority, i.e. the state; and

- Fourth, we should spend in God's way one fifth of our normal gains – income or wealth, which are gains other than windfall gains of the nature of war booties. This entitles the state to tax people's normal income or wealth at the rate of 20 percent to meet the welfare needs of the state.[3]

These directions of the Quran highlight that the proportion of our income, wealth, or gains to be spent in God's way should normally be a considerably higher fraction than the 2½ percent (of wealth), which is generally believed as the *zakat* amount. Note that such spending should go not only to the destitute and the needy but also to a multiplicity of noble causes, which we can lump together as God's cause. A substantial chunk of such causes is best handled at the state level, while others may be left for private individuals. During our Prophet's time, considerable resources in the forms of believing men and goods were mobilized for conducting war against the invading infidels.

> 9:41 Go forth (O ye who believe), equipped with light arms and heavy arms, and strive with your wealth and your lives in God's cause. That is best for you if ye only knew.

Resources mobilized in the forms of men and goods used for purposes of defense are spending in God's cause. There are many such needs that need to be met at the government or public sector level. The government should cater to such needs, and *sadaqa* or appropriate taxation should finance such needs. All those parts of government expenditure, which are meant for social welfare – feeding and rehabilitation of destitute people, provisions for unemployed workers, education, labor training, health and hospital services, and similar spending directed especially to amelioration of the conditions of the poor, and those which are meant for making available what economists call "public goods" that are best produced at the public sector level – are indeed instances of spending for God's cause. Public goods are those goods and services, the production of which, if left to the private sector alone, is grossly neglected or inadequately met. Public goods are similar to what Muslim scholars recognize as acts or goods of public interest (*muslaha*), but they are not exactly the same. Some examples of public goods are social peace and security, defense against external aggression, administration of law and justice, promotion of social, cultural, and spiritual development, economic policymaking, and general public administration for miscellaneous government functions. All such state functions should count within the purview of God's cause.

And in an impoverished developing economy, the state has a special role to play in promoting economic development, which indeed is the best way to alleviate poverty for the poor. For promoting economic development, considerable investment is needed in physical infrastructure (such as roads, highways, railways, waterways, ports, telecommunications, power and energy, information technology, etc.) as well as in human skills and education, technology and research. Promotion of such development is crucial for expanding employment opportunities, raising living standards, and, in the long run, for dealing with the problem of the poor.

It is clear that spending in God's way covers a lot more things than are currently being covered by the *zakat* or *sadaqa* system. It matters little whether one calls it *zakat* or *sadaqa*. But this system is in need of major reform in light of the directions given in the Quran and in light of recent developments in the conception of functions of a modern state. Spending in God's way then of individuals will comprise both the taxes they pay for benevolent works of the government at the government level and whatever they can afford to spend voluntarily at the private sector level on top of the taxes they pay. It should be recognized that what the government can or should do efficiently is inadequate to deal with the total problem of social inequity and to promote overall social welfare; and there is much still left to be done at the private sector or individual level. But limiting such benevolent and humanitarian spending to just 2½ percent of one's wealth will be taking a very narrow view of spending in God's way in light of the Quran. Such spending should not be limited to a proportion of just wealth alone as is generally understood in the case of *zakat*. The verses (2:267; 6:141) cited above clearly point to spending from earnings and production. Hence earnings or production could also be used as a base for such spending. And the proportion should be a flexible one depending on how much one can afford neither being too generous nor too stingy as directed in verse (25:67) cited above, taking into account what he or she has already paid to the government in the form of taxes for God's cause.

The ultimate aim of the *zakat* or *sadaqa* system should be to eradicate poverty and help people get work opportunities and become self-reliant, and not to perpetuate a beggars' class in society, which is not only degrading for them but also a nuisance in society. To the extent possible and economically efficient, such spending should be handled at the state level. Many modern developed countries have well-planned public welfare and social security systems embodying unemployment benefits, and certain medical benefits, and administered at the state level in conjunction with enterprise level retirement, lay-off and medical insurance benefits, and it is not left to the whims of individuals to cater to such welfare needs. Social security systems existing in some of the developed countries essentially exhibit the basic principles of the *sadaqa* system that the Quran propounds. The concessional aid developed countries provide and what their sponsored multilateral development financing institutions give to the developing countries is also a kind of *sadaqa* at state level on the part of the rich countries to the poor ones. Such aid should also be counted in the calculation for how much more resources the government should mobilize domestically to cater to the needs of the poor and for development and social welfare needs. The need for paying *sadaqa* at the individual level will last as long as the state cannot pay full attention to the problems of the helpless people. The state in many developing countries is almost invariably unable to take full care of the poor and the needy.

Also considering that public sector welfare systems in developing countries are found to be almost always plagued by significant corruption as available evidence suggests, there remains considerable room for charities at the private sector (NGO) and individual levels. When a believing man or woman can afford to spend and perceives the need for such spending, it becomes incumbent on him or her to do it. That is as good as his/her prayer for his/her own spiritual advancement. And a significant part of such spending should be given to reputable international charitable organizations, and international and domestic NGOs (non-governmental organizations), which engage in development and social welfare activities, and which are known to be more efficient and less corrupt than the relevant government departments.

Another point to note in this regard is that the scope of such spending should also embrace interest-free or concessional lending, which the Quran calls *qarz-hasana* (beautiful lending) (2:245; 57:11, 18; 64:17; 5:12; 73:20). In modern days, some of this concessional financing function is being performed in developing countries by developed country aid agencies and multilateral development financing institutions. The Quranic message of interest-free loans is applicable only for disadvantaged borrowers, who deserve to be treated with a humanitarian approach. The Quran also encourages the lenders to remit interest on remaining loans and postpone or write off the original loans in cases where the borrowers are in difficulty to repay them (2:278-280). In cases, which deserve humanitarian considerations, loans should indeed be extended free of interest, and where appropriate, such loans should be given as grants or alms, which is *sadaqa* in the Quranic terminology.

Conclusion

Spending in God's way should be understood in a much broader sense than the generally understood *zakat* system. It involves considerable spending on the part of a modern state for a variety of functions financed through a well-devised taxation system, besides charitable spending at the private sector (NGO) and individual levels. The best kind of spending in God's way is helping others stand on their own feet. To help another person in a way, which makes him or her look for help all the time, is inherently ill motivated and is like that of those who like to be seen by men and is of no intrinsic virtue to them (2:264). From this point of view, the modern state should take appropriate measures to promote investment and development to increase opportunities for gainful employment of unemployed people, along with crafting a well-devised social welfare and security system. At the individual level, such efforts should include saving, investment, and work that would help build infrastructure and industries for employment-generating development, along with their humanitarian spending in deserving cases.

VI. The Place of Tolerance, Plu[r]
Human Rights in Islam

> If any killeth a person – unless for murder and mischief in the earth – it is as though he hast killed the whole of humankind and if any saveth a person, it is as though he hast saved the whole of humankind. – *The Quran*, 5:32

> Darkness cannot drive out darkness; only light can do that. Hate cannot drive out hate only love can do that. – Martin Luther King, Jr.

The Western stereotyping of Islam as militant, misogynistic, and cruel might look unsurprising, given the recent scale of sectarian violence among Muslims themselves, Muslim extremists' violence against civilians in both Muslim and non-Muslim countries, and the use of archaic and harsh *shariah* rules. However, Islam, understood from the perspective of the Quran alone, is an inclusive religion that promotes peaceful intra-religious and interreligious co-existence, justice, equality, compassion, and service to humanity – far removed from the Western stereotypes.

Tolerance

In today's world, especially after the tragic events of September 11, 2001, the topic of tolerance has become perhaps the most discussed yet most misunderstood subject in Islam. Due, in large measure, to the violent extremism of a tiny group of self-declared, self-righteous Muslims, a gross misperception persists among many in America and Europe that Islam is an intolerant and violent religion. The misleading writings and utterances of some Western scholars, politicians, and religious leaders have fueled this misperception and have, indeed, contributed to a rising tide of Islamophobia.[1] This in turn has put Muslims in the Diaspora in a very delicate situation. However, the message of the Quran on this very important subject is too loud and clear to miss: There is no room for intolerance and violence in Islam.

The Quran clearly advocates religious freedom, peace, tolerance, and peaceful, and compassionate co-existence. The key message in the Quran guaranteeing full religious freedom is: "The Truth (has now come) from your Lord; let, then, him who wills believe (in it), and let him who wills reject (it)" (18:29). Islam "is, by definition, incompatible with coercion."[2] It unequivocally and emphatically proclaims: *La ikraha fiddin* – There is no room for force or coercion in religion (2:256). Islam's Prophet was strongly urged to avoid any force or compulsion in religion (10:99; 50:45; 88:21-22).

> 10:99   And had thy Lord willed, verily all who are on earth would have believed together. *Wouldst thou (O Muhammad) then force people until they become believers (muminin)?*

He was urged to tell the disbelievers: *Lakum dinukum walia din* – To you your religion, to me my religion (109:6). The Quran urges Muslims not to revile others' gods, lest they should revile Muslims' God in ignorance (6:108). It permits only defensive wars and urges Muslims to cease fighting if their enemies do so, even if their ceasefire offer may turn out to be deceitful:

> 8:61-2   And *if they (the enemies fighting you) incline to peace, then incline to it*, and trust in God, for verily He is Hearing, Knowing. And if they intend to deceive you, then verily God is sufficient for you.

The peaceful nature of Islam in fact derives from the very common root word "*salama*" of the Arabic words "*islamun*" and "*muslimun*" (the singular terms). "*Salama*" means "peace and security." "*Salama*" can also mean "surrender." We surrender to God, Who in turn has an attribute or name "*Salam*." Whichever way you look at it, a Muslim must be a peaceful person by definition. True Muslims are humble (11:23; 23:2; 25:63; 33:35); they walk in the land with humility, and when the ignorant address them they say "*Salam*" or "Peace" (25:63); they turn away from the ignorant or from their idle talks, saying "Peace" (28:55; 43:89). Noted contemporary Islamic scholar Khaled Abou El Fadl points out that these verses "emphasize the need not just for interreligious tolerance, but for cooperative moral ventures that seek to achieve Godliness on earth."[3]

In fact, there is no room for human discrimination and intolerance in Islam on the basis of race, color, sex, language, religion, political or other opinion, national or social origin, property, birth or other similar status. All men and women are equal in the eyes of God; only virtuousness determines who is nearer to Him (3:195; 4:124; 16:97; 33:35; 49:13). All the children of Adam – all men and women – deserve the same dignity:

> 17:70   And *verily We have bestowed dignity on the children of Adam.*

Although traditionally women have been treated as inferior to men among Muslims, the Quran never approved of such discrimination. It urges Muslims to look upon women with an eye of dignity, magnanimity, and equality. It states that women have rights over men similar to those of men over women (2:228). It depicts the husband-wife relationship as one of love, compassion, and complementarity (30:21; 2:187; 9:71).

While racial discrimination, or that on the basis of color, has existed in its stark form well into the twentieth century in some parts of the world – notable examples: apartheid in South Africa, and segregation in the United States, and though some vestiges of such discrimination are still to be found, Islam never approved of such discrimination, and abolished it from its conception.

According to noted contemporary scholar on comparative religion John Esposito, "Despite the recent example of the Taliban in Afghanistan and sporadic conflicts between Muslims and Christians in Sudan, Nigeria, Pakistan, and Indonesia, theologically and historically Islam has a long record of tolerance."[4] Contemporary scholar Jeffrey Lang observes that the historical record of intolerance by Christians was a sharp contrast.[5] As Mustafa Akyol notes, Saladin who reconquered Jerusalem from Christians in 1187 showed extraordinary humaneness in dealing with his vanquished enemies, which won the praise of even the Christians. This was in sharp contrast to the indiscriminate killings of all the Saracens and the Turks by Christian Crusaders in 1099 and of thousands of Muslims by the later Crusaders.[6] As Bernard Lewis puts it, "At no point do the basic texts of Islam enjoin terrorism and murder. At no point [...] do they even consider the random slaughter of uninvolved bystanders."[7]

Also worthy of note, as many writers of Islam point out, is the historical example of the Prophet Muhammad setting a precedent of peaceful and cooperative interreligious relations in Medina among Muslims, Christians, and Jews. However, the continuing sectarian strife among Sunnis, Shiites, Ahmadiyas, and intermittent clashes between Muslims and Christians, between Muslims and Hindus are matters that deserve strong condemnation from the Quranic point of view. The ideology of terrorists – the al Qaeda and other extremist groups among so-called Muslims who are perpetrating most heinous crimes against humanity – does not belong to Islam.

The Quran permits avenging any wrong done to a person

in the like manner, but at the same time encourages patience and forgiveness in lieu of revenge, as forgiveness helps a person expiate his sin:

> 5:45 And We prescribed for them (the Children of Israel) therein (in the Torah): Life for life, and the eye for the eye, and the nose for the nose, and the ear for the ear, and the tooth for the tooth, and (like) retaliation for wounds; but whoever forgoeth (forgiveth) it, it shall be expiation for him. Whoever judge not by that which God hath revealed are wrongdoers.
>
> 16:126 If ye punish, then punish with the like of that wherewith ye were afflicted. But if ye endure patiently, that is indeed the best for those who are patient.

What could be a better appeal for tolerance? The Quran has urged similar patience, generosity, and forgiveness in several other verses (2:263; 3:134; 7:198-199; 42:43; 45:14). It is a well-known historical fact that the Prophet Muhammad set a glorious precedent of tolerance when he and the Muslims accompanying him triumphantly marched into Mecca in 630 A.D. without any significant bloodshed or harm to the inhabitants who had earlier fought with the Muslims. According to the Historian von Grunebaum, "The resistance of a small group of Quraish was quickly dispelled [...]. The revolution was effected remarkably leniently. [...] even the extremist leaders were shown mercy. Looting was forbidden [...]."[8] Such political and religious tolerance in the treatment of people who had been archenemies before has no parallel in history. It is indeed a great irony that in recent years there has been a sharp surge in sectarian violence and killings between Sunnis and Shiites in Iraq, Pakistan, and Syria. The United Nations has estimated that thousands of people have been victims of sectarian violence in recent months in Iraq alone. Iran's

Foreign Minister Mohammad Javad Zarif has recently told the BBC that the sectarian violence between Sunnis and Shiites is probably the worst threat to world security.[9] This unseemly development is certainly a flagrant violation of the Quranic direction.

God considers human life sacred and forbids taking any life except by way of justice (6:151). He characterizes the killing of a human being without any legitimate reason as like the killing of all humankind, and the saving of a human being as like the saving of all humankind (5:32).

Critics have circulated misgivings about Islam on the basis of the Hadith and citations from the Quran that have been taken out of context. A few examples are as follows:

2:191 And slay them wherever ye find them.

9:5 When the sacred months have passed, slay the idolaters wherever you find them, and take them, and confine them, and lie in wait for them at every place of ambush.

9:29 Fight those who believe not in God or the Last Day, nor hold that forbidden which hath been forbidden by God and His Apostle, nor hold the religion of truth of the People of the Book.

Look, however, at the following fully cited verses, which provide the worldview of the Quran:

2: 190-3 *Fight in the way of God against those who fight against you, but initiate not aggression. Verily God loveth not aggressors. And slay them wherever ye find them, and drive them out of the places wherefrom they drove you out, for persecution is* worse than slaughter. And fight not with them at the Sacred Mosque until they first attack you there, but if they attack you (there), then slay them. Such is the reward of disbelievers. But if they desist, then verily God is Ever Forgiving, Most Merciful. And fight them until there is no more persecution, and religion is for God. But if they desist, let there be no hostility except against the wrongdoers.

These and similar verses amply illustrate the peaceful nature of the Quranic message, which never encourages aggressive wars, but allows fighting only for self-defense (2:190-193, 256; 4:91; 60:8-9). Note also that the verse (9:5) is followed by another verse, which exhorts the Prophet Muhammad to provide protection or asylum to idolaters who seek such protection (9:6). The verse (9:29) is also followed by a statement that reads "until they pay *zijya* (the poll tax)." Critics point out, however, that the idea of a special poll tax to be paid by disbelievers living in a Muslim territory to the Muslim rulers is in itself a form of religious discrimination and intolerance. However, as Abou El Fadl points out, such a levy should be understood in a historical context when "it was common inside and outside of Arabia to levy poll taxes against alien groups." The tax was in return for protection of the disbelievers. He cites the example of a case of return of the poll tax by the second Caliph Umar to an Arab Christian tribe when it could not be protected from Byzantine aggression. During Umar's time, he allowed the Christian tribes to pay *zakat* instead of the *zijya* that they regarded as degrading. Abou El Fadl further notes that the Prophet Muhammad did not collect the poll tax from all non-Muslim tribes, and he in fact paid periodic sums of money or goods to many non-hostile non-Muslim tribes. "In short," he further notes, "there are various indicators that the poll tax is not a theologically mandated practice, but a functional solution that was adopted as a response to a particular set of historical circumstances. Only an entirely ahistorical reading of the text could conclude that it is an essential element in a divinely sanctioned program of subordinating the nonbeliever."[10]

The Turkish-American scholar Edip Yuksel, in addition to the verses cited above (2:191; 9:5, 29), refers to also other verses of the Quran, which are abused by uninformed critics and enemies of Islam to portray Islam as a religion of violence, war, and terror: 3:28, 85; 5:10, 34; 9:28, 123; 14:17; 22:9; 25:52; 47:4 and 66:9. In his Reformist Translation of the Quran as well as in his new book *Peacemaker's Guide to Warmongers: Exposing Robert Spencer, David Horowitz, and Other Enemies of Peace*, he discusses these verses to effectively refute the contentions of the critics of Islam. He aptly notes:

> The Quran does not promote war; but encourages us to stand against aggressors on the side of justice. War is permitted only for self-defense (See 2:190, 192, 193, 256; 4:91; 5:32; 8:19; 60:7-9). We are encouraged to work hard to establish peace (47:35; 8:56-61; 2:208). The Quranic precept of promoting peace and justice is so fundamental that peace treaty with the enemy is preferred to religious ties (8:72).[11]

The Quran mandates that we pursue justice (16:90, 3:18, 4:58) and be firm in justice, even if it goes against ourselves, our parents, and near relatives, rich or poor (4:135). He urges us not to depart from justice even if we may have malice or enmity against anybody (5:8). This call for upholding justice is essentially a call for peace and tolerance as well. "When we achieve justice for all – women, men, black, white, yellow, brown, red, Muslim, non-Muslim – we make it possible to forge a lasting peace."[12]

Also importantly, the war-like verses of the Quran, as cited above, should be understood only in the context of a war situation where Muslims are urged to fight only for defensive purposes against those who fight with them. Indeed, as Karen Armstrong aptly notes,

> During the ten years between the *hijra* and his death in 632 Muhammad and his first Muslims were engaged in a desperate struggle for survival against his opponents in Medina and the Quraysh of Mecca, all of whom were ready to exterminate the *ummah*. In the West, Muhammad has often been presented as a warlord, who imposed Islam on a reluctant world by force of arms. The reality was quite different; Muhammad was fighting for his life, was evolving a theology of the just war in the Koran with which most Christians would agree, and never forced anybody to convert to religion. Indeed the Koran is clear that there is to be 'no compulsion in religion.' In the Koran war is held to be abhorrent; the only just war is a war of self-defense. Sometimes it is necessary to fight in order to preserve decent values, as Christians believed it necessary to fight against Hitler.[13]

Also note that, citing some Quranic verse, some allege that Islam discourages Muslims from making friends with the people of other religions. Again, this is another classic example of misgivings based on the citation of a Quranic verse out of context. The Quran does not discourage making friends with the people of other religions unless such people can be identified as real foes (60:7-9). Also, the Quran unequivocally forbids and denounces any acts of mischief, violence, or terrorism (7:56; 26:183).

Note, however, that it is the Hadith literature that contains many texts, which misguide Muslims and lead them to entertain a wrongly understood *jihadist* agenda and commit acts of violence against other religious groups. However, a proper understanding of Islam must dismiss such Hadith texts as not representing genuine Islam.[14]

Pluralism

In today's world, most nations have a diverse religious landscape that requires not just tolerance but a pluralistic paradigm that guarantees freedom of religion, freedom of expression, and freedom of association with democratic principles. The case for pluralism is reinforced in the modern context when Muslims live as minority groups in non-Muslim countries, where they like to enjoy equal treatment from the state, fair treatment from other religious groups, and freedom to practice their faith without any encumbrance. God wants us not to give away things to others that we ourselves would not like to receive (2:267). This means that we need to be as good and kind to others as we are to ourselves. This is the Golden Rule. It implies that Muslims should treat other faith groups in the same way they would like themselves to be treated by their counterparts. As pluralism advocate and activist Mike Ghouse puts it, "Pluralism is not a set of rules, it is simply the attitude of live and let live religiously, politically, culturally, cusinically [sic] and socially. [...] It is respecting the otherness of others."[15]

Islam as professed by the Quran recognizes the diversity of nations and laws (10:99; 49:13; 5:48) and underscores the need for, and the importance of, inter-communal tolerance and harmony.

> 49:13   O humankind! Verily We have created you of a male and a female, and have made you nations and tribes that ye may know one another. *Verily the most honorable in the sight of God is the one who is the most righteous.*
>
> 5:48   For each of you We have prescribed a law and a way. Had God willed, He could have made you one

community, but that He may try you by that which He hath given you. *So vie ye one with another in good deeds.*

There is a spiritual dimension to the need for a pluralistic approach to all of humanity. We all are servants of God, and we need to serve our fellow beings, regardless of color, sex, race, or religion (90:12-18). In the Quran, the Prophet was urged to invite non-Muslims to Islam with wisdom and a fair exhortation and reason with them in a nice manner (16:125). He said to them, "I am commanded to be just among you. God is our Lord and your Lord. Unto us our works, and unto you your works; there is no contention between us and you" (42:15). He made a passionate call to Jews and Christians to come to a co-operative moral agreement for the common good:

> 3:64 Say: O People of the Book! *Come to an agreement between us and you that we shall serve none but God, and (that) we shall associate no partners with Him, and (that) none of us shall take from among ourselves lords or patrons beside God. And if they turn away, then say: Bear witness that we are they who have submitted (unto Him).*

This was a constructive, pluralistic engagement with other faith communities for a common good. Harvard University Professor and Pluralism Project Director Diana Eck says that pluralism means not just diversity, but constructive inter-faith dialogue and engagement to seek understanding of one another and achieve the common good.[16]

The Quran requires Muslims to do justice even to those whom they hate (5:8, 2). Being a Muslim means that he or she should be helpful to others, no matter whoever they are. Our

Prophet gave refuge or asylum to pagans who sought such asylum, even during wartime (9:6). The *salam* verses of the Quran that ask us to turn away peacefully from others' idle talks or other talks that we may not like with *salam* or peace to the others are a call for both tolerance and pluralism (25:63, 28:55, 43:89). The Quran recognizes the sanctity of the worship places of different faith groups – monasteries, churches, synagogues, and mosques where God's name is remembered (22:40). This is a very important verse that provides a very strong support for pluralism. Historically, other faith groups were allowed to practice their faiths peacefully and their churches, synagogues, and temples were allowed to stay as they were in countries conquered by Muslims and there were few forced conversions to Islam.

Ironically, however, in recent years Muslims worldwide have reacted very adversely to certain events such as the Danish cartoons of the Prophet Muhammad, the planned and mock burning of the Quran by an individual Christian pastor Terry Jones in the United States, and the promotion of a movie that vilifies the Prophet of Islam, titled *Innocence of Muslims*. All these events were no doubt provocative, disgraceful, and disgusting. But the violent reactions that followed in Muslim countries against foreign embassies and minority faith communities were even more disgraceful. Such adverse reactions reflected the intolerant nature of many Muslims. Had they embraced tolerance and pluralism and gracefully ignored the criticism of the Prophet, the Quran, and Islam, things would have been much nicer. Recently, Muslims as well as other faith groups in the United States set an excellent example of tolerance and pluralism when they peacefully responded to anti-Muslim hate advertisements on government owned public transit systems in cities around the country.[17]

Human Rights

Tolerance and pluralism, as discussed above, and

socioeconomic justice and human egalitarianism, as discussed in the previous chapter, make the essential foundation for the recognition, promotion, and protection of human rights. The United Nations Human Rights High Commissioner's Office defines human rights as "rights inherent to all human beings, whatever our nationality, place of residence, sex, national or ethnic origin, colour, religion, language, or any other status. We are all equally entitled to our human rights without discrimination." The state has a key role to promote and protect human rights. None should be deprived of his or her rights except in specific cases with a due process. For example, a person's liberty should not be restricted unless he is found to be guilty of a crime by a court of law.

With the progress of human civilization, the end of two world wars, and that of the colonial era, man has made important advances toward tolerance, pluralism, and recognition of human rights. According to a recent United Nations report, the international community has made some notable progress in this direction in the recent past. The adoption of the Universal Declaration of Human Rights (UDHR) in 1948 marks a significant milestone toward recognition of inalienable human rights. Since then national and international laws have been enacted, and numerous international human rights instruments, including particularly a treaty to ban racial discrimination, have been adopted. Progress also includes the defeat of apartheid in South Africa.[18] Yet acts of intolerance, including acts of religious and ethnic violence, continue unabated, and slavery and slavery-like practices still exist in parts of the world. Writing in 2002, a United Nations report after the 2001 Durban Conference on Racism, Racial Discrimination, Xenophobia and Related Intolerance made these remarks:

> Despite continuing efforts by the international community, racial discrimination, ethnic conflicts and widespread violence persist

in various parts of the world. In recent years, the world has witnessed campaigns of 'ethnic cleansing'. Racial minorities, migrants, asylum seekers and indigenous peoples are persistent targets of intolerance. Millions of human beings continue to encounter discrimination solely due to the color of their skin or other factors that indicate the race to which they belong.[19]

During 2001-2009, the global situation on racial discrimination continued to remain as disconcerting as before. At the Durban Review Conference held in 2009 at Geneva, UN Secretary General Ban Ki-moon made these inaugural remarks:

> Despite decades of advocacy, despite the efforts of many groups and many nations, despite ample evidence of racism's terrible toll — racism still persists. [...] We see such intolerance in national histories that deny the identities of others, or that reject rightful grievances of minorities who might not share a so-called "official history." We see it emerging in new forms such as human trafficking, whose victims tend to be women and children of low socioeconomic status. Refugees, asylum-seekers, migrant workers and undocumented immigrants are increasingly being stigmatized if not persecuted. A new politics of xenophobia is on the rise. New technologies proliferate hate-speech.

It is, therefore, of utmost importance that nations make concerted efforts to stamp out racism from the globe and uphold and nurture human rights.

Since the time the UDHR has been adopted, the question of its compatibility with Islam has been addressed by both Muslim and non-Muslim scholars and policymakers. To put an Islamic face to human rights, the Cairo Declaration of Human Rights was adopted in 1990. This Declaration affirms human "freedom" and the "right to a dignified life" for all humanity. Yet, as Virginia University Professor Abdulaziz Sachedina rightly objects, by making it subject to conformity with Islamic *shariah*, this Declaration "fails to articulate universal appeal ... beyond the boundaries of the faith community to include all human beings."[20] He contends that Islamic scripture and theology contain the idea of *fitra* or intuitive reasoning, close to the notion of conscience, which implies "universal ethical cognition."[21] This idea then provides the standards for judging right from wrong and makes the UDHR compatible with Islam.

The UDHR would appear in effect to be a good reflector of the fundamental concerns of the Quran for humankind and for each individual's rights to a free, dignified, secure, peaceful, exploitation-free, poverty-free, and decent life. The Quran declares that all sons and daughters of Adam deserve the same dignity (17:70) and only the most righteous are the most honored in the eyes of God (49:13). It forbids us to deprive others of their basic rights (26:183). Persecution is strongly denounced (2:217). Human life is held to be most sacrosanct (5:32). This Scriptural concern for human life and dignity makes Muslims duty-bound to save all people irrespective of race, religion, color, nationality, and similar status from hunger, disease, and deprivation of basic human needs.

One important requirement to safeguard and guarantee peaceful interreligious tolerance, pluralism, and basic human rights is that the state should be faith-neutral or secular. Emory University Professor and human rights activist Abdullahi An-Naim makes a powerful, ingenious case for a secular state by arguing that religious freedom itself, as mandated by the Quran, subsumes voluntary compliance on the part of individuals and rules out use of any coercive religious edict by the state. He also points out the abuses and dangers of religious edicts used by the state. For example, the *shariah* apostasy law that makes conversion to another religion from Islam as punishable by death, as being used in some Muslim countries, is not prescribed in the Quran and runs counter to its own direction for religious freedom.[22] Secularism does not mean absence of, or animosity to, any religion. It simply works as a guarantor of freedom of religion to all faith followers. The same reasons why Muslim minorities in non-Muslim majority countries require full freedom to practice their religion are also applicable to non-Muslim minorities in Muslim majority countries. The apostasy and blaspheme laws in Pakistan and other Muslim countries, including Afghanistan, Nigeria, and Saudi Arabia that treat Muslim's conversion to another religion and defaming the Prophet, Islam, and the Quran as punishable with death are not consistent with the Quranic messages that allow full freedom of religion and freedom of expression.

The Quran mandates not only freedom of religion (18:29, 2:256, 109:6, 10:99) but also freedom of expression (4:140, 73:10). It explicitly allows human free will (13:11; 18:29; 76:3; 91:7–10), which is really the basic foundation of religion, since without free will human beings could not be made liable for their deeds. It discourages public utterance of hurtful speech except by one who has been wronged (4:148). The statement "Bear with what they say and part from them in a nice manner" (73:10) guarantees freedom and tolerance of speech.

According to the Quran, all men and women are equal in the eyes of God; only virtuousness determines who is nearer to Him (3:195; 4:124; 16:97; 33:35). The best in God's sight is one who is best in righteous conduct (49:13). There is thus no room for racial discrimination in Islam. Likewise, there is no room for misogyny in Islam, understood from the Quranic perspective. Even though women are treated as inferior to men in traditional Islam, the Quran does not approve of such discrimination. The ideal vision of relationship between husband and wife that the Quran depicts is that of mutual love and respect, mutual kindness and support, and equality and complementarity (30:21; 4:19; 7:189; 25:74; 2:228). The Quran grants women rights over men similar to those of men over women (2:228).[23] Nor is there any rationale for discrimination on the basis of any religion in name (2:62; 5:69). For that matter, no other reason, e.g., wealth or property, strength in manpower, or status or power in society, is of any value to God (9:55, 69; 10:58, 88–89; 28:76–81; 30:39; 34:37; 43:32–35; 111:2). Islam is unequivocally against slavery and slavery-like practices, human domination of one group over another group, and chauvinism and imperialism. Socioeconomic egalitarianism, as discussed in the previous chapter, is a major hallmark of Islam.

Upholding the cause of justice is critical to the protection of human rights. As mentioned before, the Quran strongly enjoins upon us justice (4:58, 135; 5:8). The Quran urges us not to bribe judges to immorally grab others' property or to distort justice (2:188). It urges us to give the right testimony even if it goes against ourselves, parents, and near relatives (4:135) and to do justice even to those whom we may hate (5:8). It urges us to give right measure and not deprive others of their rights. It urges us to maintain proper criminal justice in society – to punish people proportionately to their crimes and, where appropriate, to forgive them without jeopardizing the cause of justice.

The Quran strongly condemns the intolerance, violence, and terrorism that are currently being orchestrated by Muslim extremists in various parts of the world. In the Quran, God has clearly and strongly warned humankind against any act of wrongdoing, murder, corruption, or mischief in the land (5:32; 7:56, 74; 13:25; 26:151–152, 183; 27:48–49; 47:22–23).

The Quran guarantees private initiative and enterprise and the right to private ownership of property (2:188), subject to the understanding that it would be used also for amelioration of the conditions of the poor and disadvantaged segments of society. It envisions an exploitation-free economic system, as discussed in Chapter IX. The Quran requires us to stand and fight for human rights and against human oppression (4:75). Thus human rights abuses that are being committed from time to time by governments or religious or ethnic groups are things that deserve strong condemnation from Islam.

VII. What Makes Us Righteous?

> Verily the most honourable in the sight of God is the best in righteous conduct. – *The Quran*, 49:13

Endowed with the Divine Spirit (*ruh*) (15:29; 32:9; 38:72) and worthy of reverence even by Jinn and angels (2:30-34; 7:11), the human species has cognitive abilities that give it a distinct superiority over all other living beings. However, man is also prone to making mistakes. If he does not intelligently exercise his abilities, the consequences may not turn out to be good for him.

> 7:179 Already We (God) have cast into hell many of the Jinn and humankind, *those who have hearts with which they comprehend not, eyes with which they see not, and ears with which they hear not.* They are like the cattle; nay, they are worse! These are they who are neglectful.

Our schools and universities may produce scholars and technocrats, but they do not necessarily turn out good and wise men and women. Even scientists who do not believe in God recognize the great importance of the moral and ethical lessons that religion teaches. Indeed the very foundation for maintaining harmony and beauty in human relationships would have been severely shaken if moral values were not honoured by humankind and nurtured in society in some way. In Albert Einstein's apt words:

> The most important human endeavour is the striving for morality in our actions. Our inner balance and our very existence depend on it. Only morality in our actions can give

> beauty and dignity to life. To bring this [as] a living force and bring it to clear consciousness is perhaps the foremost task of education.[1]
>
> Our time is distinguished by wonderful achievements in the field of scientific understanding and the technical applications of those insights. Who would not be cheered by this? But let us not forget that knowledge and skills alone cannot lead humanity to a happy and dignified life. Humanity has every reason to place the proclaimers of high moral standards and values above the discoverers of objective truth. What humanity owes to personalities like Buddha, Moses, and Jesus ranks far higher than all the achievements of the inquiring and constructive mind. What these blessed men have given us we must guard and try to keep alive with all our strength if humanity is not to lose the dignity, the security of its existence and its joy in living.[2]

It is the violation of the pristine values and ethos of religion that causes human corruption, strife, and misery in the world. The twentieth century has witnessed the occurrence of two great world wars. Strife and conflicts remain unabated in various parts of the world. With all the arms build-up worldwide and arms race, and above all, with nuclear arms proliferation going apace, the world stands at a tipping point. Despite unprecedented economic prosperity and material progress the world has achieved to date, the need for strict observance of morality on the part of man or that for its effective enforcement by society has not diminished at all, but has rather increased, in modern time.

The most emphasized, recurrent theme of the Quran is that righteousness (*taqwa*) is the key to success. *Taqwa* means God-fear, God-consciousness, or moral and ethical uprightness. God-consciousness drives one to be truly and thoroughly upright or righteous. Religious practices – prayer, fasting and pilgrimage –

and also spending in God's way and living in harmony with others in society are all deeds of righteousness. But there is much more than these deeds to what constitutes righteousness. In this chapter, we turn our attention to other righteous deeds that belong to two major groups – one relating to what we believe, feel, and think with our heart and mind and the other relating to our overt actions.

Getting Our Mindset (*Iman*) Right

Whatever we do with our heart, mind, or body counts. Our beliefs and attitudes determine our personality and behavior patterns.

> 2:284   And *whether ye make known what is in your minds or conceal it, God will bring you to account for it.*

William James says, "[H]uman beings, by changing the inner attitudes of their minds, can change the outer aspects of their lives." The collective mindset of a nation determines how fast it can develop. The relative underdevelopment of the Muslim community in general in various regions of the world today is, in some significant measure, to do with the kind of mindset they generally have, which can be traced largely to the influence that has come from the Hadith literature.[3]

We need to set our metaphysical beliefs right. The Quran requires us to believe in one All-Transcending God, the Day of Resurrection (the Last Judgment or Afterlife), Jinn and angels, His revelations, and the prophets who have received such revelations (2:177; 6:100). As mentioned in Chapter I citing Fazlur Rahman, the ideas such as those of God (One God - *tawhid*) and the Judgment Day are not just intellectual postulates to be believed in, but are essential foundations for our religiomoral experience. Chapter II has outlined the rationale for the need for our belief in one God. The most significant implication of the belief in God is that we accept, or submit to, all that God represents or stands for – truth, reason, justice, knowledge, guidance, power, and all that is good, beneficial, noble, and beautiful.

Belief in God also implies belief in God's inexorable Laws, which means that we must believe in cause succeeded by commensurate effect. This is belief in a rational God, i.e., in reason. There is no room for fanaticism in religion. Thus the causal relationship does mean that what we get is according to what we earn or deserve. This point, along with the topic of divine predestination, has already been covered in some detail in Chapters I and II. Here we may make just a couple of passing remarks.

The Quran does not encourage the popular myth that everything that happens is due to fate, i.e., is predestined by God, unrelated to one's work, and that reliance on God means a blind dependence on Him. Such a belief is rather fatalism or fatalistic attitude that belies God's Laws or the logical system. Fatalism or blind dependence on God, which negates the relevance of man's own efforts is, therefore, not only a real obstacle for one's spiritual progress, but a great impediment to overall human progress and should, therefore, be shunned.

At the same time we need to note that belief in God's Laws or the logical system also implies that we need to be mentally ready to accept, and readily accept, what cannot be escaped or avoided. This is what really means accepting the given set of facts or factors, that have already been predetermined by factors, and which man must live with. The given set of predetermined facts or factors is so to say God-given or God-willed. One needs to believe in this kind of *taqdir* or predetermined fate or destiny, and this is not fatalism or predestination. However much we may detest the idea, because of hereditary, environmental, and societal reasons, such fate or destiny does play a part in human life.

Resurrection (*qiyamat*), into afterlife (*akhirat*) or the Judgment Day is necessary in order that God can reward those who are righteous and let those who do wrong get their proper recompense (10:4; 34:3-6). It has its rationale in the very conception of the evolutionary process that is at play throughout the Universe. Good deeds need to be appropriately appreciated, rewarded, and encouraged for the doers so that they can carry forward and perfect their deeds. If a man commits wrongs or follies in his life and dies before he can correct his follies, he needs to be resurrected after death to do so and complete the process of mending his follies in his afterlife.[4]

Getting our mindset right requires us to get rid of hypocrisy or pretension. The Quran condemns it in strongest possible terms: "Surely, the hypocrites are at the bottom of the fire" (4:145). God renders the actions of the hypocrites vain (47:28). A hypocrite requires much greater effort to mend his conduct and wash away his sin. Treachery is akin to hypocrisy. God does not love the treacherous (4:107; 22:38). One needs to shun pretension the way the celebrated eleventh/twelfth century Muslim thinker al-Ghazali did. Once Ghazali suffered from his existential crisis because he was "'seeking leadership and fame' [...] [and] delighted in putting people down 'out of haughtiness and arrogance and being dazzled by his own endowment of skill in speech and thought and expression, and his quest of glory and high status.'" When he realized his pretensions, he shunned them and embarked on a spiritual course of self-rectification and self-purification.[5]

Getting frustrated is another negative factor for us. Recent surge of interest in the power of positive attitude and thinking, as evidenced by many books, lectures, and courses on this subject, highlights the great importance that the nurturing of a positive attitude assumes. Frustration reflects an extreme form of dissatisfaction with one's own situation, performance, achievement, or progress, but is the wrong way of looking at the result of one's own effort. Frustration implies a complete lack of confidence in one's own self, i.e., in one's own capacity and potential, which in effect reflects a lack of faith in God Himself. None needs to despair of better days ahead or of God's spirit (*ruh*) or mercy (39:53-54; 12:87). It is none but the ungrateful or rejecters (*kafirs*) who despair of His mercy (12:87). In this context, we need also to note that, as modern medical science has brought to our attention, frustration taking the form of depression may in many cases just be a medical condition – a mental disease. In such cases, mere advice does little to alleviate their problem. Like other illnesses, such depressive mental conditions need to be medically treated with appropriate medicine coupled with other therapies, where necessary.

Feelings such as ingratitude, pride, imprudence, complacency, lust, apathy, hatred, hostility, cowardice, jealousy, greed, and generally fear, anger, bitterness, and suspicion are of the wrong kind, which retard one's spiritual development. Feelings such as contentment, gratitude, love, appreciation, and empathy are of the appropriate kind, which elevate human personality and help one evolve spiritually. Feelings of complacency or the arrogant feelings of self-achievement and smug self-satisfaction, imprudence, and pride are at the root of self-destruction. Displeasure at one's own work or achievement may inspire one to do further work, while pleasure or happiness at the plight of others is the wrong attitude.

Embracing an attitude of humility or modesty is the gateway for us to receive knowledge, get spiritual enlightenment, and make real progress. The servants of God walk on the land with humility and when the ignorant address them, they say Peace (25:63). Pride lies at the root of one's downfall and is a major stumbling block to one's pursuit of spiritual progress. The Quran declares:

31:18-9 Turn not thy cheek scornfully to others nor walk in the land with pride. Surely God loveth not any arrogant boaster. And be modest in thy conduct, and subdue thy voice, for the harshest of the voices is without doubt the braying of the donkey. (See also 17:37; 3:188; 7:146 and 57:23)

Envy or jealousy is akin to vanity or pride. It is one's feeling of discomfort at others' superiority or advantage in some respect and harboring of ill will for others. The Quran states, "Covet not the thing in which God hath made some of you excel others" (4:32). Instead of admiring, or taking inspiration from, another's superiority, the jealous person wishes ill of him, which is a wrong attitude. Such a person feels bad at others' fortune and good at others' misfortune. By being jealous, one shuts the door of one's own spiritual progress. Jealousy in its naked form often leads one to commit wrong deeds and serious crimes. The Prophet Joseph's brothers did not like that he should be loved more by their father, and this jealousy led them to throw infant Joseph into a pit (12:8-9, 15). Jealousy makes one blind to see that another person can be superior and can bring a higher truth. Such jealousy led many in the past to become disbelievers in a new religion brought by a prophet, or to differ on matters of religion, and be divided into different groups (45:17). It is also out of jealousy of one another that Muslims have also become divided into different sects, despite God's clear directive to the contrary (3:103, 105).

Removing hatred or malice against others from our minds is a heavenly quality (7:43, 15 47). The Quran describes Heaven or the heavenly state as one where there is, among other things, no hatred or malice, but only feelings of brotherhood or love in the hearts of the dwellers (7:43, 15:47). It is not hatred but love and empathy, which is conducive to spiritual evolution. Hatred may make one blind to see reason and justice. God warns us not to take as friends those people who nurture hatred (3:118).

Undue fear cripples a man in his pursuit for progress, whether material or spiritual. British political thinker Edmund Burke said: "No passion so effectually robs the mind of all its powers of acting and reasoning as fear."[6] President Franklin D. Roosevelt of the United States once said: "Let me assert my firm belief that the only thing we have to fear is fear itself; nameless, unreasoning, unjustified terror which paralyzes needed efforts to convert retreat into advance."[7] True believers need not be cowards, as they have nothing to fear. They do not have to fear the criticism of others (5:54). God has warned us against fearing people rather than Him (4:77). As noted in Chapter III, God's promised heavenly state for the righteous believers is that of no fear and no grief. Fear comes from devilish thoughts and activities (3:175).

We need also to deal with anger. Anger prevents one from taking a dispassionate look at things. Like hate, it hurts our spiritual pursuit. Anger often leads one to forget sanity. It can damage a noble cause. The Quran describes the righteous believers as those who restrain anger (3:134). God rewards those who depend on their Lord, keep away from great sins and indecencies, and forgive even when they feel angry (42:36-37). God removes rage from the hearts of the believers (9:14-15).

One needs to be moderate and considerate in one's demeanor to others. God commands moderation, not excesses (20:81). God characterizes greed as immoderate conduct (33:19; 68:13; 74:15). This Quranic message about greed is echoed by what one writer said: "The lust of avarice has so totally seized upon mankind that their wealth seems rather to possess them, than they to possess wealth."[8] Egregious greed lies at the root of busts in capitalist economies.

Too much suspicion is not good. Suspecting something, which is not really true, is a manifestation of one's ignorance, meanness, or malevolent attitude. Nothing could perhaps be more embarrassing to one than suspecting a friend to be a foe or to misunderstand him. God has strongly warned us against too much suspicion, spying, and backbiting. And suspicion taking the form of a slander is a grave sin in the eye of God (24:23).

> 49:12 O ye who believe! Avoid much suspicion; for verily suspicion in some cases is a sin. And spy not; nor speak ill of one another behind their backs. Would one of you like to eat the flesh of your dead brother? Ye abhor that. So be careful of (your duty to) God.

A man's goal in life should be self-reliance or independence, though at birth and during childhood and formative years, he needs to be brought up, supported, and nourished by others. Independence is a godly quality (35:15; 47:38; 3:97). It is hardly becoming of a man to seek others' help to do a thing, if he can do it himself. This should not, however, be interpreted to mean that we are not indirectly dependent on others' work and help all the time. This indirect dependence is unavoidable, as all in society are interdependent in some way or other. The independence we need is that from seeking unilateral help from others without a *quid pro quo*, i.e., which amounts to begging. Dependence in the form of begging is a curse, degrading to human soul.

Feelings of contentment, gratitude, and appreciation are good virtues. One needs to be contented with what one has or gets. Gratitude springs from contentment. Whoever is grateful to God for all that he gets or enjoys in life is grateful for his own soul, i.e., for his own spiritual benefit (31:12). God loves the grateful (39:7). He gives more to people who are grateful to Him (14:7). God does not love the unfaithful and the ungrateful (2:276; 22:38). This also does imply that a person needs to show proper recognition or appreciation of others' work, which essentially amounts to expressing gratitude to God.

It is indeed a pitiable sight that Muslims are found to engage in bitter internecine and sectarian suspicion, animosity, violence, and killing in various parts of the world. One shudders to think how Sunni and Shiite Muslims are killing one another on an alarming scale in Iraq! The brotherhood of amity and love that once characterized the Muslim *ummah* has long been found missing among Muslims. They have forgotten, and are not paying enough attention to, the clear, invaluable message of their Holy Book.

Getting Our Other Actions Right

Just as other religions do, Islam teaches us the fundamental moral values of truthfulness, honesty, justice, and kindness. The true servants of God are truthful, just as God is. They always keep their word (2:177; 3:17; 13:20; 33:23). God advises us to be correct or straightforward in our words (33:70), to establish and uphold justice, and not hesitate to testify truthfully even against ourselves, and our parents and relatives, whether they be rich or poor (4:135), and to never mix truth with falsehood nor knowingly conceal the truth (2:42). God admonishes us to be with, or to stand for, those who are truthful (9:119). He wants us to keep our firm pledges when we make them (16:91). He wants us to restore trusts to their owners, and judge justly between people (4:58). He curses those who, among other things, break their promise after confirming it and make mischief in the land (13:25).

By lying we not only deceive others, we also deceive ourselves. Thereby we undermine the value of our words and lose our credibility. That way we degrade and lose our own self and lose the right to command love and respect of others. Falsehood and dishonesty carry the germs of all kinds of injustice, mischief, and corruption. It is a great pity and travesty of religion that we find people galore who appear as religious, yet who do not even

What Makes Us Righteous?

slightly hesitate to tell lies, who are not straightforward in their talk, and who are basically dishonest. They are obviously not truly religious. Dishonesty may manifest itself in various forms: insincere speech, insincere work, deliberate misinformation, deliberate improper judgment, and deception and corruption of all kinds.

While we need generally to keep our promises, at the same time we should not make our unjust or unjustifiable promises a barrier for doing good or make them for deceiving others. The Quran warns:

> 16:94 Make not your oaths a device of deceit between you, lest a foot should slip after being firmly planted; and ye should taste evil because ye debarred (men) from the path of God, and yours will be a grievous punishment.

God enjoins upon us justice, fairness or equity, and kindness in all of our actions and behavior (16:90, 76; 5:8; 42:41-42; 2:188; 17:34; 49:9; 4,127, 135; 58; 55:9; 60:8; 65:2). It forbids wrongful devouring of others' property and willful bribing of judges in order to grab others' property (2:188). It condemns unjust grabbing of orphans' property in particularly strong terms, and likens this to the swallowing of fire into one's bodies (4:10). It admonishes man not to go near to orphans' property except with good intentions (17:34) and to manage their property with fairness and restore such property to them when they become adults or attain understanding (4:5-6).

The Quran testifies that among the People of the Book (the Jews and the Christians), there are such honest people as can be trusted with a heap of treasure, while there are others who cannot be trusted even with a single coin; they will not return it unless one is after them. They do so mistakenly thinking that they have no duty to the gentiles. They have no such warrant from God, and they knowingly lie concerning God (3:75). This verse is a pointer to Muslims that there are good and honest people in other communities as well and that Muslims also have no warrant from God to think that they have no duty to other communities or to brand all people of other communities as untrustworthy.

God wants us to be kind, generous, and forgiving as far as possible (2:263; 3:134; 7:198-199; 42:43; 45:14), even when we can legitimately take revenge for any wrongs done to us (5:45; 42:40). We need to be good and kind to our parents, relatives, orphans, the poor and the needy, the neighbors – whether relatives or strangers, fellow-travelers and the wayfarers, and the slaves (4:36; 6:151; 17:23-24; 2:83, 215; 4:36; 19:14, 32; 29:8; 31:14-15; 46:15; 71:28) and we need to speak kindly to humankind (2:83). We have a special duty to our parents. Indeed God wants us not to say even "Fie" to them, or to show any indication of annoyance with them. Man generally gives preference to his own children over his parents. But the Quran says:

4:11 Your parent or your children: Ye know not which of them is nearer unto you in usefulness. (See also 46:15)

Parents, however, must not be obeyed if they misguide and insist on associating partners with God; yet we need to treat them well and live with them with kindness (31:15).

As noted in Chapters 2 and 3, living morally is a critical precondition for one's spiritual development. Along with honesty and integrity, a vital trait of character of a righteous person is decency in his sexual conduct. It is a major area deserving our attention, an area where man fails the most and where he needs to be guided the most. Chastity, restraint in married life and learning to love without any touch of lewdness – these are the valuable lessons one can learn from the Quran as criteria or norms for sexual decency (17:32, 5:5, 79:40-41, 7:28). The Prophet Muhammad was strictly exhorted by God not to pay attention to that with which man enjoys worldly life (20:131). He was also urged by God to give similar advice to his wives (33:28). Neither he nor his wives, who were like mothers to the believers, thus could be perceived to have cared much for worldly, carnal pleasures (20:131; 33:28-34; 60:12; 66:3-5).

The Quran advises man to remain chaste as long as he cannot afford to get married (24:33). It asks believing men and women to lower their gaze and guard their modesty (24:30-31). It urges believing women to put on proper dresses to cover their private parts and bosoms, except what is ordinarily apparent and not to display their beauty and strike their feet in such a way as may look or sound like invitation to indecency (24:31; 33:59). It urges sexual restraint in married life (5:5; 79:40-41). It wants us not to go near to acts of indecency, whether open or secret (6:151] and to avoid sin, whether open or hidden (6:120). If somebody commits a sin, and then blames it on the innocent, he carries the burden of both a false charge and a flagrant sin (4:112).

Adultery or fornication (*zina*) is a great sin in the sight of God (17:32). The Quran makes such acts punishable in a stern manner (4:15-16; 24:2-4) unless the committers of such a sin repent sincerely and mend their conduct (4:16-17; 24:5). It is ironic that the laws in western countries enacted by legislatures do not consider consensual premarital or extra-marital relationship as punishable fornication, which the Quran does. It is reckless sexual behavior that is primarily responsible for the spread of the HIV[9], the virus that causes the AIDS[10] disease. This disease is a modern-day scourge in many countries – especially in Africa, where it has already turned into an alarming epidemic, not only causing a heavy toll of death and immense human suffering, including turning a huge number of children into orphans, but also having enormous adverse impact on overall economic and social development.

Doing any harm to others includes discourteous or harsh treatment, or doing any acts of mischief, violence, torture, injury, and killing. The Quran teaches us to be duly polite to others in conversation and arguments (2:83; 16:125; 29:46), to greet or salute others or to return the salutation, if possible with an even better greeting (4:86; 24:27, 61; 25:63; 33:56), to be duly polite and respectful to those who are superior (2:104; 4:46; 24:62-63; 33:56-57; 58:11; 49:1-5], to enter a house not without the due permission and greeting of its inmates (24:27-29), to seek permission to enter rooms of couples at specified private times (24:58-59), and not to ridicule or mock others (49:11; 23:110).

God's direction to us that we should return the greeting of others with even a better greeting, or with a similar greeting in the least, conveys a deeper message calling for maintaining cordial human relationship that we need to foster among ourselves. Building such relationship in society is precisely the way we can create an environment of durable peace, friendship, and harmony in society.

We should duly respect and obey those who command knowledge and legitimate authority (4:59). Indeed, a good measure of our respect to the superiors is whether we listen carefully to what they say and whether we sufficiently respond to their sound advice. We should not ask too many questions, which hardly make any sense or which, if answered, may cause trouble (5:101-102).

The yardstick by which we can judge whether we are being rude or unfair to others is that of whether or not we are crossing or transgressing the limits of decency. A conscientious person can judge when he is transgressing the limits in his conduct. If he really transgresses the limits, he can feel it, and feels sorry for it. Thus, when the Prophet Moses in his youth wrongfully sided with a person of his own tribe in his quarrel and fight with another

What Makes Us Righteous? 139

person and accidentally killed that person, he could realize that he transgressed the limits and became deeply repentant for his action and asked for God's forgiveness, and vowed to never again side with a wrong person (28:15-17). The Prophet Muhammad possessed an excellent and extra-ordinary character, which is well worth emulating by all believers (33:21; 68:4-6). He could realize – get inspiration from God – if he had, by mistake, any lapse on his part in his conduct with others, which he rectified instantly, e.g., his lack of sufficient attention to a blind man (80:1-11), and his concealment of something in his mind for fear of men when he was trying to bring about a rapprochement in the marital relation of Zaid with Zainab (33:37), because of which he was inspired by God not to fear men, but fear God (33:37).

Among other righteous deeds, which we need to be aware of, and do, when the context arises is the bequest that we should leave for our parents and near relatives when death approaches us. Leaving a written bequest or will before death to parents and near relatives according to reasonable usage is a solemn duty prescribed for us by the Quran (2:180-183, 240; 5:106-108). This provision for making a will before death provides a special opportunity for the dying person to make any special considerations for his near relatives who are poor and disadvantaged or for other poor people he may have in mind. The laws of inheritance at death prescribed by the Quran also provide for making a special accommodation for the needs of the poor, including poor relatives, in our property.

> 4:7-8 Men shall have a share in what parents and kinsfolk leave behind, and women shall have a share in what parents and kinsfolk leave behind, whether it be little or much – a share ordained [by God]. And when at the time of distribution (cf inheritance), relatives, orphans, and the needy are present, give them (out of the

property) and speak to them kindly.

If some of the near relatives are poor relative to the others, this consideration should enable the poor ones, including the females, to receive a larger share of the property than the usual distribution rules prescribed in the Quran would warrant.

The Quran states that there is some good in both intoxicants and games of chance, but the evil in them is greater than their good (2:219). Drinks that cause intoxication and trigger irrational and immoral behavior are admittedly not desirable by any norms of civility. Gambling is bad precisely because it often does irreparable damage – material, mental, or spiritual – to the persons who lose the stakes. Drunken driving is a source of accidents and is prohibited by law in many countries. God advises us not to go near to prayer when we are intoxicated and do not understand what we say (4:43). Going to prayer when one is out of one's mind makes no sense. Drugs that cause intoxication, hallucination, or distortion of perception, the use of which is currently so widespread in many countries, also fall in the same category as intoxicants, and hence need to be avoided for both health – both physical and mental health – reasons and good behavior.

Good food is necessary for good health. We need to eat wholesome food and avoid food that may cause us problems. The things God has forbidden us to eat include only meat of animals that die of themselves (carrion), blood, pork, and meat of animals that are sacrificed to entities other than God (2:172-173, 5:3; 6:3-5, 121, 145; 16:115-116; 22:30). The reason given in the Quran for forbidding pork is that the swine is unclean (6:145). Dead animals, the meat (carrion) of which is forbidden, also include the dead through either strangling, beating, falling from a height, or the dead through goring by horns and partially devoured by wild animals (5:3).

Note, however, that whoever is driven by necessity, for him eating the forbidden food is no sin, if he eats it not craving it and not exceeding the limit. For those who go on a pilgrimage to the Holy Kabah, gaming of animals is forbidden during the pilgrimage; but gaming of the sea and its food are lawful (5:95-96). The Quran also mentions of animals with claws or undivided hooves, and some specified fat of oxen and sheep that were prohibited particularly for the Jews. Such prohibitions were specially imposed on them as a measure of punishment to them on account of their rebellion (6:146).

God has warned men against forbidding food that was not forbidden by Him (5:87; 10:59; 16:116). In the past some people unfairly prohibited some food without any divine authority (6:119, 138-139, 143-144). As in the past, despite the clear Quranic direction to the contrary, the Hadith literature mentions some additional foods as unlawful (*haram*) (e.g., the meat of domestic asses as in *Sahih Muslim*, Book 021, Number 4769 And 4772, meat of hedgehog as in *Sunan Abu Dawud*, Book 27, Number 3790, and uncooked garlic as in *Sunan Abu Dawud*, Book 27, Number 3819).

Providing for Criminal Justice

The Quran provides for forgiveness of certain sins or crimes of those who repent and mend their conduct, but at the same time it provides for stern punishment of those who persist in their sins or crimes. Human behavior, which is inimical to decent human and moral values, cannot be allowed even a passive endorsement by society in the name of human rights. Tolerance and human rights must of necessity go with certain obligations on the part of men and women. For the sake of peace, morality, and justice, those who are persistent perpetrators of mischief, violence, tyranny, immorality, and injustice in society need to be dealt with harshly.

The Quran provides for exemplary punishments when the criminals do not repent their sins or crimes, and mend their conduct. One example of such punishments is for war crimes. Those who fight against God or godly values and commit serious crimes like murder and persecution deserve to be dealt a harsh punishment – either killing or crucifixion, or cutting of their hands and feet on alternate sides, or expulsion from the land (or imprisonment) (5:33). Only those who can be exempted from such severe punishment are those who repent (and, by implication, desist from such crimes) before they fall into the hands of those against whom they were fighting (5:34). The traditional interpretation of another verse (5:38) provides another example of an exemplary punishment: cutting off the hands of a thief, whether male or female, for the crime of stealing. However, modern interpretation such as that of Edip Yuksel and others suggests that the punishment for stealing should be limb marking, not limb cutting, which would be a humiliating punishment for the thief.[11] Note however, whether limb cutting or limb marking, such a dire or mild punishment can be waived and the culprit can be forgiven if he or she repents and mends his or her conduct (5:39). Also, the Quran provides for retaliation by capital punishment for deliberate killing without any valid justification – retaliation by the successors of the killed or, by implication, by the judicial system, but it also states that if the successors of the killed make any remission, then a lighter punishment according to usage should be given and compensation should be made to the aggrieved party (2:178-179). There is provision for still lighter punishments or expatiation in the case of accidental killings (4:92).

The Quranic law is thus quite flexible. It is not always necessary then – it is not a hard and fast rule – that a killer, a persecutor, or a mischief-monger, or a thief has to be given the extreme capital or corporal punishment. Those who are the custodians of justice in society need to judge whether the culprits are those who really regret their misdeeds, or whether they are confirmed miscreants in society. The Quran provides for a wide range of choice for them, which can shift from an extreme punishment to a very light one or outright forgiveness. That means that the appropriateness of a particular punishment should be decided by not only the nature of the crime but also by the type of the criminal. This can be illustrated by the example of two boys, one of whom is less naughty than the other. For the same crime, the less naughty boy deserves a lighter punishment than the naughtier one. A simple word of rebuke may be a sufficient punishment for a certain crime for some people. On the other hand, a more responsible person doing a misdeed deserves a greater punishment than a less responsible one doing the same misdeed. That is the reason why the slaves or servants, or those who possess less intelligence or sense, need to be treated more generously and punished less harshly (4:25). By the same token, the mentally ill or deficient persons need to be treated generously. At the same time, in a more civilized society, where crimes are less frequent, punishments can afford to be lighter than in another society, where crimes are more widespread. That is why more and more civilized societies can afford to move further and further away from crude and severe punishments. The criteria to judge which system of justice dispensation is appropriate are whether the punishments being applied are proportionate to the wrongs done and whether such punishments are sufficient deterrents to future crimes. Interpreting Shah Wali Allah, Iqbal aptly notes, "The [particular] Sahri'ah values (ahkam) ... (e.g., rules relating to penalties for crimes) are in a sense specific to [a particular] people; and since their observance is not an end in itself they cannot be strictly enforced to the case of future generations."[12] Eminent contemporary Muslim thinker and scholar of Islamic law Khaled Abou El Fadl notes:

The law helps Muslims in the quest for Godliness, but Godliness cannot be equated to the law. The ultimate objective of the law is to achieve goodness, which includes justice, mercy, and compassion, and the technicalities of the law cannot be allowed to subvert the objectives of the law. Therefore, if the application of the law produces injustice, suffering, and misery, this means the law is not serving its purposes. In this situation, the law is corrupting the earth instead of civilizing it. In short, if the application of the law results in injustice, suffering, or misery, then the law must be reinterpreted, suspended, or reconstructed, depending on the law in question.[13]

Thus the particular forms applied of the Quranic principles can be flexible depending on particular circumstances. This is evident from the following verse of the Quran:

16:126 And if ye punish, let your punishment be proportionate to the wrong that has been done to you; but if ye endure patiently, verily it is better for the patient.

The rigid application of the so-called *shariah* law, which is applied in some Muslim countries, does not, therefore, stand justified in light of the Quran. The Quran does not say that the thief's hands must always be cut off, or that the adulterer and the adulteress must necessarily or always be flogged, or that the killer must always be hanged. Though the Quran provides for flogging of the adulterer and the adulteress (24:2), this should be interpreted as an extreme punishment applicable in cases that do not deserve leniency under any consideration.

In another place, the Quran clearly allows for either punishment or forgiveness in case the guilty persons repent and mend their conduct:

4:16 And as for the two of you who are guilty thereof (of indecency), punish them both. But if they repent and make amends, then leave them alone; for God is Ever Forgiving, Most Merciful.

Media reports covered sensational stories of *shariah hudud* punishments such as stoning of adulteresses and amputations of hands and feet in some countries such as Afghanistan under the Taliban, Saudi Arabia, Iran, Sudan, and Nigeria in recent years. With the ousting of the Taliban regime, the situation in Afghanistan has now changed. Human rights activists denounced these punishments. Though such punishments are not applied in most modern Muslim states, with the rise of orthodox Islamic political tendency, they were reintroduced in the late twentieth century in Pakistan, Iran, Sudan, Afghanistan, and Nigeria.[14] It is indeed regrettable that following the Hadith, the *shariah* courts in these countries, especially Nigeria and Iran, are rigidly applying, or are trying to apply, the punishment of "stoning to death" to those who are guilty of adultery, a punishment that is not in the Quran. Hadith supporters insist that there was a verse calling for this punishment in the Quran, which was inadvertently omitted. But this must be a preposterous claim. Also striking is the fact that such a barbarous and brutal punishment is often meted out to the women involved in such a crime, as their crime is often easier to prove. Another example of a *shariah*-prescribed brutal punishment is killing for apostasy of a Muslim, i.e., of a Muslim converting to another religion, a punishment that is against the very spirit of the Quran, which guarantees full religious freedom and tolerance, and which emphatically proclaims that there must not be any compulsion in religion (See 18:29, 76:3, 2:256 and 10:99 cited earlier).

A recent case in point was that of Abdul Rahman in

Afghanistan, who was declared by the *ulama* an apostate fit for killing, because he converted to Christianity. He was being tried by a court by Afghanistan's *shariah* law, even though, with US-led forces, the country was wrested from the Taliban rule. Under intense pressure of international outcry, his life was spared when the court dismissed his case on technical grounds that he was not mentally fit to stand trial. But the life of Abdul Rahman still remained under threat in Afghanistan. It was good that he got refuge in another country. Abdul Rahman's case highlights the point that it is some Muslim countries or societies where lamentably there is no full religious freedom. Needless to say, the sooner such anti-Quranic punishments are banished from society, the better for society and civilization.

According to Khaled Abou El Fadl, the current practice of Islamic or *shariah* law suffers from the deficiencies of both "a lack of competency [on the part of those who apply it] in the usage of legal objectives and methodologies [of *shariah*]" and the non-development of such objectives and methodologies "to meet contemporary advances in epistemology, hermeneutics, or social theory. In the contemporary age, Muslims end up with a rather ironic and painfully nonsensical paradigm."[15]

As noted above, the Quran provides for some harsh exemplary punishments. Sometimes it may be necessary to apply some of these punishments – if these are deemed necessary to maintain peace, decency, and harmony in society. There is evidently need for introducing harsher, and more effective punishments in countries where corruption and indecency are found to be widespread. But such punishments need to be only selectively and cautiously applied in order not to exceed the extent, which proves sufficient to deter the crimes that we address to eliminate. What we always need to bear in mind is that religion is for us; we are not for religion. God has forbidden us to commit excesses in the name of religion (4:171; 5:77). God is not unduly harsh to humankind. He first sends lighter punishments to see if human beings return from their sins and, when such punishments prove ineffective, He sends the heavier ones (32:21).

Some Concluding Remarks

To become a truly righteous person, and a good Muslim, it is sufficient for us to live according to the guidance provided in the Quran, which is most comprehensive and detailed (2:2; 17:9; 10:57; 16:89). It is not necessary for any religion to spell out everything. God has given us conscience by which we can often judge what is conscionable, right, or decent, and what is unconscionable, wrong, or indecent. It is our responsibility to strive to clear our conscience, purify it, and work according to it for our success, as the Quran itself proclaims (See 91:8-10 cited earlier).

Man is evidently in a state of loss, unless he establishes faith in, and rapport with, God (which essentially means faith in godly values), leads a righteous life, and enjoins on one another truth and patience and perseverance (103:2-3). Righteousness or goodness leads to further guidance or goodness (19:76; 42:23):

> 42:23 And whoever earns any good, We add further good for him. Verily God is Ever Forgiving, Appreciative.

Ahmad beautifully expounds this idea:

> Body and mind generate feelings and also discrimination between what is good and what is evil. Now, every being is prone to good as well as evil. When one gives goodness the upper hand, the evil gradually loses its edge and sustains defeat after defeat and in the long run conceals itself within goodness itself to cut out the ignomiuy of defeat. Then its motive power rather contributes to the expansion of goodness itself [...]. [Likewise,] when a person gives evil the upper hand,

goodness in the long run hides itself in the folds of evil out of shame and even then from within, it warns lest the person turn too bad.[16]

The righteous people are foremost in good deeds (23:61). They are the most civilized creatures (98:7). They are worthy successors (*khalifas*), or inheritors of the earth (6:165; 21:105). And God has promised them the ruler-ship of the world, as they establish the rule of law (or religion), peace, and security (24:55). It is they who create Heaven in the earth, and their afterlife will be still better (16:30, 97).

In a nutshell, believers will do well to heed this wise advice of the Eastern sage Shah Aksaruddin Ahmad:

> Be in Love with God;
> And go along the Path of the Messenger.
> The Path of the Messenger is the Path of the Quran;
> Find the Path in the Quran;
> And serve God, your Lord.
> Fear not Hell;
> Crave not Heaven.
> Being only His lover,
> Care for Him alone; rely on Him alone.
>
> To serve God is to serve humankind,
> Be they disbelievers, polytheists, hypocrites,
> Or be they even sinners.
> Leave it to the Creator of creation to judge;
> It's not your right to judge.
> Seek your own salvation;
> Seek just your own salvation.[17]

VIII. Marriage, Divorce, the Status of Women, and the Treatment of Slaves

> He created from among yourselves your mates that ye may find rest in them, and He placed love and mercy between you. Verily in this are signs for those who reflect. – *The Quran*, 30:21

Marriage

The Quran does not approve of free-style living. It recommends marriage as the proper institution for intimate relationship between a man and a woman. An ideal marriage binds two souls with mutual understanding, love, and mercy (30:21). If both husband and wife live together with such feelings for each other and can keep alive these feelings, such a living becomes a source of constant delight and happiness for each other, and can also turn into a springboard for mutual progress. The Quran asks men to find abundant good in their spouses (4:19). Unlike an animal, a human being needs a matrimonial bond to make a respectable, responsible, and durable family. The family in turn creates a sound basis for procreation of children, who need the loving care and support of a family for their proper upbringing. Such families in turn make the very bedrock of a sound and prosperous civilization. The Quran states:

> 16:72 God hath made for you spouses from among yourselves and through them hath given you children and grandchildren and hath made for you provisions of good things.

A relationship based on cohabitation without marriage stands on a very shaky ground. Reluctance to marry may simply mean that the couple wants to shirk their responsibilities of husband and wife. This relationship can, and is often found to, break up at any time without imposing any obligation on either party. The Quran describes spouses as garments for each other (2:187). Just as men and women need clothes to cover shame, for comfort, a shield against cold and heat, and for adornment, so husband and wife need each other to mutually complement themselves with protection, comfort, and support. Indeed, a man and a woman are endowed with diverse qualities in which they excel each other, and their union culminates in a mingling of such qualities to enrich their living in diverse ways.

To ensure propriety, decency, and happiness in family relations, the Quran forbids one to marry specified close relatives and two sisters at a time (4:22-4). It recommends marriage between persons of similar nature and qualities. Good men or good women need to find respectively good women or men as their spouses. The Quran states that the believing men and women are protecting friends of one another; they enjoin what is right and forbid what is wrong (9:71). That is why God ordains that believing and chaste men and women should marry respectively from among believing and chaste women and men. Idolaters and adulterers, or idolatresses and adulteresses are not lawful respectively to the believing and chaste women or men. For a believing boy or girl, a believing slave girl or boy is better to marry than an unbelieving free girl or boy, even though the latter may be more attractive (2:221 and 24:3). The Quran states:

> 24:26   Vile women are for vile men, and vile men are for vile women. Good women are for good men, and good men are for good women.

If matches in marriages are done properly, wives become in a way reflections of their husbands, just as children are the reflections of their parents. Wives of pious men can expect to have the same pleasant fate of their lives as their husbands (43:68-73).

The Quran, as the Bible, disapproves of same-sex (gay or lesbian) relationship. The homosexual people during the Prophet Lut's time were dealt with a Divine punishment (7:80-84). Such relationship is not an ideal family environment for children who need the love and warmth of both parents. Also, such relationship closes the door to procreation of progeny of their own blood, which is most often another important reason for marriage (16:72, 42:11). Yet, same-sex relationship is gaining increasing social acceptance, inasmuch as ridiculing it makes room for undue human discrimination. Currently, a number of European countries, Canada, Argentina, South Africa, and sixteen states and the District of Columbia in America permit legalized same-sex marriage. Overall though, the heterosexual marriage relationship will continue to remain the predominant social norm.

The spirit of the Quranic message suggests, as does Catholicism, that abstinence is better than artificial measures to control birth. Nor does the Quran approve of the abortion of unintended unborn children, unless it can be justified on wife's legitimate health issues or other complications. Nowadays, artificial birth control measures are widely practiced everywhere and are being advocated and extensively used as a way of controlling population growth. This is being done out of the Malthusian fear that population growth tends to outstrip food production in the world. Though Malthus has been proved wrong long ago, the practice of artificial birth control continues apace, mainly to improve the living standards of families, whether rich or poor. The Quran discourages us to kill children or to take life without justice out of fear of poverty (6:151). The proliferation of artificial birth control measures for use in premarital and extra-marital sexual activities has indeed become a familiar, but unseemly and disgraceful outcome of relationships outside wedlock. This is encouraging promiscuity, giving rise to a growing problem of single mothers, and to a rising trend of couples or women seeking abortion of unintended unborn children from relationships before marriage or outside marriage. In some regions of the world, especially in China and Northern India – in China encouraged in significant measure by a one-child, and just recently introduced relaxed but still very restricted, state policy – wide-scale abortion of unborn baby girls has led to worrying levels of gender imbalance – males far exceeding females.[1]

In some countries, population growth is rather unduly decelerating, or population is declining in absolute terms, where birth control obviously does not make any sense. But where the need for checking high population growth is felt as in many poor developing countries, such control can be encouraged by encouraging abstinence on the part of couples, by encouraging late marriage, and by encouraging education and employment of women in dignified jobs. God has indeed urged those who cannot afford to marry because of financial reasons to postpone their marriage and remain chaste until their financial condition becomes affordable (24:33).

According to verse (5:5) as well as other verses of the Quran (4:4, 19-21; 2:236-237; 33:50), it is incumbent upon a man to give a dowry, according to his means, to his wife, and not the other way round. The practice of dowry giving by a woman's family to her husband, which is found to be prevalent among some groups of people in some regions, is contrary to what the Quran prescribes. Such a practice often creates enormous financial distress for many poor families and therefore, should be strongly discouraged by the state.

The Quran makes a man squarely responsible for bearing the financial burden of his wife and children after they are born. If one cannot afford to marry a free (or, by implication, more

Marriage, Divorce, the Status of Women and the Treatment of Slaves

expensive) woman, he should consider marrying a maid (or, by implication, less expensive woman), and failing even that he should remain unmarried and chaste until he becomes financially solvent to afford a wife (4:25; 24:33).

That man takes responsibility for financially supporting his wife is also mentioned in verse (4:34). However, this should not be taken to mean that a wife should not be allowed to engage in a dignified paying job, should she find one, to supplement the family's income. Women can certainly play some role in making both ends meet, in making a comfortable living, and in shaping a financially better future for their family. Husbands should not stand on their wives' way to seek such roles, unless the work is undignified, and unless such work seriously interferes with family management, including the caring for their children. Both husband and wife should work shoulder to shoulder, if necessary, to make their life materially and spiritually more worthwhile and rewarding. And in modern times, it has been hard for many impoverished families in many, both poor and developed, regions of the world to provide nicely for their livelihood without both husband and wife working.

Monogamy is the natural, ideal choice for a man. Polygamy (polygyny) is not a normal, ideal, or desirable family relationship. It most often destroys the peace and tranquility of family relationship, creating anguish and suffering for the incumbent wife. The Quran permits polygyny, but only in some restricted cases. The restrictions are that husband must be financially solvent enough to support the additional wife or wives and that he should be able to do justice to more than one wife. Unless both conditions are satisfactorily met, one should refrain from considering taking more than one wife. The following verse deserves a close attention:

4:3   If ye fear that ye will not be able to deal justly with the orphans (in giving them their wealth), marry of the women who seem good to you, two, three or four; and if ye fear that ye cannot do justice (to more than one), then just one, or that (the slave girl or captive) whom your right hands possess. This will be more appropriate, that ye will not do injustice.

In another verse, the Quran states: Ye will not be able to do justice between (your) wives, however much ye wish (4:129). This verse underscores the point that it is indeed very hard to accord just treatment to multiple wives. Monogamy is, therefore, always the preferred option. It is striking that the Quran mentions marrying more than one wife only in the context of how we should treat orphans. Polygamy is, however, generally interpreted to extend to taking wives from general women, not simply from orphans, including prisoners of war or slave girls. God's law needs to accommodate possible situations in society, when women outnumber men, for example after warfare when men are killed in substantial numbers, and there remain a greater number of widows or unmarried women than that of unmarried men. In such situations, it will be in the interest of social harmony and welfare to allow one man to take more than one wife. The mandatory restriction of one wife to one man as in some faiths such as Christianity as practiced will in such situations force some women to remain unmarried for life. That cannot be a just social arrangement. Also, a mandatory monogamous requirement may also encourage divorcing of the current wife to take another wife or encourage adulterous extra-marital behaviour in society, which would also be an unhealthy outcome for society. Thus to encourage morals and harmony to prevail in society, it will be in the fitness of things that polygyny is allowed in society.

Polygamous behavior is generally looked down upon in a modern Muslim society, and its practice is found to be waning with more education, greater urbanization, and greater mobility of people within countries and across countries. Some Muslim countries, notably Turkey, Tunisia, and Iran under the late Shah, in effect outlawed polygyny, which was rather too radical. In many other Muslim states, polygyny "has been hemmed in by legal restrictions, and has become socially unacceptable in the urban middle and upper classes, as well as economically impractical for the urban lower classes. Polygamy is now very rare outside the Arabian peninsula, where men have the means and the opportunity."[2]

There is some misperception in certain quarters surrounding the Prophet Muhammad's multiple marriages. We need to note that he married a fifteen year-older Khadijah and lived with her alone for twenty-four years until her death. His other marriages took place in his later years in special circumstances. Several of his wives included aged war widows of his friends who left many children, some being past the age of sexual behavior. Two of his wives were Aisha and Hafsah who were daughters respectively of his close associates Abu Bakr and Umar. He married Zainab, the divorced wife of his adopted son Zaid. The Prophet first hesitated but later decided to marry Zainab (33:37). To suggest that the Prophet took so many wives in order to satisfy his physical need would indeed amount to estimating the Prophet far below what he deserves.[3] As discussed in Chapter 2, in order to rise to the spiritual height that he did, which earned him the qualification of a great character (68:4-6), Prophethood and nearness to God (53:1-8), and the status of an ideal deserving to be emulated by all God-loving people (33:21), he could not afford to care for the mundane pleasures.

The Prophet remains an ideal and an inspiration for all men and women (33:21; 68:4-6). Each and every Muslim and non-Muslim needs to ponder hard how he rose to such spiritual eminence that enabled him to receive a Great Book of Divine revelation, which describes him as a mercy (*rahmat*) for the whole universe (9:61; 21:107; 28:46) and a light-giving lamp (*munir*) to all humankind (33:46). Evidently, a personality that earned this unique honor could not be other than one who had conquered his animal nature. After all, prophets and God's devout servants are the human models to project before humanity a pattern of life that is modeled on the divine image.

The Quran encourages the marriage of unmarried people:

> 24:32 And marry (i.e., cause to get married) those among you who are single and virtuous ones from among your slaves, male or female. If they are in poverty, God will provide them of His grace. And God is Ample-Giving, Knower of Things.

Also, the Quran notes that the monasticism that the followers of the Prophet Jesus invented was not approved of by God, even though they did this practice only for seeking God's pleasure, since they did not really observe it with the right observance (57:27). God did not prescribe celibacy for them; they impose it on themselves but all of them do not observe the limits. In religion, celibacy is not essential nor is marriage. While marriage is not essential, it does not follow that religion should make it mandatory for any to remain a male bachelor or a female celibate for all his or her life. Stories of scandalous sexual abuse that have come to light in recent time about numerous Catholic priests involved are a stark reminder that the Catholic Church is trying to do something that is hard to comply with. But God does not task a soul beyond its normal capacity (2:285; 6:152; 7:42; 65:7). Islam does not approve of any system of priesthood. No one needs a priest in order to be religious – to get one's salvation.[4]

Divorce

The Quran provides clear guidance on how a husband should proceed with divorcing his wife, should it be deemed necessary when the relationship between husband and wife becomes too sour to continue. It also provides guidance on how a wife can seek justice when she has grievances against her husband. If one follows the Quran's advice regarding divorce very carefully, it should become crystal clear that God wants us to proceed very carefully and gradually with separation and divorce. First of all, we should note that a mere uttering by a husband that he has divorced his wife, if he has not really meant it seriously, is no true word of divorce. A husband may say to his wife "I divorce you" in a fit of anger, but does not stick to it when he cools down. It is indeed very unfortunate that in Muslim society, because of wrong teachings from religious teachers around them, there have been instances of instantaneous happenings of divorces just on the basis of uttering of the divorce word three times at a time. But the Quran says that God does not hold us responsible for the mere utterance of oaths or words:

> 2:225 God will not take you to task for what is unintentional in your oaths (words) but He will take you to task for what your hearts have meant. God is Ever Forgiving, Most Forbearing.

The first stage to proceed on the course towards a divorce is waiting for four months. This waiting is required for the husband if he is determined or serious about divorcing his wife. The Quran states:

> 2:226 Those who forswear (definitely intend to divorce) their wives should wait four months, if then they change their mind (and return), God is Ever Forgiving, Most

Merciful.

If after this waiting, a husband firmly decides on a divorce, he can proceed with the divorce. After this divorce, the wife is required to wait three (monthly) courses (the period of *iddat*). A clear message of the Quran is that the husband would be justified to take back his divorced wife in case she is pregnant and if both agree to this effect. They are required not to conceal if the wife is pregnant. Both husband and wife have similar rights over each other. Look at the verse below:

> 2:228 Divorced women shall wait, keeping themselves apart, three (monthly) courses. And it is not lawful for them that they should conceal that which God hath created in their wombs if they are believers in God and the Last Day. And their husbands have the right to take them back in that case if they desire reconciliation. And they (wives) have rights similar to those (of men) over them in kindness.

For those women who do not expect to have menstrual courses, or for those who are not having courses, the period of waiting (*iddat*) for the divorced wife is three months. And for those women, who know they are pregnant, the waiting period for the divorced wife is till the birth of the child (65:4). God exhorts those who intend to divorce their wives to do so keeping an eye on the waiting period. God advises them not to drive their wives out of their houses, unless they commit flagrant indecency:

> 65:1-2 O Prophet! When ye intend to divorce your wives, put them away for divorce for their (prescribed) period, and count the period, and be careful (of your duty) to God, your Lord. Drive them not out of their houses, nor

should they themselves leave unless they commit open indecency. ... Then when they have reached their term, take them back with kindness, or part with them with kindness, and take for witness two just men among you, and establish right evidence for God.

The Quran requires that the word of divorce should be pronounced twice, and after that the husband is free either to retain the divorced wife or release her in kindness (2:229, 231). It is not lawful for the husband to retain his divorced wife to her hurt (2:231).

Verse 2:230 speaks about the remarrying of the divorced wife by her former husband, if she has married another husband, and states that the remarrying is not lawful unless the second husband has divorced her. The verse reads as follows:

2:230 And if he hath divorced her, she is not lawful unto him thereafter until another husband she hath married (after the divorce) hath divorced her. (In that case) it is no blame for both of them if they return to each other, and if they think they can keep within the limits (imposed by) God. And these are the limits ordained by God, which He maketh plain for a people who know.

The meaning of the verse is clear. If the divorced wife marries another husband, it is quite sensible that she cannot remarry her former husband unless and until her second husband divorces her. This is common sense, and stands perfectly to reason. The verse should not be read to imply that the divorced wife has to marry another person, and that that person needs to divorce her to make it possible for the original husband to get her back. Unfortunately, the verse has been translated and interpreted in this latter wrong sense, which represents a glaring example of how some of the verses of the Quran have been grossly misrepresented by our learned religious scholars (*ulama*), who have been influenced by traditional interpretations offered by the Hadith. According to them, the remarriage of husband and wife is not possible unless the divorced wife has married another person, and until that person has divorced her. That precludes the remarriage of husband and wife, if the divorced wife does not, or refuses to, marry another person. The remarrying of former husband and wife has thus been made conditional upon, first, marrying of the divorced wife to another husband, and second, on the break-up of that marriage. This is the so-called infamous *hilla* (or *halala*) system, which has caused great harm in our society by imprudently leading to break-up of many happy marriages and destruction of many happy lives! The Quran clearly admonishes those who divorce their wives not to force them out of their houses before their term expires and to make a choice between taking their divorced wives back or parting with them when the term expires, as in verse (65:2) cited above.

The Quran also explicitly warns us not to create any obstacles on the way of remarrying of the divorced wife with her husband:

> 2:232 And when ye have divorced women, and they have reached their term (*iddat*), *place no difficulties on the way of their remarrying of their husbands, if it is agreed between them in kindness.* This is an admonition for him who believeth in God and the Last Day. That is more virtuous for you, and cleaner. God knoweth and ye know not.

This is clear Quranic advice. Such remarriage and reunion should not be made subject to any additional condition. Yet, it is ironic that our *ulama* have chosen to mislead Muslims. Does it not ever occur to our common sense that we should not force a divorced wife to marry another husband against her will? Only in case she willingly marries another person, she cannot be lawful to her former husband unless her current husband divorces her. And why should one ever anticipate that a person would marry the divorced wife of another person just for the sake of divorcing her? All this looks ludicrous. Yet, such an inhuman and vile practice is found to exist in Bangladesh, parts of India, and Iran. Notably in the Iranian city of Qom, "there are men who make a living as 'one-night husbands': they marry thrice-divorced women, consummate the marriage, and divorce them the next day, so that the women can now lawfully go back to their families."[5]

The Quran has repeatedly urged us to reflect on the verses and apply our sense. Also, importantly, God urges the husband, after he has divorced his wife and the wife has reached her waiting period, to either live together with his divorced wife in kindness or to part from her in kindness, and not to treat lightly the divine advice (2:231). Even though the current marriage laws in some countries have largely, if not wholly, taken care of the Quranic instructions,[6] yet the vested interest groups try hard to re-impose the notorious *halala* system. The conscious people in society should firmly stand against such monstrous attempts.[7]

The Quran warns those who divorce their wives that they should treat their wives in a just and humane manner, that they should not take back anything they have given their divorced wives, that they should bear the living expenses of the divorced wives if they are pregnant and, after delivery of their children, bear the expenses of the suckling of their children (2:231; 4:19-21; 65:6; and 2:233). At the same time, the grievances of wives who are mistreated by their husbands need also to be appropriately addressed. The Quran urges us to take appropriate measures to address such cases of grievances and in case a dispute occurs between husband and wife and is not amicably settled between them, they should engage arbiters from both husband and wife's sides to settle such disputes (4:35).

It needs also to be noted that in Muslim societies, men are often found to initiate divorce, and women's rights to divorce their husbands are practically limited. Such discrimination is, however, unwarranted in light of the very spirit of the Quran's message.

The Status of Women

In traditional interpretation of Islam and much in line with the Hadith, women are accorded a much inferior status to that of men. The Quran, however, provides a much more humane view of women's rights and privileges. It gave them "legal rights of inheritance and divorce; most Western women had nothing comparable until the nineteenth century."[8] Bestowing upon women their proper rights and privileges was nothing short of a revolution in the prevailing social milieu of the time. The changes that the revelation of Islam brought about include prohibition of female infanticide, abolition of women's status as property, establishment of women's legal rights to inheritance, changing marriage from a proprietary to a contractual relationship with women's rights to a dowry, allowing women to retain control over their own property, granting women financial maintenance from their husbands, and controlling the husband's free ability to divorce. However, while ideas favoring gender equality flourished in the West, patriarchal interpretation adopted at medieval times in classical Islam continues to date in traditional Islam. This development, however, runs counter to the spirit of the Quran's message in regards to women.

Unlike the Biblical notion that Eve was created out of Adam's rib (Genesis, 2:21-24), the Quran rather reminds us that we all originate from the same source – the same *nafs* or soul or cell, and that our mates are created of the same kind so that we may incline to them:

7:189   He it is Who did create you from a single *nafs*, and from it did create his mate that he might incline unto her. (Also see 4:1)

Thus being of the same source, man and woman are on a par with one another. Also, the Quranic expressions that everything has been created in pairs (36:36; 51:49; 53:45) and that a man and a woman are just parts of the same pair also underscore the necessary complementary and equal nature of the relationship between a man and a woman. The Quran has accorded women rights over men similar to those of men over women:

2:228   And they (women) have rights similar to those (of men) over them with justness, and the men are a degree above them.

The above verse and another verse at (4:34) give some edge to men over women. The latter verse cites the reasons why men have some edge over women, which are that men are responsible for maintaining, protecting, and financially supporting the other. Contemporary reformist Muslim scholars have rightly observed that "the edge" referred to in verses 2:228 and 4:34 just reflects "men's socioeconomic responsibilities for women" and does not indicate any superiority of men over women in general. They point out that the Quran itself distinguishes between two types of messages: those that are "universal principles" and those that respond "to specific social and cultural contexts or questions [that] were subject to interpretation (3:7). They believe that those verses that assign greater rights to men ... reflect a patriarchal context in which men were dominant and solely responsible for supporting women."[9] Noted Islamic scholar Khaled Abou El Fadl very aptly puts it, "men and women equally qualify for God's grace and reward. The authority given to men over women is not because they are men but because, in a particular historical context, men financially provided for women. But if the circumstances change, and women share financial responsibility with men, authority must be equally shared between the two as well."[10]

Gender equality in Islam in fact follows from the very conception of God as Gender-Neutral. God never discriminates between a man and a woman – men and women equally qualify for His grace and reward for virtuous deeds (33:35). In His sight, the most virtuous person, whether male or female, is the most honored (49:13). A woman may indeed excel a man in virtuousness and in various qualities (4:32). Pharaoh's wife was a pious woman – an example to others and far superior to Pharaoh in foresight and work (28:9; 66:11. The Quran also emphatically proclaims:

> 3:195 Their Lord hath heard their prayer (and saith): Never do I cause the work of any to be lost, be ye male or female – ye are one from another. (See also 4:124; 16:97)

The expression "ye are one from another or members of one another" in verse (3:195), which recurs in another place of the Quran (4:25), is also a reminder to men that women are of the same human status as themselves. Furthermore, the verses (30:21 and 2:187) underscore that it is love and mercy that should characterize the relationship between husband and wife. The verse (9:71) describes believing men and women as protecting friends or supporters of one another in virtuous deeds, who enjoin what is good and just and forbid what is bad. Husband and wife are in need of each other; they need to respect each other in a similar way. Husbands should be conscious of their obligations to their wives and responsive to their needs (2:233, 240-241; 4:19-21). Likewise, wives should also be conscious of their obligations to their husbands and responsive to their needs (60:12). All these verses depict the ideal vision of the relationship between men and women – one of equality and complementarity.

Also, it is important that wives are conscious of their rights over their husbands. If wives fear mistreatment or desertion from their husbands, the Quran provides that they should have a mutual marriage settlement or agreement as a cushion against such possible mistreatment, and such an agreement is a best guarantor of their rights (4:128). The way women can best understand their obligations and protect their rights is through letting them get proper and sufficient education. The opportunities and access to education should be equally available to both boys and girls. It is ironic that in Muslim communities in particular in many regions and countries, female education is grossly neglected, and the existing education facilities are not equally available to boys and girls. As a result the literacy rate among the females is deplorably low in some countries such as Pakistan and Afghanistan. This situation needs to be remedied with great urgency and utmost effort. The relative neglect of girls' education in Muslim countries goes against the Quran's emphasis on knowledge acquisition for all, male or female. Another important and practical way Muslim women's status can be lifted would be to empower them economically by supporting them with opportunities to earn income independently and to enable them to become business entrepreneurs. One good way would be to provide them access to micro-credit facilities along the model of the Grameen Bank of Bangladesh which benefits women the most.[11]

God exhorts men to treat women with dignity and honor – not to forcibly inherit women against their will, not to pressure them to give back what has been given them, not to take back anything from their wives' dowries (4:19-21). Even at the time when a man divorces his wife, God urges him to take care so as not to cause any injury to his divorced wife (2:231). And the Quran makes the husband fully responsible for financially supporting his divorced wife during pregnancy, and both her and their child during the two years of nursing the baby (2:233). Indeed, the virtuous are those who, among other things, wish to see their spouses and their children as a source of comfort for them, and pray to God for such an effect (25:74).

The virtuous men's wives need to be or are, in general, virtuous as well (33:28-34); they go to Heaven along with their husbands (43:68-70). The respectable men's wives are respectable also with rare exceptions. The Prophet's wives are like mothers to all of his followers (33:6). The purport of all this is that women are not to be treated as inferior to men and their status and rights should be regarded as similar to those of men.

The Quranic verse 4:34 has been traditionally interpreted as giving husbands the authority to beat or scourge their wives in case of open rebellion (as a matter of last resort after trying the methods of admonishing them first, and then of leaving them alone in bed). However, many modern Muslim scholars point out that the expression *"adribu-hunna"* in the verse does not necessarily mean "strike or scourge them." According to Reza Aslan, this expression (which is an extension of *daraba* including the object "them") can also mean "turn away from them," "go along with them," and remarkably, even "have consensual intercourse with them."[12] Edip Yuksel and his colleagues, in their *Quran: A Reformist Translation* have translated this particular text as "separate them" and not as "beat them."[13] According to Jeffrey Lang, "From a purely rational standpoint this alternative interpretation ['turn away from them"] seems preferable to the traditional one ["beat them"], for with regard to the latter it is hard

Marriage, Divorce, the Status of Women and the Treatment of Slaves

to see how inflicting physical punishment on the wife would lessen her resentment of her husband. If anything, one would think that beating her would accomplish just the opposite. ... This [alternative] interpretation of *udribu* also fits with the non-violent character of all the other recommendations [of 4:34-35], including the fourth step of bringing in family conciliators."[14] The usual interpretation of this verse marks the influence of traditions. However, if we grant that women have just rights over men as men have over women as the Quran demands (2:228) and if we are to maintain propriety and dignity in our mutual behavior, as implied by the Quranic verse: "Live with them in a manner that is dignified" (4:19), the verse above should be interpreted along more compassionate lines. Scourging or beating is undignified and inconsistent with the broader message of the Quran.

Indeed, it is beneath good taste and it hardly befits a decent man that he should hurt, injure, or torture his wife in any way, as the Quran explicitly forbids one to injure his wife even when he decides to divorce her (2:231). In the admonition particularly given to the Prophet Muhammad in verse (33:28), God exhorts him to bid goodbye to his wives in a fair manner, if they choose this worldly life. There is no talk of punishing them in other ways.

The other term used in the verse (4:34) is *quanitat* that has been usually rendered as "obedient" (to the husband). Regarding this Amina Wadud contends that this word implies "good" rather than "obedient" and that this word is used with regard to both males (2:238, 3:17, 33:35)) and females (4:34, 33:34, 66:5. 66:12).[15] It describes a characteristic or personality trait of believers towards Allah. They are inclined to be co-operative with one another and subservient before Allah.[16] Also note that many Muslim scholars interpret the verses (2:228; 4:34) to denote general superiority of men over women. As Amina Wadud rightly points out, this interpretation is mistaken since the preference of men over women in this context is because of the particular conditions of men having larger financial ability and responsibility to support women; it is not an unconditional preference and hence it cannot be construed as indicating any general superiority of men over women.[17] Wadud further notes that the Quranic *tafsir* (exegetical works) done mostly by men reflect their own prejudices towards women and do not display the overall Weltanschauung or worldview of the Quran in terms of "emulating certain key principles of human development: justice, equity, harmony, moral responsibility, spiritual awareness, and development. [...] The Quran clearly rejects any [...] notion of the 'inherent' evil of woman. It explicitly demands respect for her 'inherent' good as potential child-bearer (and primary nurturer). It places her on absolute par with man in terms of the spiritual potential (to know and serve Allah) and the potential to attain Paradise."[18]

Indeed, God is unforgiving to those who, among other things, make an unfair discrimination between husband and wife:

> 6:139 And they say: That which is in the bellies of such cattle is reserved for our males, and is forbidden to our wives; but if it is still-born, then they (all) have shares therein. He (God) will punish them for such (false) attribution (to Him).

The ninth-century Mutazilite scholar al-Jahiz was much ahead of his time in declaring, "Any reasonable person cannot say, the women are above men or lower than men by a degree or two or more. [...] It is true impotence for a man to be incapable of fulfilling the rights of fathers or uncles unless he disparages the rights of mothers and aunts."[19]

The Quran does, however, make some exceptions to the treatment of men and women in a few cases such as in the case of distribution of inherited property from deceased parents, children or other relatives and in the case of taking them as witnesses for dispensation of judicial justice in business dealings. But such exceptions cannot be considered as real discrimination between men and women, as these are required to maintain proper balance and equity between men and women in property ownership and use, and to ensure justice in business dealings in a social context where men, and not women, shoulder full financial responsibility, and where women do not have the same level of business knowledge as men. The Quran requires that when parents leave behind property at death, a son should get twice as much as a daughter by way of inheritance (4:11); the surviving father gets twice as much as the surviving mother (4:12); and the deceased parent's parents, if they are still living, also get according to the rule that the father gets twice as much as the mother (4:11). Such distinction prescribed in the Quran for distribution of property between men and women is made precisely due to the fact that for the most part, when a daughter gets married, she gets financial support mainly from her husband, and when a son gets married, he needs to take full responsibility for supporting his wife and children, including sometimes supporting the surviving parent. In such circumstances, it should be logical that the male gets a higher share of the inherited property from relatives. But "the rules of law that apply to women", as Abou El Fadl aptly notes, should not be regarded as "static and unchanging. The Islamic law has to keep changing forward to achieve the moral objectives expressed in the Qur'an. To achieve justice, there has to be a constant effort to achieve a more authentic proportionality between the duties and rights of Muslim women. So, for instance, if within the social dynamics of time, women carry a financial responsibility equal to [that of] men, it is more consistent with Shari'a to allow women an equal share to men in inheritance."[20]

    Apart from the inheritance case, the other case where the

Quran makes some distinction between men and women is where testimony is taken for making contracts for financial transactions. The Quran requires two men as witnesses, and in case two men are not found, one man and two women can substitute for two men as witnesses (2:282). It is only in the case of financial transactions that the Quran makes this distinction for making testimonies. Contemporary scholars think that such discrimination is in order in a context when women are less informed than men in financial matters. Thus the Quran states that two females are required because if one of them forgets, the other may remind her (2:282). "Some contemporary female [Muslim] scholars have argued that the requirement of two female witnesses demonstrates the need for women to have access to education, both secular and religious, in order to receive the training and experience to be equal to men in a business environment – something that has not been prohibited by the Quran. In light of the right of the women to own property and make their investments, this interpretation is in keeping with broader Quranic values."[21]

A first significant effort for Muslim family law reform covering marriage, divorce, and inheritance through reinterpretation of the Quran, and to liberate women advocating their rights, education, and access to social life and the professions was made by Qasim Amin, an Egyptian and a disciple of Muhammad Abduh, through his remarkable book in Arabic titled *The Liberation of Woman* published in 1899. The book, translated in Turkish and other languages, "evoked a very strong reaction from the traditionalist establishment in Egypt and elsewhere ... [but] had a considerable impact, more especially on the rising generation of women."[22] Qasim Amin's efforts in Egypt were paralleled by similar efforts by Mumtaz Ali, a disciple of Sir Sayyid Ahmad Khan, in India. As Esposito notes:

> Both focused on the plight of Muslim women as a primary cause of the deterioration of the family and society. [...] Qasim Amin criticized lack of education, child marriages, arranged marriages, polygamy, and easy male-dominated divorce as causes of the bondage of Muslim women. Ali took a similar position. Ali refuted the antifeminist Quranic exegesis of some classical legal scholars, maintaining that their interpretations did not reflect the meaning of Quranic texts but the customs and mores of the exegetes' own times. Fundamental reforms were required. These ideas informed the positions of the feminist movements and political elites a generation later in the 1920s and 1930s.[23]

Despite notable reforms made in recent years in Muslim marriage and divorce laws in a number of countries, the plight of Muslim women still remains deplorable in many parts of the world. As Reza Aslan notes, a feminist movement has been under way throughout the Muslim world in modern time in trying to regain women's equal status in light of the Quran. '[A] whole new generation of contemporary female textual scholars [...] have been laboring toward a gender-neutral interpretation of the Quran [...]. As Shirin Ebadi proudly declared while accepting the 2003 Nobel Peace Prize for her tireless work for defending the rights of women in Iran, "God created us all as equals. [...] By fighting for equal status, we are doing what God wants us to do."'[24]

In the early Islamic community in Medina, women played important roles. Aslan adds, "The so-called Muslim women's movement is predicated on the idea that Muslim men, not Islam, have been responsible for the suppression of women's rights. For this reason, Muslim feminists are advocating a return to the society Muhammad originally envisioned for his followers. Despite differences in culture, nationalities, and beliefs, these women believe that the lesson to be learned from Muhammad in Medina is that Islam is above all an egalitarian religion. Their Medina is a society in which Muhammad designated women like Umm Waraka as spiritual guides for the *Ummah*; in which the Prophet himself was sometimes rebuked by his wives; in which women prayed and fought alongside the men; in which women like Aisha and Umm Salamah acted not only as religious but also as political – and on at least one occasion military – leaders; and in which the call to gather for prayer, bellowed from the rooftop of Muhammad's house, brought men and women together to kneel side by side and be blessed as a single undivided community."[25] As Esposito notes, women in this early Islamic community not only fought in battles but also "nursed the wounded during the time of the Prophet. They were consulted about who should succeed Muhammad after his death. Women also contributed to the collection and compilation of the Quran[,] [...] owned and sold property, engaged in commercial transactions, and were encouraged to seek and provide educational instruction[.] [...] The second Caliph, Umar Ibn al-Khattab, appointed women to serve as officials in the marketplace of Medina."[26]

The way women are required to dress in some Muslim societies is often seen as a reflection of men controlling women - "a symbol of women's inferior status"[27]. The veil (*burqa*), the headscarf (*hijab*) or *chadar*, which many Muslims wear, has become a subject of intense religious and political debate in recent time. Many Muslims view the recent ban on the wearing of *burqa* or *hijab* covering the face in several countries as an infringement on human rights, while the governments imposing the ban argue that this goes against their secular tradition. They also argue that such veiling in public places creates problems for security officials to properly identify them. Many Muslims view it as part of the modesty requirements stipulated by the Quran (24:31) and in line with the directions made to the Prophet's and believers' wives and daughters (33:59). Note also that the Quran stipulates modesty requirements also for men (24:30). Wearing a veil was not a general practice of Muslim women during the Prophet's time. In fact veiling did not become a widespread vogue in the Muslim world until three to four generations after the Prophet's death.[28] What the Quran directs, and what is really important, is that Muslim women should wear decent and dignified dresses so as not to evoke men's invitation to indecency (33:32-33). The Quran allows leaving parts of the body uncovered that are normally apparent such as head, face, hands and feet. It specifically mentions the private parts and bosoms for covering by the dress; it does not mention head, face, hands and feet for covering by the dress (24:31). Guarding modesty requires believers to maintain purity of attitude in mind, and decency of behavior with persons of the opposite sex. This is obviously more important than using a veil (*burqa* or *hijab*), which is not always found to be a good reflector of one's decency of behavior with persons of the opposite sex. Veiling thus should not be viewed as an essential Islamic dress.

Women should be allowed to enjoy same political rights as men. The Quran approvingly refers to the Queen of Sheba as a head of state, which illustrates the point that women have the necessary capacity, judgment, and expertise to take on important state responsibilities. It is encouraging to see that several countries in the contemporary Muslim world (Pakistan, Turkey, Indonesia, and Bangladesh) have had or have women Presidents or Prime Ministers.

It is the Hadith, not the Quran, that has denigrated the status of women with derogatory passages about women.[29] The fact of the matter is that all such Hadith texts are fabricated – fabrications made in a male-dominated and misogynistic society and are misleading to humankind. It is ironic that Muslim fundamentalists or puritans, toeing the Hadith, display a particularly demeaning attitude toward women, treating them "as a constant source of danger, and vulnerability for Islam," and going "as far as branding women as the main source of corruption and evil."[30]

Indeed, as Bernard Lewis points out, the emancipation of women in Muslim countries has been a most problematic challenge in the face of a strong resistance from traditional conservatives and radical fundamentalists, who view such liberation as mere Westernization, distinguished from modernization, and "a betrayal of Islamic values".[31] No doubt, as Lewis identifies, the degrading way women are being treated in many Muslim countries and regions – their rights of access to education and work in public place being suppressed, their social and political rights being curbed and their personal freedom being curtailed relatively to the rights and privileges enjoyed by the males – has been a major cultural factor holding back modernization and development of these countries.[32] But this cultural snag is not a fault line with Islam if understood in light of the Quran alone; it is due to the misleading influence that has come from the Hadith.

The Treatment of Slaves: Free or Marry Them, Not Enjoy Them in Captivity

With the progress of civilization, stark and large-scale forms of slavery have been largely banished from the earth. However, slavery and slavery-like practices still exist today in parts of the world. The Quran strongly urges believers to free slaves and characterizes this act as an integral part of righteousness and as a greatly virtuous deed (2:177, 90:12-13). The Quran puts a high premium on the freeing of slaves (90:12-13, 5:89, 58:3). The Prophet Muhammad himself set noble examples by personally ensuring the freedom of an African slave Bilal and making his slave Zayd his own adopted son. He also married a Coptic Christian slave girl.

If to free slaves is part of righteousness, then truly righteous people cannot have slaves and enjoy them in captivity. Indeed, slavery is a most dehumanizing institution. A good Muslim will never enslave a person, but will rather free him or her, or keep him or her as an equal member of his family. As Fazlur Rahman rightly points out, as noted earlier, the Quran's emphasis on manumission should not be interpreted as retaining the institution of slavery and earning merit by freeing them, but rather as abolishing it altogether.[33]

Slavery has existed in human society from time immemorial. Moses' people were slaves and victims of torture perpetrated by Pharaoh's folks and it was Moses who liberated them from Pharaohs' folks. Even though the Quran, revealed in the seventh century, came with a clarion call for freeing slaves, slavery has significantly existed in Saudi Arabia and much of the Muslim world well into the twentieth century until it was officially abolished. It has been widely practiced in the developed countries such as the United States even in the nineteenth century.[34] The Ottoman Sultan Abdulmecid abolished slave trade in the nineteenth century. Tunisia, which was part of the Ottoman Empire, abolished it in 1846. This was seventeen years before the United States banned it. Interestingly, in October 31, 1863, the Mayor of Tunis Husayn Pasa wrote a letter to the American Consul General Amos Perry, urging the Americans to rethink their stance on the issue of slavery for the sake of "human mercy and compassion."[35] The 1865 Emancipation Proclamation (1863) and Union victory (1865) freed almost 4 million slaves in the United States.[36] The United Kingdom abolished it in its empire at the beginning of the nineteenth century and treated slave trading as an international crime. In its own territory, Muslim *shariah* courts also do not apply rules relating to slavery, as they recognize that times have changed when slavery should not exist, just as these courts do not apply such aspects of *shariah* as corporal punishments for crimes and those relating to apostasy. It took up to the late twentieth century for slavery to be abolished in the Middle East, with rare local exceptions, e.g., the Ottoman and Tunisian abolitions of slavery cited above.[37] In one form or another, slavery still persists in various countries including developed countries. News reports suggest existence of clandestine or overt human trafficking in women and children from less developed or impoverished to more developed or rich regions of the world. The long-running troubles in the Darfur region of Sudan led to a spate in slave trade.[38]

The Quran provides a clear direction that one should consider marrying from among slave girls, should he find it difficult to marry a free woman (4:25). It also states that one should marry slave girls, giving them proper dowry if they demand it, or free them to get married, not to own and enjoy them in captivity without marriage (4:25, 24: 32-33). The Quran exhorts us not to take any as paramours or concubines (4:25; 5:5). It speaks of marrying orphans (4:3), not enslaving them. It urges believers to give deeds of emancipation to those slaves who ask for such a writing if they know any good in them, and give them out of their riches, and not to compel them to prostitution (24:33). So it follows that the Quran strongly encourages us to set slaves free and marry them, rather than take them as legal partners in conjugal life without marrying them. One is likely to get the impression from the last part of verse (24:33) that God is lenient or forgiving to those who force slave girls to prostitution. Such an interpretation of the verse, however, would be rash and inappropriate, since to think that God is forgiving to those who violate His advice is wrong. It is far beneath the taste of decent, righteous people that they should enjoy girls in captivity, let alone compel any of them to prostitution, especially since the Quran specifically mentions freeing of slaves as part and parcel of righteousness.

The Quran's call for essential human egalitarianism

precludes any form of human domination over other humans. Slavery and slavery-like practices should no longer remain as a relic of the past. Such practices do not belong to the present or the future.

IX. Implications of the Quran's Message for the Economic System

(O humankind!) Give full measure; and be not of those who give less. And weigh with right scales. And wrong not men of their things (or rights), and act not corruptly in the earth, making mischief. – *The Quran*, 26:181-183

Principles and Elements of the Quran-based Economic System

The Quranic message for justice, equity, fair play, and care for the poor and needy people in society has profound implications for the economic system. For an economy to be vibrant, some preconditions that need to be fulfilled include social harmony, political peace and stability, decent living conditions for the labor force, a supportive government with a good legal system, efficient and corruption-free service providers, and freedom for all men and women to uninterruptedly pursue their economic goals. Islam, properly understood, embraces the elements of modernity that define the western economic system – the ideas of liberty, competition, free enterprise, integrity and business ethics.

A careful study of the relevant Quranic guidelines points to some broad and important implications for the economic system as follows:

- The most preferable economic system is neither pure capitalism nor pure socialism, but a capitalist system with a socialistic overtone to care for the basic needs and welfare concerns of the poor and disadvantaged people in society;
- It should be an equitable economic system without stark economic inequalities;

- Trading is permissible and should be free and fair, subject to appropriate qualifications; and
- The system should be freed from all kinds of exploitation, including market distortion through manipulation.

As stated earlier in this book, the Quran's focal emphasis is on the establishment of an order of socioeconomic justice and essential human egalitarianism in society. The Prophet Muhammad himself was an orphan and a needy person, and when he found shelter and became free of want he was strongly urged by God not to be oblivious of the needs of the orphans and the needy (93:6-10). The Quran thus emphasizes distribution, but at the same time it lays down certain broad guidelines that point to the need for an efficient production and marketing system in the economy to support what we might say is the most important objective of human endeavor, i.e., moral and spiritual uplifting of all men and women in society.

According to the Quran, some of the essential elements or principles of an ideal economic system would include the following:

- Respect for private property ownership;
- Respect for individual economic freedom, initiative, and enterprise;
- Recognition of the need for recording of loan and debt dealings, for respecting contractual obligations, and for requiring return of trusted properties;
- Providing for an equitable distribution of wealth and income and allowance for social security, social welfare and common good;
- Taking measures to curb exploitation or monopoly power

and promote market competition;

- Allowing free play of economic forces, i.e., freedom of work, initiative and enterprise, freedom of production, free movement of factors of production and goods and services with some exceptions (See below); and

- Promotion of social and economic development conducive to an environment for both spiritual development and supportive material development.

The Quran acknowledges the inviolability of private property. It urges us not to encroach upon others' property (2:188). It advises us to approach orphans' property with a good intention, not with an intention to grab such property (17:34), and to work as custodians of such property until the orphans can be trusted to manage their property themselves (4:5-6). This also implies that in cases where some valuable national property is found to be mismanaged by its owner(s), the state has a right to entrust its management to others who are more efficient, while giving the owners their due after deduction of the reasonable management fees. The Quran cautions against taking excessive management fees and urges well-off managers to part with any fees to manage such property (4:6). This is a clear direction for avoiding any form of exploitation and for humanitarian treatment wherever this is needed.

Note that the respect for property also translates into ensuring necessary individual freedom, initiative, and enterprise for earning income and acquiring wealth for their livelihood. The call of the Quran "when the prayer is ended, then disperse in the land and seek of God's bounty" (62:10) is a clear mandate to individuals to pursue their efforts for earning their livelihood. This is approval for the capitalist or private enterprise system of production and trading. However, the Quran also makes us conscious about the need for distributive justice. We can own and possess wealth, but subject to the understanding that everything after all belongs to God (2:284) and we are only caretakers of wealth. The relatively affluent amongst us need to care adequately for the needs of the poor and needy people, as discussed in Chapter V.

Recording of contracts and honoring them are essential important aspects of businesses and services that involve time element. They are not necessary in the hand-to-hand trade of merchandise. The Quran mandates recording of loan and debt operations and, by implication, similar business and service operations that involve the time factor, and urges honoring of such contractual obligations (2:282). It also directs the trustees of trusted properties to return such properties to their owners (2:283, 4:58). One of the reasons why developed countries in the world are more developed than the less developed countries is precisely the fact that business ethics is much more strictly observed and legally enforced in the former countries than in the latter. The emerging economies, which include most Muslim nations, are plagued with widespread corruption and their legal environment is also not well developed.

The neo-classical position that market-clearing activities under laissez faire leads to an optimal solution is valid only when the given distribution of income and wealth in society is sacrosanct or optimal. If, however, the given wealth and income distribution is considered to be highly or significantly inequitable, there should be a prior redistribution of such wealth and income. For example, there are countries, where the existing distribution of land resources is highly unequal, which requires redistribution in favor of the landless. Thus from the point of view of creating equitable opportunities for access to resources for all men and women and from the point of view of making maximum possible contribution to the production and welfare potential of an economy, where existing distribution of land and other resources is found grossly unequal, a redistribution of such resources should be carried out.

The Quran strongly condemns hoarding (3:180). Hoarding in goods hurts an economy by creating artificial scarcities. Accumulation of wealth *per se* has no merit in God's sight (34:37). Rather accumulation and concentration of wealth in fewer hands creates an inequitable distribution of income and wealth, which eventually proves to be counterproductive to the economy, as it curbs effective demand and hurts the development of productive resources. This is probably reflected in the metaphor used in the Quran that such wealth will work as a burdensome collar tied to the necks of the owners of such wealth on the Resurrection Day (3:180).

The Quran rules out any kind of human injustice, exploitation, or cheating of any kind, whether it is individual, societal, religious, sectarian, political, or economic (16:90, 5:8, 26:181-183, 17:35). Economic policies, activities, or transactions that are not justified by the norm of justice should be considered as not permissible in Islam. A just and exploitation-free economy conceived by Islam has far-reaching implications. Some are as follows:

- There should be competition in economic dealings – in trading (selling or buying) of anything (goods, services and factors of production such as capital, land and labor), and appropriate measures should be taken to curb monopolistic behavior and elements found in any such dealings;

- There should be no hurdles or obstructions to the free production and free flow and movement of goods and services and factors of production, including capital, labor, knowledge, and technology within a country as well as across the borders of countries, excepting for some goods that can be restricted on religious and health grounds or for strategic reasons;

- Work in the work place should be judged by quality or efficiency of work alone and there should be no discrimination by sex, race, creed, color, or geographical origin. If concessions are to be made for disadvantaged groups, these should be made in a policy-neutral way that does not affect the production system or the allocation of resources. This would require that the social safety net or subsidization programs, if undertaken by the state, should be financed by the state's general budget from general government tax revenue, not by taxes on or subsidies for specific economic activities;[1] and

- Economic policies should be directed to ameliorating the material and spiritual conditions and pursuits of all men and women, to removing distortions in all economic activities, and to creating an environment conducive to private enterprise, growth, and development.

Since it will take us much beyond the confines of this chapter to elaborate on these implications, it may suffice here to make some brief observations as follows:

- Islam advocates an appropriate synthesis of both capitalistic and socialistic systems. The socialistic features that need to be incorporated in a predominantly capitalistic system are appropriate social security and safety net measures, embodying the charity system and social welfare programs that the Quran prescribes, as discussed in Chapter V.

- Islamic principles call for abolition of all controls and

taxes on production and trade of all goods and services except for goods that qualify for a prohibition on religious, medical, or strategic defense grounds. Controls and licensing create vested interests and artificial scarcities and scope for corruption and exploitation. Production or trade-specific non-tax controls and taxes distort the allocation of resources by artificially discouraging the production of affected specific goods and services. Likewise, production or trade subsidies also distort the allocation of resources by artificially encouraging such production or trade.

- By the same token, there should be no non-tariff and tariff restrictions or subsidies on imports and exports of any country. Modern economic theory and also available empirical evidence on the effects of trade liberalization and other globalization measures worldwide suggest that free trade fosters maximum economic growth and welfare of all countries, including developing countries.

The world will be a much better place if existing protectionist practices and tendencies in both developed and developing countries are significantly reduced and phased out as quickly as possible. This calls for co-operation and support on the part of all countries for multilateral trade reform programs being conducted through the auspices of the World Trade Organization (WTO). The recent 2013 global trade deal reached in Bali among 159 countries is a modest achievement in the right direction. More needs to be done, especially on trade liberalization through tariff reductions. Opposition to free trade and globalization that comes from certain quarters on fears of losses of jobs in previously protected industries and less growth of developing countries is largely misperceived. However, any adverse effects on employment that may follow from a free trade situation can be effectively tackled by additional safety measures, as recent and ongoing donor-supported policies and practices of developing countries suggest. The fear of any loss of economic growth is simply misplaced, since it is protection that causes a net loss of economic growth.

The state should take appropriate effective measures to curb monopolistic practices of both suppliers (or sellers) and buyers of any goods and services as well as of factors of production such as labor, land, and capital. That means that the government should endeavor to ensure competitive pricing of the following prices:

> Prices of all goods and services;
> Wages of labor;
> Rent on land; and
> Interest or return on borrowed and lent capital.

And the state should also take the responsibility of putting in place appropriate economic policies and measures to ensure an environment that is conducive to economic development with reasonable price stability. The State should also make use of pro-active policies to promote and accelerate economic development to alleviate poverty and create employment for the unemployed. Inflation is a hidden and regressive tax on the poor and deflation is damaging to development. The state needs to ensure a reasonable price stability to avoid too much price increase, which is unjust to the poor and at the same time it should not allow price inflation to go below a certain level that may trigger deflation, recession, or depression, which is more damaging to an economy.

Islamic principles are thus basically oriented to the promotion of a free market competitive economy. The Turkish journalist and author Mustafa Akyol also shares the idea that Islam really promotes a capitalistic orientation of the economy rather than a heavily socialistic one. He views the positions generally taken by Muslim scholars, proscribing the use of interest in modern finance and supporting a socialistic orientation of the economy, as ideas that are harming the interests of Muslims. Akyol argues that Islam is really compatible with a free capitalistic economy, not socialism. "It is true that the Koran has a strong emphasis on social justice and this has led some modern Muslim intellectuals to sympathize with socialism and its promise of a 'classless society.' A careful reading of the Koran would work against such 'Islamo-socialism,'" he writes.[2]

Indeed the Quran urges us to compete one with another in all good work:

5:48   So vie ye one with another in good work. Unto God is your goal.

By implication, competition in good work should be extended to all economic activities. The best and most effective way to eliminate monopolistic behavior or exploitation is to ensure competition in all economic activities and transactions. Note, however, that competition must be a fair one in the sense that it must not be cutthroat competition at below cost price, which is sometimes resorted to by unscrupulous businessmen to gain monopolistic control of the market. This cannot be approved of by religion. The state should assume the responsibility to enforce sound and effective competition rules for the market.

But at the same time Islam requires a well-devised safety net or social welfare program to safeguard the interests of, and cater to the basic needs of, the poor and disadvantaged groups in society. It also requires state promotion of economic and social development to effectively solve the problem of the poor and the unemployed. If the distribution of economic resources is grossly unequal, Islam requires some appropriate redistribution of such resources, especially of land So, in nations where stark inequality of resources, especially land, is found as in many countries, it will be advisable to carry out appropriate redistributive land reform in such countries. There is also a need for the state to shoulder a major part of the required spending for welfare or benevolent activities for the poor and disadvantaged groups in society, which is *sadaqa* in the Quranic terms. Also the state needs to take a great deal of responsibility to devise an appropriate tax and expenditure system to cater to the needs of public goods and services, which if left to the private sector alone will risk being grossly neglected or inadequately met. All such state functions should count within the purview of God's cause. And, as already mentioned in Chapter V, in an impoverished developing economy, the state has a special role to play in promoting economic development, which indeed is the best answer to alleviation of poverty for the poor.

Monopoly in production, selling or buying of any goods and services and factors of production leads to an undue constriction in their production and supplies causing monopolistic pricing of such goods and services. That demands abolition of all existing controls or barriers that impede competition in such activities, e.g., existing barriers or difficulties to, and controls on, new entry to business by aspiring entrepreneurs. However, in the case of production, even with full removal of existing controls and barriers to production, the very nature of the scale of production can create monopolies, both at private sector and state levels. In such situations of what are known as natural monopolies, the government needs to resort to effective taxation measures to siphon off monopoly profits with some qualification. The qualification relates to the need for retention of a sufficient incentive to technological innovation. Technological innovation plays a very significant role in fostering growth and in reducing the costs of production, in reducing the prices that consumers pay, and thus in improving human living standards. A proper synthesis or compromise needs to be struck between mopping up excess profits from the production and distribution system and retaining a sufficient incentive for those who innovate.

Monopolistic sellers charge higher than normal prices; monopolistic buyers (monopsonists) cause the sellers to sell at lower than normal prices. Both such sellers and buyers cause exploitation, which needs to be tackled by appropriate policy response, but not through direct price control or regulation. Price regulation has been proven to be an inappropriate policy instrument because of its possible adverse effects on the allocation of resources. Economists advocate appropriate taxation in the case of both monopolies and monopsonies, which does not artificially affect production on specific lines.

In sum, the Quranic guidelines and their implications as analyzed above suggest an economic system that is ideal in all respects. It embraces, where necessary, redistribution of productive resources in a way that is not grossly unequal in the first place; promotion of competition and effective curbing of monopolistic practices that cause exploitation; promotion of private initiative and enterprise and technological innovation; institution and implementation of effective safety-net programs; and promotion of economic development with reasonable price stability that is conducive to social and spiritual development.

Riba vs. Interest Used in Modern Finance

The earlier edition of this book with a different title covered this topic in some way.[3] Later this discussion was developed into a full paper and presented to a conference at Princeton University.[4] Here the principal points are summarized.

A major conclusion of the paper is that the Quranic ban on *riba* does not really apply to interest that has come to play a vitally important role in the modern economy. A second observation is that though Islamic banks have come into existence and are, on a significant scale, operating worldwide, these institutions have not been able yet to fulfill its basic and avowed objective, i.e., to go without interest, except only in a very marginal sense.

A concern for establishing social justice and fairness underlies the Quranic ban on *riba* or usury. During the time of the Quran's revelation, the borrowers were laden with unbearable debt because of the extortionate nature of the *riba* that used to double and redouble on non-repayments, as mentioned in 3:130. This pre-Islamic Arab practice obviously needed to be condemned on equity or humanitarian grounds. That is precisely the reason the Quran warns the lenders, in 2:278-280, to give up the remainder of any *riba* payments due from the borrowers, to be content with just capital repayments, and to postpone repayments or, better still, to write off the loans by way of *sadaqa*, if the borrowers are in financial hardship. This *riba* should not be equated with interest that has come to be used in modern finance. During the time of the revelation, *riba* was charged on loans extended generally to people who did not engage in commercial trading or production. The individual lenders in the past usually did not consider the plight of the people whom they lent money.

As some modernist scholars, notably Fazlur Rahman, have shown, interest used in modern finance is substantively different from *riba* and works like any other economic price. Rahman observes that, in the pre-Islamic Arabian practice, the initial payment of interest itself for a certain period of time "was not usurious and was, therefore, not considered *riba* . What made it *riba* was the increase in capital that raised the principal several-fold by continued redoubling. [...] [I]n case the debtor was unable to pay, the term of payment was extended with an enormous increase in the principal amount." He further argues, "When the entire system was banned, the milder cases within that system were also naturally abolished since the system itself was tyrannical. It cannot, therefore, be argued that since the Qur'an abolished even the milder cases, it must be concluded that the bank-interest of today also stands condemned; this is because the bank-interest of today is a separate kind of system." He aptly argues that in the modern economic system, "interest occupies the same place as price and performs the all-important function that any price-mechanism performs, viz., of regulating the supply and demand of credit and rationing it among the customers. If the rate of interest, i.e., the price of loaning money, is reduced to zero, then we are faced with a limited supply and an infinite demand. It would become impossible to control the rationing of credit available, so to say, and to assign priorities." He criticizes Abu Ala Mawdudi's contention that interest is simply a matter of haggling and speculation on the part of the lender and the borrower, a contention that betrays Mawdudi's ignorance about how modern finance works.[5]

Several other modern scholars associate themselves with the distinction between *riba* and interest. Imad-ad-Dean Ahmad of the Minaret of Freedom Institute cites people's time preference – the fact that goods and money are valued by people more at present time than at a future date – as the cause for interest to arise and argues that any unconscionable overcharging, whether on an interest rate or on a spot price, is *riba*, but market interest is not *riba*.[6] Yusuf Ali, in a commentary in his most popular Quran translation, says, "My definition [of *riba*] would include profiteering of all kinds, but exclude economic credit, the creature of modern banking and finance."[7] Muhammad Asad, Muhammad Pickthall, M. H. Shakir, and Edip Yuksel and his colleagues also translate "*riba*" as "usury" in an excessive sense, meaning that interest used in business transactions in the structure of modern credit and banking does not qualify as *riba*. Other scholars who also align themselves with this modern view of interest include author Imam Feisal Abdul Rauf and the Turkish author and columnist Mustafa

Akyol. Rauf rightly points out that the invention and use of interest was one of the pillars of capitalism, which, together with the development of limited liability corporate businesses and the growth of liberalism, was instrumental in dramatically changing the economic fortunes of the Western world, while the Muslim world lagged far behind. "The strict prohibition on charging interest still prevails in the Muslim world and has largely prevented it from robustly developing the financial market's institutions of banking, capital markets, and stock exchanges, the foundations of capitalism. Neither could the Muslim nations effectively control their own monetary policies, since raising and lowering interest rates is the chief way a nation's central bank controls inflation and the amount of money in circulation."[8] Mustafa Akyol thinks that, among all Muslim countries, only Turkey most developed and modernized its economy by shunning the orthodox Muslim thought that Sayyid Qutb and Abul Ala Mawdudi promoted.[9]

Indeed the Quran's sanction of trading (and implicitly profit) and condemnation of *riba* are predicated on the notion that profiting from trade is normal and legitimate, while *riba* is exploitative. Note, however, that trading can also be exploitative, where the seller can dictate the price (seller's market), or where the buyer can dictate the price (the buyer's market). Exploitative or monopolistic trading gives rise to excessive or extortionate profit, which the Quran certainly does not approve of. Extortionate interest or usury (i.e., *riba*) is analogous to extortionate profit. Both deserve the same condemnation. If exploitation elements are stripped from both trading and usury, they should stand on the same footing. So it follows that interest, which can be conceived of as exploitation-free is not really disapproved of by the Quran. The Quranic message of interest-free loans is applicable only for disadvantaged borrowers, who deserve to be treated with a humanitarian approach. This is *qard hasana* or a beautiful loan that the Quran talks about in several verses (2:245; 57:11, 18;

64:17; 5:12; 73:20). The Quran even encourages the lenders to write off the original loans in cases where the borrowers are in difficulty to repay them (2:278-280).

Also, the very Quranic concern for maintaining justice *(adl)* means that interest should be used to compensate lenders and bank depositors in a just and fair way. Abolition of nominal interest on loans extended in business transactions will rather result in inflicting injustice on the bankers and depositors who fund the banks. A distinction also needs to be drawn between nominal and real (i.e., price-adjusted) interest. Zero nominal interest would mean a negative real interest in an inflationary situation and a positive real interest in a deflationary situation, hurting or benefiting the lender respectively, and doing quite the opposite to the borrower. In the real-world, generally inflationary, situation, providing no nominal interest on bank deposits – so-called zero-interest in Islamic Banking terminology – thus makes little sense, as it hurts the depositors.

The phenomenon of inflation is just one factor that gives rise to interest. A second factor is people's time preference – valuing goods and money at the present moment more than at a future date. If, for example, a person would like to exchange $100 today for $110 a year after, his rate of time preference would be 10 percent. Interest plays an essential vital role in helping individuals allocate their income into present consumption and future consumption (i.e., saving) by bringing their time preference at the margin into equilibrium with the interest rate. A third, and perhaps the most important, reason for interest to arise is a return or profit that can be earned on capital invested in any economic activity such as trading, production, or provision of any service. A producer would like to borrow money to use in his enterprise so long as he earns a return at the margin higher than, or at least equal to, the rate of interest he pays on borrowed capital. The higher is the return on capital, the higher will have to be the interest rate to be in equilibrium with the rate of return situation.

In both second and third cases, interest plays a vital role in allocating resources – in the second case between consumption and saving, and in the third case, between different uses of capital. In the third case, interest also plays the role of a rationing device, rationing the uses of resources to the limit of the available resources. The scarcer the available amount of capital, the higher is the interest rate that will serve as an appropriate rationing device.

Modern economic theory shows how interest plays a pivotal role in allocating productive resources in the most efficient manner. It plays an equilibrating role in bringing all economic forces to work in a systematic, symbiotic way toward an equilibrium situation where the marginal rate of return or profit on capital as well as the marginal rate of time preference is equal to the prevailing rate of interest. Economic policymakers also use interest as an effective policy tool to ensure that an economy does not get overheated to generate undue inflation, or it does not slide into a recession with deflation. Interest is also used as a vital reference rate in the appraisal of government and public sector projects. Interest plays the role of the opportunity cost of capital and is an integral part of the calculus of many economic decision making activities. This interest thus plays a very beneficial role in the modern economy. It is not really banned by the Quran.

The other related question is whether Islamic finance institutions have been able to get rid of interest. The label "Islamic" used with these institutions is inapt, not simply because interest used in modern finance cannot really be condemned as unIslamic, but also because the very principle which justifies their existence in the first place, namely that they should do away with interest, is found, on scrutiny, to be largely violated in practice. These institutions have largely failed to get rid of interest, in part, because the interest-free principle is hard to realistically apply except in equity (as in *mudaraba* and *musharaka*) financing, which is only marginally used by these institutions due to difficulties and risks involved in such financing and, also in part, because just equity financing does not work for a stable banking industry.

The products offered by Islamic banks to implement the interest-free idea are called *mudaraba* (passive partnership) and *musharaka* (joint venture) contracting. Other major products offered fall in three major groups: markup or cost-plus *murabaha* (sales-based products), *ijara* (lease-based products), and *sukuk* (bond financing). *Murabaha* and *ijara* in turn have some sub-groups. *Murabaha* contracts include *bai al-inah* (sale and buyback), *bai salam* (deferred delivery sales), and *istisna*. *Bai salam* and *istisna* are used to fund goods that are yet to be produced or properties that are under construction.

Though not much empirical information is available on the operation of these banks, available evidence suggests that their various products, cloaked in Arabic terminology, mimic, for the most part, the services performed by conventional banks. Their real involvement in interest-free operations is limited to equity investment in only *mudaraba* and *musharaka* contracts, which operate on a profit and loss sharing (PLS) basis. However, these contracts accounted for only 5.2 percent of the total Malaysian Islamic bank financing at end-2012.[10] Another study of nine Middle Eastern (MENA) countries for 2008 shows that *mudaraba* and *musharaka* (PLS) financing was significant only in Saudi Arabia. It was absent or considerably insignificant in other MENA countries – completely absent in Kuwait and Yemen and very insignificant in UAE and Jordan. Much of the investment – 75 percent on average – went into the *murabaha* mode, followed by *ijara*.[11]

The reasons for Islamic banks' low PLS or equity financing are clear. There are inherent difficulties that banks face in engaging in equity financing. The banks lack needed expertise in project selection and evaluation and requisite business experience for equity investment. Also, business entrepreneurs are often reluctant to share all information with their bankers, in part, also because of their concern that this might make them exposed to tax authorities' watchful eyeing of their activities. That means that information that the concerned parties have about the PLS projects is asymmetrical, which necessarily makes Islamic banks more averse to financing such operations as involve risk and uncertainty than short-term trade or other businesses that assure certain returns.

In *murabaha* financing, the bank is to first buy the goods from the seller and possess them for a period, thus assuming liability, as in a normal trade, and then sell them back to the buyer who wanted the goods with a profit margin on the price. However, in practice, the bank does not take possession of the goods and there is virtually no holding period involved. Thus the loan advanced by the bank is much like a normal loan of a conventional bank and the profit margin, in an annualized form, is akin to interest.

In the case of another popular instrument used, *ijara* financing, the bank collects rent with a profit on the property leased out to the buyer of, say, a vehicle or a house or some durable equipment. Let us say, the bank enters into a partnership with a person who wants to buy a house. The bank pays, say, 80 percent of the house price and the individual 20 percent. The bank rents its share of the house back to the individual until it is fully paid for, collecting rent with profit over the interregnum period. The profit collected, on an annualized basis, is little different from conventional mortgage interest. The name change does not alter the essential nature of the charge.

Likewise, *sukuk* (bond) and other products of Islamic banks also are essentially similar to parallel products of conventional banks and involve interest.[12]

"Whether the product is dressed up in Arabic terminology, such as Mudarabah, or Ijarah, if it looks and feels like a mortgage, it is a mortgage and to say anything else is semantics."[13] The Turkish-American professor at Duke University Timur Kuran, who is considered a leading authority on Islamic economics, is a strong critic of Islamic finance. He "argues that Islamic finance is a faith-based fabrication that sits awkwardly in a modern business school."[14]

Conclusion

The Quran calls for a just, fair, and exploitation-free egalitarian economic system, with minimal distortions in economic activities. One important implication of the Quranic directions is that there should be an equitable distribution of economic resources, especially land, if it is found to be starkly unequal in a society. An important message of Islam is that none should fully enjoy his or her own fruits of labor but share them with his or her fellow beings through an appropriate distribution system.

Interest has become an unavoidable, integral part of the modern economy. It plays a very powerful role as an economic development and monetary policy instrument and as an essential device for efficient allocation of productive resources. Islamic banks do not really avoid interest except in *mudaraba* and *musharaka* financing, but this financing mode is not much used, in part because heavy reliance on such financing does not assure good returns to them. Islamic banks use a reference rate that is called a profit rate. But this is essentially interest in nature. But their overt non-embracing of interest deprives the Muslim economies of a very powerful tool that can help promote economic development, assure price stability, and strengthen banking, capital markets, and stock exchanges.

X. The Hadith is Unreliable
Earlier Hadith Criticism and Theological and Historical Tests of Hadith Authority and Authenticity

> These are God's signs (or revelations) that We recite unto thee (O Muhammad) with truth. Then in which Hadith (story), after God and His revelations, will they believe? —*The Quran*, 45:6

Though the Quran uses the term "Hadith"[1] in a number of its verses, the Hadith in its popular sense refers to traditions attributed to the Prophet Muhammad – his alleged sayings and stories of his practices. Though the Hadith and the Prophetic *sunnah* are not exactly the same thing, the Hadith is considered to be the main vehicle through which the so-called Prophetic '*sunnah*'[2] – the example of the Prophet embodied in his statements, actions, and overt or tacit approvals or disapprovals – has been conveyed. The Hadith and related literature[3] have greatly influenced Muslim beliefs and practices and shaped the development of Islam, as we know it in its various forms. The vast majority of Muslims have come to revere the Hadith literature as the second essential source of religious law and guidance after the Quran.[4] Any question, therefore, about its authority or reliability is likely to be generally greeted by a Muslim with amazement and shock. However, it is time they looked at this question dispassionately to determine whether what they believe to be reliable is really so. It is time this question was settled decisively once and for all.

Generally, those who portray Islam in a good light do so by tapping its "best traditions."[5] The issue, however, is not really about choosing between good and bad traditions; the issue is really about whether we can still afford to continue with traditions that may often misguide us. The Hadith is open to criticism from the perspectives of all conceivable criteria: theological, historical, and objective as follows:

- Theological: This is a test really of the authority of the Hadith beside the Quran as a source of religious law and guidance. This question will be looked at from the point of view of what the Quran itself says about it.
- Historical: This is a question of reliability or authenticity of the Hadith from the point of view of its historical basis.
- Objective: This test looks at how reliable or truthful are the Prophetic accounts in relation to the Quranic text, reason, or scientific truth.

We will turn to these points, but before that it would be in order to note earlier Hadith criticism.

Earlier Hadith Criticism

Aisha Musa's recent work[6], which explores earliest extant discussions on the authority of the Hadith, shows that opposition to the Hadith as a competing source of religious authority started practically from day one of their recording. Such opposition predates Al-Shafii (d. 204 AH/820 CE)[7] and is found in a text that Muslim tradition holds to be a letter from the Kharijite Abd Allah Ibn Ibad to the Caliph Abd al-Malik in 76/695.[8] Though the authorship and dating of this letter are in some dispute, it still predates al-Shafii and its importance as a challenge to the authority of the Hadith remains undented. A key passage of this letter criticizes the Kufans for taking "Hadiths" for their religion abandoning the Quran. "They believed in a book which was not from God, written by the hands of men; they then attributed it to the Messenger of God."[9]

The opposition to the Hadith to which Al-Shafii responds "in his *Kitab Jima al-Ilm* was much as he has portrayed it. Both Al-Shafi'i and Ibn Qutayba (d. 276 AH) refer to the opponents of the Hadith as Ahl al-Kalam. Al-Shafii's work responded to a group that rejected all Prophetic reports and for this rejection their basic argument was that God declares the Quran as an explanation of everything (16:89).[10] In relation to Al-Shafii's position on Wisdom and obedience to the Messenger, they suggested that "the Wisdom is found only in what God has revealed (i.e., the Qur'an); so that whoever submits to that is obeying the Messenger. ... [O]beying the Messenger meant obeying only the Qur'an that God has sent down to him, and that when the Qur'an mentioned the Book together with Wisdom, the Wisdom was the specific rulings of the Book."[11] We find echoes of such arguments in modern Quran-alone or Quran-only movement. Al-Shafii also mentions a group that accepted only those reports that are in agreement with the Quran.[12] Ibn Qutayba dealt with criticisms of particular Hadiths. Musa notes, "Both Al_Shafii and Ibn Qutayba indicate that the objection to Prophetic reports was widespread. Al-Shafi'i states that so many people presented so many arguments to him that he could not exactly remember who said what. Ibn Qutayba makes it clear in his introduction that the opponents of the Hadith had written books containing scathing criticisms of the proponents of the Hadith. To date, none of these books has come down to us."[13] Musa's research demonstrates that opposition to the Hadith as an authoritative scriptural source of law and guidance has not been influenced by modern, Western, orientalist ideas about Islam, but is very much an Islamic development from within – "an inherently Muslim response to inherently Muslim concerns."[14]

Daniel Brown notes that the principal argument of Ahl al-Kalam was that the Hadith does not accurately reflect the Prophetic example, as the transmission of Hadith reports was not reliable. The Prophetic example, they argued, "has to be found elsewhere – first and foremost in following the Qur'an." And according to them, "the corpus of Hadith is filled with contradictory, blasphemous, and absurd traditions."[15]

Musa mentions also two other early groups such as the Khazimiyya and Haruri. The former accepted only laws that were suggested by the Quranic text or those transmitted by consensus among Muslims; the latter took the Quran and not the *Sunnah* as the basis of their religious practices. In nearly two centuries after Ibn Qutayba's time, opposition to the Hadith could be discerned again.[16]

Mutazilites, who represented one of the earliest rationalist Muslim theological schools, and are the later Ahl al-Kalam, also viewed the transmission of the Prophetic *sunnah* as not sufficiently reliable.[17] The Hadith, according to them, was mere "guesswork and conjecture [... and] the Quran was complete and perfect, and did not require the Hadith or any other book to supplement or complement it."[18] After Mutazilites, as Azami notes, many early Muslim writers criticized Bukhari's work concerning 80 narrators and 110 individual accounts of Hadith. Of these critics, he mentioned the names of two fourteenth century scholars: Abdur Rahman b. Abu Bakr Suyuti (author of *Tadrib ar-Rawi*, ed. by A. R. Latif, Cairo, 1379) and Ibn Hajar (author of *Hadyal-Sari*, Cairo 1383).[19] However, such early Hadith criticism became suppressed and drowned under opposition by the established *ulama* and their supporters, often with state support.

The trend of opposition to the Hadith re-emerged in the late nineteenth century in the Indian sub-continent as part of a reformist program in Islam. The first such major challenge to the Hadith came from Sir Sayyid Ahmad Khan (1817-1898). He viewed the Hadith as an obstacle to reform and "questioned the historicity and authenticity of many, if not most, traditions, much as the noted scholars Ignaz Goldziher and Joseph Schacht would later do."[20] According to him, the transmitters of Hadith (*rawis*) often engaged in transmitting Hadith according to the sense rather than the exact words of the Prophet. This widespread practice resulted in textual variations among traditions on the same subject, "differences that go well beyond the wording and affect the meaning. As a result, he contends, one can be sure in very few instances that traditions accurately portray the Prophet's words and actions, even if they can be shown to have originated during his lifetime."[21] About Hadith compilers' capacity to judge the character of Hadith transmitters of several past generations involved in oral Hadith transmssion, Sayyid Ahmad Khan further notes, "it is difficult enough to judge the character of living people, let alone long dead. The *muhaddithun* [Hadith scholars/transmitters] did the best they could, but their task was almost impossible."[22]

"Debates in Egypt at the turn of the twentieth century were touched off by an article 'a-Islam huwa ul-Qur'an Wahdahu' ('Islam is the Qur'an Alone' that appeared in the Egyptian journal *al-Manar*."[23] This article was authored by Muhammad Tawfiq Sidqi (d. 1920). "Sidqi held that nothing of the Hadith was recorded until after enough time had elapsed to allow the infiltration of numerous absurd or corrupt traditions."[24] At the theological level, he argued that the Quran was sufficient as guidance: "'what is obligatory for man does not go beyond God's Book.' Thus the Qur'an explains itself as 'the book which explains all things' (16:89), and God Himself bears witness that He has 'omitted nothing from the Book' (6:38) [...] obedience to the Prophet [...] Muhammad's authority [...] is strictly limited to implementing the Quran."[25] "If anything other than the Qur'an had been necessary for religion," Sidqi further notes, "the Prophet would have commanded its registration in writing, and God would have guaranteed its preservation."[26] Mahmud Abu Rayya, whose book on the Hadith was published in Cairo in 1958, viewed the Hadith as unreliable.[27] Abu Rayya regarded the absence of recording of Hadith in written form in more than one hundred years after the Prophet's death as a major obstacle to the authenticity of the Hadith.[28]

It is also worth noting that in the early twentieth century, in the generation following Sayyid Ahmad Khan (in India) and Muhammad Abduh (in Egypt), there emerged a self-designated Ahl-i-Quran group who argued along Sidqi's theological lines. They "came to view adherence to Hadith as the cause of Islam's misfortunes;" and "argued that pure and unadulterated Islam is to be found only in the Qur'an," which alone is "a reliable basis for religious belief and action."[29] This movement was represented by Abd Allah Chakralawi (d. 1930), Mistri Muhammad Ramadan (1875-1940), Khwaja Ahmad Din Amritsari (1861-1936), and Muhammad Aslam Jayrajpuri (1881-1955).[30] In Bangladesh, Maulana Akram Khan (1869-1968)[31], a noted journalist and biographer of the Prophet Muhammad, taking examples from *Bukhari* and *Muslim*, showed that Hadith texts (*matn*) could be incorrect or unacceptable, even if the chain of transmission (*isnad*) was regarded as sound.[32]

Ghulam Ahmed Parwez (1903-1985) of Pakistan (originally of the East Punjab, India)[33] was one of the first major Hadith critics of modern time. According to him, the treatment of the Hadith or *sunnah* as a divinely inspired source in Islam was fundamentally flawed. He refuted Shaffi's contention that the expression *"hikmah"* in the Quran (2: 129) referred to the Prophet's *sunnah* by contending that this expression is used in a general sense of "wisdom".[34] If the Hadith was divine revelation (*wahy*), Parwez argues, then why was it not preserved in the same way as the Quran? In sharp contrast to the case of the Quran, he notes, "No steps were taken by the Prophet or by his immediate followers to preserve the integrity of *Hadith*."[35] He also contended that unreliability of Hadith transmission "undermines its validity."[36] Thus, according to him, there could not be any *shari*ah (or *sunnah*) aside from the Quran. This contention has been termed as heresy by Mawdudi's Jamaat-i Islami group, even though Mawdudi himself is regarded by some as a critic of the Hadith in some way. Regarded as the founder of the anti-Hadith movement in the Indo-Pak sub-continent[37], Parwez was declared an infidel (*kafir*) by the *ulama*. Another Muslim scholar, a contemporary of Parwez, who did not accept the unquestioned authority of the Hadith was Ghulam Jilani Barq[38] who contended that only such Hadith was acceptable which did not conflict with the Quran and which did 'not repudiate morality or human experience.'[39]

Another notable work in this direction in recent years is that of an Egyptian-American scholar Rashad Khalifa (1935-1990).[40] Some of his earlier work on Islam such as that on a mathematical miracle about the Quran along with his admirable, easy-to-understand English translation of the Quran[41] drew international acclaim from the Muslim world, which he soon lost with his anti-Hadith stance. Using mainly theological arguments, his fundamental thesis was that it s the Quran alone that fully defines Islam. The Quran is complete, fully detailed and explained, and also the best and only legitimate Hadith. The Prophet's job was simply to deliver the Quran, and nothing else. He was forbidden even to explain it. "Obeying the Prophet" means obeying the Quran. Following the so-called Hadith amounts to following the Hadith of those who collected and compiled them; it does not mean following that of the Prophet. Following the so-called Hadith has led Muslims to insult as well as idolize the Prophet. A progressive deterioration of the Muslim *ummah* began with the appearance of the Hadith. Rashad Khalifa, however, complicated his position by declaring himself as a Messenger of God, even though he maintained that the Quran is the final Message from God brought by the Prophet Muhammad. An assembly of *ulama* in Saudi Arabia declared him an apostate, which apparently led to his assassination in 1990. However, the movement triggered by him did not end with his assassination, but got rather reinvigorated. Some of his followers or admirers, notably Edip Yuksel and Layth Saleh al-Shaiban, have been playing key roles in an ongoing Quran-only movement (See below for some elaboration).

Another notable recent piece of work along this line is that of Kassim Ahmad[42] of Malaysia. His work rejected the Hadith as a basis for theology and law, and states that "the Hadith are 'sectarian, anti-science, anti-reason and anti-women'."[43] He contends that the Prophet brought only one book, the Quran, not two books. He raises the pertinent questions: why it took 250-350 years for the Hadith to be compiled and why the Sunnis have collections different from the Shi'ites. He analyzes the factors such as power struggles and theological disputes that led to Hadith compilation and draws a close parallel between the appearance of and reliance on the Hadith and the decline and backwardness of Muslims?[44] The Malaysian government proscribed Ahmad's book in 1986, and the country's established *ulama* have declared him as "the enemy of Islam."

The Bangladeshi writer Panaullah Ahmad makes some terse, forceful comments on the Hadith, scattered in his book *Creator and Creation* published in 1986,[45] which dismiss the Hadith effectively as an authority for religious law and guidance. According to him, the "chequered history" of Hadith recording, collection, and compilation "due to bribery, sabotage," and a long lapse of time from the Prophet's death points to its "grave shortcomings." He continues, Islam does not entertain "monarchical imperialism and any state or even priestly interference" with the Divine code, but examples of such interference abound in the Hadith. This has resulted in numerous Hadith texts that give up or negate "parts or key points of the Quran [...] or clouding of the real issues." In the process, the Hadith has become "more a detractor of the Quran and the Prophet than a real guide [...] Non-compilation by the Prophet's contemporaries during his lifetime, non-systematization for about two centuries, concoction and ingenious forging of reports by pseudo-enemies and faulty transmission – all contributed to a spurt of spurious Hadith that led to clouding of the real issues; and so practice of religious principles affected by this inimical process tended towards rigidity rather than elasticity so beautifully inherent in God's revelation [...] [This] has contributed to regimentation of thoughts and ideas." Being "more or less confined to the ritual aspect of Islam," it "tended towards regimentation not only in thought but also in habits." It has painted the Prophet and some of his illustrious wives in ways that go beyond the "bounds of propriety. [...] It has given four schools of thought, which stultify the Quran itself (II-176 Baqra, VI-159 An'am)."[46]

    A vigorous ongoing movement to reform Islam along the teachings of the Quran alone is being led by the Turkish-American scholar Edip Yuksel. As a first key step, he along with his colleagues Layth Saleh al-Shaiban and Martha Shulte-Nafeh came out in 2007 with their "Quran: A Reformist Translation" – second, to my knowledge, after Rashad Khalifa's, which is a landmark contribution toward getting an understanding of the Quran largely free from the undue influence of the Hadith literature and the sectarian teachings of traditional Muslim clerics. Their commentary in this translation powerfully demonstrates why we should trash all the Hadith books. It also contains a manifesto for Islamic reform along the Quranic lines alone, which is also separately published. Another key figure reinforcing this Quran-only movement is Ahmed Subhy Mansour, an Egyptian-American and a former Al Azhar University professor, whose works in both Arabic and English are available both in traditional print media and on the Internet (See Ahl Al-Quran international website http://www.ahl-alquran.com/English/main.php; in Arabic *www.ahl-alquran.com*).

    Aisha Musa's *Hadith as Scripture: Discussions on the*

Authority of the Prophetic Traditions in Islam, 2008 is also a significant scholarly contribution to the ongoing debate over the authority of the Hadith as a scriptural source of religious law and guidance. This work reviews arguments that have been employed both for and against the authority of the Hadith in early Islam and finds resonance of the early anti-Hadith arguments in modern discourses. Importantly, it lays bare the weaknesses of the pro-Hadith arguments.[47]

A new compilation of contributions from many contemporary reform-minded Muslim scholars, *Critical Thinkers for Islamic Reform*, published in 2009, is a first major effort at group level to spearhead the ongoing Quran-only or Quran-mainly movement. The Quran-only movement is also being importantly aided, in this Internet age, by numerous website writings, blog and forum discussions and those on social media sites such as the Facebook, Twitter, and Linkedin, and freely available online anti-Hadith books and articles. These and other recent developments such as the negative stereotyping of Islam amid the recurrence of violence and terrorism orchestrated by Muslim extremists have spurred what appears to be an unprecedented surge in interest and curiosity among both Muslims and non-Muslims to know what genuine Islam is about. It is evident that the Quran-only movement is showing new signs of life and gaining a new momentum.

It is also in order here to note that the call for *ijtihad* (independent reasoning or reinterpretation) and rejection of *taqlid* or blind imitation of the past made by many modern scholars is essentially a call for rejection of the unquestioned authority of the Prophetic traditions. The pioneers of this movement include figures such as Jamal al-Din al-Afghani (1838-1897) and his disciple Muhammad Abduh (1849-1905) in the Middle East, Muhammad Iqbal (1875-1938) in South Asia, and many contemporary scholars especially in America and Europe among who are Abdulaziz Sachedina of the University of Virginia, M. A.

Muqtedar Khan of the University of Delaware, and Tariq Ramadan of Oxford University. These reformist thinkers stress the role of *ijtihad* in Islam to respond to the demands of modernity and to revive the inner dynamics and creative character of Islam. The closing of the door of *ijtihad* by the 10th or 12th century, according to the Indian-Pakistani Poet-Philosopher Iqbal, put Islam in "'a dogmatic slumber' that resulted in five hundred years of immobility due to the blind following of the tradition."[48]

Non-Muslim modern Western scholars have also seriously questioned the historicity and authenticity of the Hadith, which became a legitimate source that undermined Islam in their eyes. Noted among these Hadith critics are Sir William Muir[49], Alois Sprenger[50], Ignaz Goldziher[51], Joseph Schacht[52] and G.H.A. Juynboll[53]. Muir and Sprenger were the first Western scholars to question the reliability of the Hadith literature as a historical source.[54] Muir contended, "the Qur'an alone represents a reliable source for Muhammad's biography," and it accurately portrays "his own thought":

> The Coran [Quran] becomes the groundwork and the test of all inquiries into the origin of Islam and the character of its founder. Here we have a store-house of Mahomet's own words recorded during his life, extending over the whole course of his public career, and illustrating his religious views, his public acts, and his domestic character.[55]

He regarded the Hadith literature as "plagued with corruptions and of limited value as a source for the earliest history of Islam. Muir completely discounted the value of classical Hadith criticism based on an examination of the chain of transmission, the *isnad*. He insisted that the text of the tradition itself, the *matn*, 'must stand or fall upon its own merits.'"[56]

The Hungarian scholar Ignac Goldziher "has documented numerous Hadith the transmitters of which claimed were derived from Muhammad but which were in reality verses from the Torah and Gospels, bits of rabbinic sayings, ancient Persian maxims, passages of Greek philosophy, Indian proverbs, and an almost word-for-word reproduction of the Lord's Prayer."[57]

Joseph Schacht, "the most influential modern Western authority on Islamic law [...] on the basis of his research, [...] found no evidence of legal traditions before 722 [CE], one hundred years after the death of Muhammad. Thus he concluded that the *Sunna* of the Prophet is not the words and deeds of the Prophet, but apocryphal material originating from customary practice that was projected back to the eighth century to more authoritative sources – first the Successors, then the Companions, and finally the Prophet."[58]

G.H.A. Juynboll's work is a powerful critique not only of the authenticity of the Hadith, but also of scholarly works, which have attempted to support notions of the authenticity of the Hadith. In criticizing the *isnads* (chains of narrators) he quite bluntly states:

> I am skeptical as to whether we will ever be able to prove beyond a shadow of a doubt that what we have in the way of 'sound prophetic traditions' is indeed just what it purports to be.[59]

Juynboll cites numerous Hadiths with which persons such as Sa'id ibn al Musayyab (d. 93 AH/711 CE) and Hasan al Basri (d. 110 AH/728 CE) and several other companions and successors of the Prophet could be rightfully credited, but which "he contends later evolved into prophetic traditions that can be found among the Six Books."[60]

The Theological Test

The *ulama* present various arguments in support of the authority of the Hadith as a second source of Islam. These arguments could be grouped as follows:

- God urges us to obey His Messenger and follow his example;
- The Hadith is also some kind of revelation from God, which the Prophet followed;
- The Quran is not sufficient for us; it does not explain everything; e.g., *salat* is not explained fully by the Quran; and the Hadith makes it easier to understand the Quran.

Do these arguments really stand to scrutiny? Let's analyze below.

The Argument: God Urges Us to Obey His Messenger and Follow His Example

This is a basic argument used by Hadith advocates right from Al-Shafii's time. Many Quranic verses are cited to support this argument. A sample is as follows:

3:31-32	Say (O Muhammad): 'If ye do love God, then follow me; God will love you and forgive your faults, and God is Ever Forgiving, Most Merciful.' Say: 'Obey God and the Messenger; but if they turn away, then verily God loveth not those who disbelieve.' (See also 4:59 and 8:20)
4:80	He who obeyeth the Messenger indeed obeyeth God.

> 59:7 Whatever the Messenger giveth you, take it and whatever he forbiddeth you, refrain from it.
>
> 33:21 Indeed in the Messenger of God ye have an excellent example for him who looketh unto God and the Final Day, and remembereth God much.

However, from these and similar Quranic verses, it is not possible to conclude with certainty that they point to the need for accepting the Hadith as a separate source of religious law and guidance. The verse 59:7, in particular, has been used partially out of context; the full verse shows that the above statement relates to the distribution of war booties and has nothing to do with the acceptance of the Hadith. As we have seen, the early opponents of the Hadith such as Ahl al-Kalam and Mutazilites as well as their modern counterparts such as Rashad Khalifa and others have effectively argued that obedience to the Prophet or of his example should not be viewed as separate from following the Quran. The Hadith supporters have interpreted following God as following the Quran and following the Prophet as following the Hadith. However, the verses (3:31-32; 33:21) noted above clearly imply that we should love and follow the Prophet as a way of loving and following God. That these verses do not point to the need for following the Hadith becomes more evident when we consider other verses of the Quran, which emphasize the need for following the Quran alone. First look at the following verses where God refers to the Prophet's sayings as nothing different from those revealed as the Quran:

> 69:40-43 It is the SAYING of an Honoured Messenger. It is not the saying of a poet; little ye believe. Nor is it the saying of a soothsayer; little ye heed. It is a Message revealed from the Lord of the Universe.

More verses emphatically call for following the Quran alone. The Prophet himself emphasized, "I follow naught except what is revealed unto me" (6:50; 46:9) and God advised him and us to do the same (6:155; 45:6; see also 7:3). Also, he was asked to admonish his people only with the Quran (50:45). Another verse cautions us against believing in anything other than God's revelation (45:6). So if we just follow the Quran, we really follow him as well. And it is also noteworthy that the Prophet used to recite the Quran to people around him (62:2; 75:16-19). He did not need to explain it to them, as he was barred from doing that; the burden of explanation was on God Himself (75:18-19).

The Prophet, of course, also said things to his people around him, which were not just recitations from the Quran. During his lifetime, it was incumbent upon the Muslims living around him that they respond to what he said to them and obey him closely, as evident from the verse at (8:20), where God urges believers who hear the Prophet not to turn away from him. Only those around him could hear him. For us and other people of succeeding generations who are not around him, the only meaningful way for responding to him and not turning away from him would be to carefully follow the revelations that he has brought us.

Another relevant point to note is that the Prophet was asked to emulate God's nature (30:30) or God's path, as God is always on the straight path – *sirat im-mustaqim* (11:56). This really means that the Prophet's *sunnah* should not be viewed as separate from that of God, which He has spelled out in the Quran. In fact, God has characterized the content of the Quran as the most consistent and best Hadith (39:23). Thus if we follow the Quran, we also follow both God's and the Prophet's *sunnah*. Note also that the Prophet was specifically urged by God to judge only by the Quran, and not follow any personal desires (6:114; 4:105; 5:48-49). And the Quran also unequivocally proclaims that those who do not judge by what has been revealed from God are disbelievers (*kafirs*) (5:44), wrongdoers (*jalims*) (5:45), or rebellious (*fasiqs*) (5:49). This clearly means that the Quran alone should be used as the basis of religious law in Islam.

And, importantly, the fact that there was not much compiled Hadith during over two centuries after the Prophet's death, which the Prophet's companions and other Muslims during that long period of history could follow, also highlights the point that the Hadith is after all not of much religious significance to Muslims.

Indeed, the Quran best mirrors the conduct of the Prophet. It gives specific references to what he was and what he did, what he personally believed (2:285; 42:15), how he prayed (26:218-219; 52:48-49; 73:2-8, 20), and about his actions that God disapproved of (80:1-11; 33:37; 66:1, 93:7), which he, of course, corrected. How he rose to the status of a Prophet that enabled him to receive comprehensive divine guidance and attain *miraj* (ascension) (17:1, 53:5-18) point to things that men of understanding who have aspiration to attain spiritual progress need to ponder. There are references in the Quran about the Prophet's wives, too (33:32-34; 33: 28-34; 60:12; 66:3-5). In a way the whole Quran is a reflection of, or about, what the Prophet did and said in his life and about how he conducted himself in various situations. Also importantly, God proclaims in the Quran that the Prophet's sole duty was to deliver this Book to humankind (5:67, 92, 99; 13:40; etc.): "But if ye turn away, then know that Our Messenger's duty is only to deliver (the Message)" (5:92). Apparently because Muslims have been giving a lot of importance to other spurious teachings rather than to the Quran, the Prophet is going to lament to God on the Day of Judgment that his people have treated the Quran as a forsaken thing (25:30).

Also, all of the Prophet's personal ways of living may not carry religious significance for other contexts – for example, what he did with his beard or hair, how he cleaned his teeth, what dress he put on, how he slept, what particular foods except the forbidden ones he liked and ate, and so on. Indeed trying to follow everything that the Prophet did without trying to explore and understand their underlying reasons has no real meaning for us. Blind imitation of a person or of the past is "*taqlid,*" which has been dismissed by many Islamic scholars as inappropriate. It is like idolizing a person like a god. Such idolizing is what God has strictly forbidden us (3:79-80). Indeed the Quran does not want us to follow everything the Prophet did, since he also made mistakes (9:43; 80:1-10; 33:37; 66:1), which he, of course, corrected. Furthermore, when particular physical and socioeconomic environments differ, human needs and things that suit them best also differ. Even human body needs, and accordingly food needs, differ from person to person, and from time to time as well as in different health conditions for the same person. The same food may not suit everybody; many are found to be allergic to specific foods (e.g., even normal milk that contains lactose is unsuitable to those who are not lactose-tolerant). The Quran itself recognizes the diversity of nations and tribes (49:13; 2:60). For every one of us God has established a law and an open way; if God had willed He could have made us one nation, but He will try us in what He has given us (5:48). Thus even if the Hadith could succeed in giving us the real Prophet, it still would not have validated the need to follow him in every bit of detail. So an attempt to sanctify everything the Prophet did or said as *sunnah* for us cannot be considered as relevant or appropriate. As Kassim Ahmad remarks:

> It is unreasonable and unthinkable that God would ask the Muslims to follow the prophet's personal mode of behavior, because a person's mode of behavior is determined by many different factors, such as customs, his education, personal upbringing and personal inclinations. The prophet's mode of

eating, of dress and indeed of general behavior cannot be different from that of other Arabs, including Jews and Christians, of that time, except regarding matters which Islam prohibited. If the Prophet had been born a Malay, he would have dressed and eaten like a Malay. This is a cultural and a personal trait which has nothing to do with one's religion.[61]

From whatever point of view one likes to consider, the need for the Hadith has no legitimate basis. The Quran does not validate its authority as a source of religious law and guidance.

The Argument: The Hadith is also a Kind of Divine Revelation

This argument originates from Muhammad b. Idris al-Shafii (d. 204 AH/820 CE) who granted the Hadith the status of a second form of divine revelation (*wahy*) in the form of "*hikmah*" (wisdom) mentioned in the Quran along with the Book (62:2). However, the group referred to as Ahl al-Kalam, even during al-Shafii's time, effectively refuted his position on Wisdom and obedience to the Messenger, stating that the Wisdom is found only in the Divine revelation, i.e., the Quran; so that whoever submits to that is obeying the Messenger; obeying the Messenger meant obeying only the Quran that God has sent down to him, and when the Quran mentioned Wisdom together with the Book, the Wisdom specifically meant the rulings of the Quran itself. As Aisha Musa rightly points out, al-Shafii also fails to address the Hadith opponents' point that the Quran is an explanation of everything.[62]

The flaws in al-Shafii's arguments have provided the basic ground for the challenge to the scriptural authority of the Hadith to continue and gain traction in modern time. As we have seen above, Ghulam Ahmad Parwez effectively refuted al-Shafii's argument by saying that "*hikmah* or wisdom" is meant in a general sense and cannot be characterized as specifically meaning the Prophet's Hadith. This contention has support in the fact that all prophets essentially undergo spiritual transformation and they all bring to humankind wisdom and insight into religion and spirituality. Their revealed book is the main vehicle of such wisdom. But apart from that it is also true that their followers and associates during their lifetime did have an extra advantage to have some access to such wisdom. Note also that the verse (62:2) refers specifically to the inhabitants of Mecca, who were in clear error, to whom the Prophet came. That the expression "the Book and the *hikmah*" used in the Quran need not specifically mean the Prophet's Hadith is supported by the fact that the same expression is found to have been used also in the case of other prophets, Jesus, the house of Abraham and John (3:48, 79, 81; 5:110, 4:54; 19:12). Also note that God characterizes the Quran itself as a Book of wisdom (10:1; 31:2; 36:2; 43:4). So it cannot be held with certainty that the expression "*hikmah*" at verse (62:2) unequivocally refers to the Prophet's Hadith. Rather all these verses reinforce the idea that "wisdom" refers to general "spiritual or religious knowledge and insight" that prophets are usually endowed with, and those who came in close association with such persons benefited the most from such wisdom. But this does not necessarily lend support to any Hadith hypothesis.

The Quranic verse at (53:3), which says that the Prophet did not say anything of his own desire, is also taken to mean that everything he said was divinely inspired. So whatever he said outside the Quran is meant as referring to his Hadith. This argument is also flawed, since this verse could and should be interpreted to precisely mean that he has not uttered anything of religious significance that is not in the divinely inspired Book, the Quran, as supported by the verse (69:40-43) cited above. It further begs the question at the very outset: if the Hadith is also some kind of revelation from God, how is it that it is not included in the Quran, or even not compiled by his close associates? "The absence of written records brings into question the revealed status of *sunna*; if *sunna* was *wahy* [revelation] it certainly would have been recorded in writing. [...] neither the Prophet, nor his Companions, nor the early Caliphs considered anything to be revelation except the Qur'an."[63] The question also arises of why it took well more than one hundred years after the Prophet's death to discover this perceived truth that *sunnah* is also divine revelation.

In fact the Quran affirms that it is the disbelieving or wrongdoing people who used to fabricate sayings in God's name even during the Prophet's lifetime:

> 3:78 And verily there is a party among them who distort the Book with their tongues, that ye may think that it is of the Book, but it is not of the Book. And they say: It is from God; but it is not from God. And they invent a lie against God, while they know it.

And during the Prophet's time there were also illiterate people who did not know the Quran except from hearsay and those who used to write with their own hands and say that those writings were from God (2:78-79). These verses and the verse at (3:78) strongly indicate that the tendency to fabricate sayings in God's name or, by implication, in the Prophet's name has been there ever since the Prophet's lifetime. These verses lend strong support to the point that the Hadith that came long after the Prophet's demise can claim little credibility, let alone claim the status of divine revelation.

The Argument: The Quran is Not Sufficient and Easy; It Does Not Explain Everything

It is indeed ironic that it is Muslims, who are influenced by the Hadith, who think that the Quran is not sufficient or easy as guidance. The *ulama* usually employ this argument in favor of the

Hadith. But by so doing they do in effect doubt or contradict the Quranic claims that it explains everything and that it's easy to follow.

> 16:89 And We have revealed unto thee (O Muhammad) the Book explaining everything, a guidance and a mercy and good news for those who have surrendered (to God, i.e., who have become Muslims).
>
> 54:17 And We have indeed made the Quran easy to learn; then is there any that will learn? (See also 6:114; 54:22, 32, 40.)

The revealed Word of God is, as it has been meant to be, clear, accessible, and readily comprehensible. The Quran is self-contained and must be understood by its internal logic and interpreted by its own verses, without any external aid. Inayat Allah Khan Mashriqi, the founder of the radical Khaksar movement in India, notes:

> The correct and the only meaning of the Qur'an lies, and is preserved, within itself, and a perfect and detailed exegesis of its words is within its own pages. One part of the Qur'an explains the other; it needs neither philosophy, nor wit, nor lexicography, nor even Hadith.[64]

The Quran is comprehensive; and all the requirements for belief and practice in religion are contained in it. It is a fully sufficient guidance for humankind.

> 17:9 Surely this Quran guideth unto that which is most right and giveth good news to those who believe and do

good work that theirs will be a great reward.

Thus if God says He has made the Quran easy enough to learn or understand, it is incomprehensible why our *ulama* should dispute it. On the other hand, it is also true that the Quran is a Book of wisdom, and that how far one succeeds in deciphering the wisdom of the Quran depends on one's capacity to understand, which, in turn, is a function of one's level of intelligence, knowledge, and wisdom. What turns out to be the real beauty of the Quran is that as one gets wiser and wiser, one can find and extract deeper and deeper meanings from the Quranic message. As mentioned in Chapter 1, there are some verses in the Quran, which are allegorical and not easily comprehended by all. Only those who are grounded well in knowledge, i.e., spiritually advanced, understand them. The fact that there are some verses in the Quran, which are not understood or well understood by some readers, does not warrant them to take recourse to the Hadith. Is there any evidence that the Hadith has made clearer those verses of the Quran, which are not easy to understand? Rather on the contrary, the available evidence suggests that the Hadith has made confusion more confounded (See the next chapter).

Indeed, the Quran has been revealed with so much clarity and elaboration and, in many cases, with repetitions of the same verses, that it hardly needs any explanation from an external source. To become a good and wise Muslim, one does not need any other document, just as Muslims during the two centuries after the Prophet's death did not need any.

The contention, or concerns, of the *ulama* that the Quran does not give sufficient details of the *salat* system that Muslims practice have been addressed in Chapter IV. What we need to realize is that whatever has not been categorically mentioned in the Quran concerning anything should not be regarded as essential elements of Islam. Whatever religious practices God wants us to follow are adequately and lucidly described and explained in the Quran. Even minute details of admonitions have not been left untouched. Rather, the Hadith has corrupted the *salat* practice, as discussed in Chapter IV, as other practices (See also the next chapter).

Also, as some commentators have argued, certain religious rituals such as *salat* and *hajj* were already there, and have come down to us from generation to generation through our fathers and forefathers. They were copied and carried forward from the time of the Prophet Abraham (21:73), whom the Prophet Muhammad followed (3:95; 2:135; 4:125; 16:123). Such practices or *sunnah* do not require any reference to the Hadith.[65]

The Historical Test

The historical basis of the Hadith is at best tenuous. Some of the historical points such as (1) the reported prohibition of the Prophet himself on Hadith writing, and honoring of the same position by his immediate followers, (2) the long time gap between the Quran and the Hadith, and the accompanying lack of proper records of the deeds and sayings of the Prophet, and (3) flawed oral transmission due to weakness of the human sources including their imperfect memories add well to effectively dismiss the Hadith altogether as untrustworthy. To this list one may add (4) the influence of the ruling regimes, of people with wealth and power of the time, and of the disputing theologians on Hadith collection, recording, selection, and compilation, and finally (5) the weakness of the criteria used to judge authenticity of individual Hadith texts.

The Positions of the Prophet and his Companions on Hadith Writing

Kassim Ahmad notes: "Notwithstanding the conflicting

versions of *Hadith* that say otherwise, historical facts [...] prove beyond any shadow of doubt that there were no *Hadith* collections existing at the time of the Prophet's death. History also proves that the early caliphs prevented the recording and dissemination of Hadith."[66]

The *ulama* take it for granted that the Prophet gave his blessing to the collection and writing of his Hadith. Mazhar Kazi reports that in his farewell address the Prophet declared, "Convey to others even if it is a single verse from me."[67] This is taken as a go-ahead for Hadith dissemination. However, the statement here more meaningfully appears rather to point to the revealed Quranic verses, not his own words, since he was the messenger of God's message and mercy for the whole universe (68:52; 21:107) and his message, which was nothing but the Quran, needed to be conveyed to all humankind.

Aisha Musa notes that three collections of Hadith contain a report narrated seven times, with only minor variations in textual content, by Abu Sa'id Khudri refer to "a direct command from the Prophet prohibiting his followers from writing down anything on his authority other than the Qur'an and ordering those who had done so to erase what they had written."[68] One such report finds place in *Sahih Muslim* (Book 042, Chapter 17, Number 7147). There are similar other Hadith reports, e.g., one from *Abu Dawud*, and another from *Taqyid* by al-Baghdadi confirming the Prophet's prohibition on Hadith writing, and direction for erasure of any Hadith.[69] Musa also notes that al-Baghdadi's reports on the authority of Abu Sa'id Khudri, Abu Huraira, Zayd ibn Thabit, and others confirm the Prophet's objections to writing.[70] In one report, Abu Huraira quotes the Prophet as saying, addressing some companions who were writing Hadith, "Is it a book other than the Book of God that you want? The two communities before you went astray only because they wrote some books for themselves along with the Book of God."[71] Evidently, the Prophet was aware of the dangers of writing down his traditions beside the words of God. There are, however, also other reports that temper this position of the Prophet, saying that the Prophet later permitted Hadith transmission and writing.[72]

Whatever historical reports we seem to have about the position of the Khulafai-Rashidun (the Righteous Caliphs) on the Hadith suggest that they also discouraged its compilation. According to one report, the first Caliph Abu Bakr burned his own notes of Hadith (said to be some 500), after being very uneasy about these notes.[73] "According to Jayrajpuri, because the Companions (of the Prophet) so often disagreed with one another Abu Bakr forbade the collection of Hadith."[74] Caliph Umar ibn al-Khattab is well known and well documented for his strong opposition to the transmission and recording of the Hadith.[75] He is reported to have cancelled his initial plan to compile Hadith, apprehending its possible adverse impact in the form of neglect of the Book of God – the Quran. During his caliphate, "the problem of Hadith forgery was so serious that he prohibited Hadith transmission altogether."[76] Umar reportedly also arranged for burning of all available Hadith. The position of Uthman and Ali also appears to have been lack of any overt effort to collect any Hadith for dissemination purposes.

Hazy or conflicting historical reports about the early period of Islam notwithstanding, the fact remains that there were no written records of Hadith during the lifetime of the Prophet as well as during the rule of the four Caliphs. This is despite the fact that "several documents of the Prophet, such as the Medina Charter or Constitution, his treaties and letters, had been written on his orders."[77] This amply proves the point that if the Prophet had wished, he could have made arrangements for recording of his Hadith as a separate religious document, just as he did in the case of the Quran. The stark fact is that he did not wish such recording, and his discouragement of Hadith recording was honored by the four Caliphs and remained in force apparently for some thirty years after the Prophet's death, but was ignored later. According to one report, a Hadith in Abu Dawud, the Ummayad ruler Muawiya wanted a Hadith to be written in the presence of one of the Prophet's most noted scribes Zayd ibn Thabit, but when Zayd reminded him of the Prophet's prohibition on Hadith writing, he (Muawiya) erased it.

As Iqbal notes in his celebrated work *The Reconstruction of Religious Thought in Islam*, even Abu Hanifah, regarded as "one of the greatest exponents of Muhammedan Law in Sunni Islam [...] made practically no use of [...] traditions," even though there were collections available at that time made by other people no less than thirty years before his death. Nor did he collect any Hadith for his use, unlike his peers Malik and Ahmad ibn Hanbal. Thus, according to Iqbal, "if modern Liberalism considers it safer not to make any indiscriminate use of them [traditions] as a source of law, it will be only following [the example of Abu Hanifah]."[78] "In reaction to a situation [where huge numbers of forged Hadith reports were in circulation] that was virtually out of control, Abu Hanifah approached *Hadith* with the assumption that very few could be proved *sahih* [authentic]."[79]

The Long Time Gap and The Lack of Proper Records

The long time lapse with which the Hadith surfaced after the Prophet's death raises questions of its reliability that can never be satisfactorily resolved. Muslim and non-Muslim historians and scholars all point out that there were no written records of the Prophet's sayings and deeds during the first century after his death, and not much Hadith writing – and not any Hadith book that gained respectability later on by the Muslim community at large – during the long two centuries after the Prophet's death.[80] The Hadiths that gained acceptance as *sahih* or authentic such as those collected and compiled by Bukhari (d. 256 AH/870 CE),

Muslim (d. 261/875), Abu Dawud (d. 275/888), Tirmidhi (d. 279/892), Ibn Majah (d. 273/886) and Nasa'i (d. 303/915) – all came more than two hundred years after the Prophet's death. The compilations accepted by the Shiites came even later. They were all based on oral transmission from generation to generation through chains of transmitters (*isnads*) numbering seven to even one hundred in the chain. Even written records of the past traditions were not good enough. As the historian MacDonald notes that one danger in written records "was evidently real ... the unhappy character of the Arabic script, especially when written without diacritical points, often made it hard if not practically impossible, to understand such short, contextless texts as the traditions."[81] "There was fierce opposition to the written records of traditions for a long time also on the theological ground that this would lead to too much honoring of the traditions and neglect of the Quran, a fear that was justified to a certain extent by the event."[82]

    The big question is: Why did the compilations come after such an inordinately long lapse of historical time after the Prophet's death? Kassim Ahmad legitimately asks: "Why was the official compilation not made earlier, especially during the time of the righteous caliphs when the first reporters, i.e., the eye witnesses, were still alive and could be examined?"[83] Because of the long time lag one can hardly be sure that the accounts are genuinely those of the Prophet Muhammad. How can one be so certain that the chain of narrators through the oral transmission has been successful in transmitting the same message *ad verbatim* from generation to generation, when even in the same generation, or say, even in the same year or month or day, people are often found unable to exactly reproduce one's utterances?

    The scholars of Hadith (the *muhaddithun*), "no matter how dedicated, were simply too distant from the time of the Prophet and forgery had become too rampant for authentic *Hadith* to be recovered."[84] Some anecdotes of the *muhaddithun* suggest that they could not prevent forged Hadith from being circulated even in their own names.[85] It is also worth noting that there were enemies of Islam and pseudo-Muslims who wanted to sabotage the propagation of true Islam by attributing false statements or reports either to God, or to His Prophet, right from the Prophet's lifetime. Evidence that there were such people who directed their efforts to diverting attention from the mainstream Islam and to causing dissension and divisions in the Muslim *ummah* even during the Prophet's lifetime is provided by the Quran itself:

> 9:106-7 And there are those who put up a mosque by way of mischief and disbelief, and in order to cause dissension among the believers, and as an outpost for those who fought against God and His messenger before. They will indeed swear: 'Our intention is nothing but good'; but God beareth witness that they are certainly liars. Never stand there (to pray). A mosque whose foundation was laid from the first day on piety is more worthy of your standing therein, wherein are men who love to purify themselves. God loveth those who purify themselves.

Here it refers to some people who put up a mosque to cause dissension among Muslims. Such people were evidently not well-meaning Muslims. Thus, forgers had been active even during the Prophet's lifetime. Forgery had been rampant during the caliphate of the Prophet's immediate successors, and it "only increased under the Umayyads[86], who considered Hadith a means of propping up their rule and actively circulated traditions against Ali, and in favor of Muawiya. The Abbasids[87] followed the same pattern, circulating Prophetic Hadith, which predicted the reign of each successive ruler. Moreover, religious and ethnic conflicts further contributed to the forgery of Hadith."[88]

Flawed Oral Transmission Due to Human Sources

Since the Hadith was preserved and transmitted primarily orally, both by default and design, the transmission process was as good as the human sources involved in the process. The oral transmission was preferred to written records by the Hadith scholars, because written records to be credible required direct attestation by living transmitters of Hadith who could vouch for their credibility. The question is: Was this transmission process reliable enough to give assurance that what we get as words or reports of deeds of the Prophet are genuinely those of the Prophet?

Also note that Hadith reports originating from all narrators do not command the same credibility. Hadith reports that are reported to have originated from two of the companions of the Prophet, Anas b. Malik and Abu Huraira are especially suspect. Anas lived long (about hundred years), because of which it was convenient for Hadith forgers to list him as an originator.[89] "Aisha criticized Anas for transmitting traditions although he was only a child during the life of the Prophet."[90] Aisha was reported to have criticized also Abu Huraira and Ibn Abbas joined her in this criticism.[91] Abu Huraira was originator of a very large number of Hadith texts (more than 5000), even though he converted to Islam in less than three years before the Prophet's death. According to some reports, the second Caliph "Umar called Abu Huraira a liar,"[92] and reprimanded him for his questionable conduct. During Muawiya's rule, he reportedly lived in his palace in Syria.[93] His memory was poor, but the Bukhari compilation provides reference to his poor memory being miraculously cured by the Prophet (*Sahih Bukhari*, Vol. 1, Book 3, #119, also repeated at Vol. 4, Book 56, #841, also repeated by another narrator with a somewhat different text at Vol. 1, Book 3, #120), a claim that might not be true. And legitimately, a question also arises: how sure can one be that the later transmitters (who are known as *rawis*, some of whom were *tabiun*, i.e., companions of the companions of the Prophet, or *tabi-tabiun*, i.e., companions of the *tabiun*) in the *isnad* attributed Hadith texts to the original companion of the Prophet accurately without any mistake, even with full good intentions? Any mistake made by anyone of the narrators of any Hadith in the *isnad* involved would necessarily make its transmission flawed and its accurate attribution to the Prophet difficult.

There are even some Hadith texts in *Bukhari* that suggest that even the Prophet used to forget things (*Sahih Bukhari*, Vol. 1, Book 5, #274, Also Vol. 1, Book 8, #394)! Surely the less reliable human agents involved in Hadith transmission were more likely to forget and make mistakes. The authenticity of Hadith breaks down on this count alone. It definitely relies on too many unproven assumptions.

The Influence of Power Struggles and Theological Rivalries on Hadith Writing

The Umayyad and Abbasid rulers actively promoted Hadith writing. According to a historical tradition, Ibn Shihab al-Zuhri (d. 742 CE) was the first individual to record (in writing) the Hadith, but under duress – under orders from Caliph Hisham, "who became the first traditionist [*sic*] to violate the Prophet's prohibition on recording Hadith in writing. Al-Zuhri is reported to have said: 'We disapproved of recording knowledge until these rulers forced us to do so. After that we saw no reason to forbid Muslims to do so.'"[94]

About the power struggles and theological rivalries that led to forging of Hadith in circulation, MacDonald notes:

[T]he Umayyads, who reigned from AH 41 to AH 132, for

reasons of state, [...] encouraged and spread—also freely forged and encouraged others to forge—such traditions as were favorable to their plans and to their rule generally. This was necessary if they were to carry the body of the people with them. But they regarded themselves as kings and not as the heads of the Muslim people. This same device has been used after them by all the contending factions of Islam. Each party has sought sanction for its views by representing them in traditions from the Prophet, and the thing has gone so far that on almost every disputed point there are absolutely conflicting prophetic utterances in circulation. It has even been held, and with some justification, that the entire body of normative tradition at present in existence was forged for a purpose.[95]

One example of Hadith fabrication given by Goldziher is that by Ummayad caliph Abd al-Malik also known as Malik b. Anas[96] who was an important collector of Hadith is as follows:

When the Umayyad caliph 'Abd al-Malik wished to stop the pilgrimages to Mecca because he was worried lest his rival 'Abd Allah b. Zubayr should force the Syrians journeying to the holy places in Hijaz to pay him homage, he had recourse to the expedient of the doctrine of the vicarious *hajj* to the Qubbat al-Sakhra in Jerusalem. He decreed that obligatory circumambulation (*tawaf*) could take place at the sacred place in Jerusalem with the same validity as that around the Ka'ba ordained in Islamic law. The pious theologian al-Zuhri was given the task of justifying this politically motivated reform of religious life by making up and spreading a saying traced back to the Prophet, according to which there are three mosques to which people may take pilgrimages: those in Mecca, Medina, and Jerusalem. [...] An addition which, apparently, belonged to its original form but was later neglected by leveling orthodoxy in this and related sayings: 'and a prayer in the *Bayt al-Maqdis* of Jerusalem is better than a thousand prayers in other holy places,' i.e. even Mecca or Medina. Later, too, 'Abd al-Malik is quoted when the pilgrimage to Jerusalem is to be equated with that to Mecca.[97]

Contemporary Muslim scholar Jeffrey Lang cites another example of a politically motivated Hadith. The following Hadith report in *Sahih Bukhari*, "which so succinctly exonerates the first three Caliphs [after the Prophet's death] in the precise order of their reigns, certainly sounds like it was invented to refute their detractors."[98]

> On the authority of Abu Musa: the Prophet entered a garden and bade me guard its gate. Then a man came and asked leave to enter. And [the Prophet] said: Let him enter, and announce to him [that he will gain] Paradise. – And lo, it was Abu Bakr. Thereafter another man came and asked leave to enter. And [the Prophet] said: Let him enter, and announce to him [that he will gain] Paradise. – And lo, it was 'Umar. Thereafter another man came and asked leave to enter. And [the Prophet] remained silent for a while; then he said: Let him enter, and announce to him [that he will gain] Paradise after a calamity that is to befall him. – And lo, it was 'Uthman ibn 'Affan.[99] (Similar texts in *Sahih Bukhari*, Vol. 5, Book 57, # 42, 44)

Lang provides two examples of Hadith fabrication in the area of theological disputes. One point of contention is that "[...] the legitimacy of *ijma* (consensus) as a source of Islamic Law was much debated during Imam al Shafi'i's time, who defends it in his *Risala*, Yet al Shafi'i, a leader in the Hadith party, was apparently unaware of the famous statement of the Prophet, "my community will never agree on an error" (al Tirmidhi), which establishes its validity. Another point of contention among al Shafi'i's colleagues is whether prophetic *sunnah*s on issues unmentioned in the Qur'an are binding. This time, however, al Shafi'i is able to call upon a made-to-order Hadith:

> Narrated Abu Rafi: The Prophet said: 'Let me not find any one of you reclining in his couch and saying when a command reaches him, "I do not know. We shall follow [only] what we find in the Book of God." (*Abu Dawud*)[100]

Lang also cites the example of the stoning of married adulterers introduced by the Hadith, but which conflicts with the Quran, and which did not go unchallenged in early Islam. He further notes:

> There are numerous examples like these in the tradition literature of seemingly made-to-order Hadiths that provide unequivocal proof for the correctness of various juridical stances that were taken in long-standing legal debates. If these traditions are genuine, it is surprising that these debates persisted so long – often into the late second and third Islamic centuries – and that these extremely convenient traditions are not cited in earlier works that discuss the topics they address.[101]

> The *rijal* and other Hadith related literature describe [...] motivations behind Hadith fabrication. Political, sectarian, partisan, prejudicial, and self-aggrandizing aims were frequently behind Hadith deception. Most often Hadiths were manufactured and manipulated to lend prophetic authority to customs, opinions, doctrines, or party planks that were unconnected to his [the Prophet's] teachings and behaviors.[102]

About questionable Hadith authentication, contemporary Iranian-American scholar Reza Aslan comments as follows:

> By the ninth century, when the Islamic law was being fashioned, there were so many false Hadith circulating through the community that Muslim legal scholars somewhat whimsically classified them into two categories: lies told for material gain and lies told for theological advantage. In the ninth and tenth centuries, a concerted effort was made to sift through the massive accumulation in order to separate the reliable from the rest. Nevertheless, for hundreds of years, anyone who had the power and wealth necessary to influence public opinion on a particular issue – and who wanted to justify about, say, the role of women in society – had only to refer to a Hadith which he had heard from someone, who had heard it from someone else, who had heard from a Companion, who had heard it from the Prophet.[103]

Thus according to Aslan, one basic reason behind the distorted Prophetic traditions was that those who took upon themselves the task of projecting Islam – "men who were, coincidentally, among the most powerful and wealthy members of the *ummah* – were not nearly as concerned with the accuracy of their reports or the objectivity of their exegesis as they were in regaining the financial and social dominance that the Prophet's reforms had taken from them."[104]

The Novel Criteria Used to Judge Authenticity of the Hadith

The Hadith believers boast of certain criteria that were used by the compilers to screen out fake Hadith and select authentic Hadith, listed in annex to this chapter. These criteria are euphemistically labeled as "the science of the Hadith" (*ilm al-*

Hadith) or the science of accepting and rejecting narrations (*ilm al-Jarh wa al-Ta'dil*). However, on close scrutiny, these criteria are not fool-proof to establish undisputed authenticity of Hadith accounts, as evidenced by the inclusion in so-called *sahih* Hadiths of numerous texts that are "vulgar, absurd, theologically objectionable, or morally repugnant"[105] (See the next chapter for illustrations). These criteria, as an anonymous writer remarks, are:

> [A] system of guidelines which numerous scholars, both Muslim and non-Muslim alike, have clearly shown to be seriously inadequate – if not a complete farce, as these standards are broken on numerous occasions in even the 'best' collections of Hadith. This of course makes the authenticity of the Hadith dubious at best – a situation with serious ramifications for the Islamic *sharia* and the religion of Islam as a whole [when, of course, understood in terms of the Quran and the Hadith together].[106]

The criteria relate to the *isnad* and *matn*. However good such criteria might look on paper *prima facie*, they are inherently grossly inadequate for the following reasons:

1. The subjective nature of judgments by individual Hadith compilers about the character of the numerous narrators involved;

2. The multiplicity of *isnad* narrators involved spanning several generations and possible problems associated with *isnads*;

3. Possibility of human error committed by narrators involved due to communication, human memory, or other problems;

4. The sheer vast number of *matn* texts involved;

5. Observed biases of the compilers in their choice of narrators and choice of texts; and

6. Flaws in the criteria themselves.

The basic question that needs to be judged first is that it is the compiler like Bukhari, Muslim, etc., who is judging the character and qualifications of the narrators, and whose judgment could easily go wrong. It is beyond anybody's comprehension how it was possible for one to ascertain with full accuracy that a narrator had not lied or not made any unintentional mistake in stating things, even if he was known to be pious or virtuous by some traditional standards. As Jayrajpuri aptly notes, "Honesty and dishonesty are internal qualities which cannot be known with any certainty by observers. As a result, *ilm al-rijal* [the knowledge of men] is only an approximate *qiyasi* [science], and one can never be absolutely certain that one's judgment about a transmitter is correct."[107] Also, as already noted earlier citing Sayyid Ahmad Khan, judging the character of contemporary people is difficult enough; accurately judging that of the transmitters of earlier generations must have been very hard indeed, if not totally impossible, especially when the transmitters involved were so numerous and the period covered was so large. As contemporary Muslim scholar Jeffrey Lang aptly notes, "All things considered, it seems that a major drawback of classical Hadith studies is that judgments on the veracity of one set of data – the Hadith reports - are based on a second set of data – the *rijal* reports – that we have no compelling reason to believe is more reliable than the first, quite the opposite."[108]

The criteria of classical Hadith judgment are subject also to criticism that there was always the possibility of forging of the *isnad*, and such forging, according to some reports, took place on just as large a scale as the forging of contents. For forgers, there was always a great incentive to attribute reports to most trustworthy authorities.[109] It appears that *isnad* tampering occurred in various ways: *isnad* invention and theft and, most frequently, *isnad* manipulation, which involved "'tampering with *isnads* in order to make them appear more reliable than they are in reality.'[110] It consisted either of interpolating the name of a trustworthy transmitter or eliminating the name or names of discreditable transmitters from the *isnad*, or both of these."[111] This practice of what is called *tadlis* was widespread; and it consisted of *ihala* (transfer) of traditions from a dubious to a reliable *isnad*, *wasl* or *tawsil* (connecting) of missing links in the *isnad* by interpolating some names of authorities, and *raf* (raising) a tradition to the level of a more prestigious authority, mostly the Prophet, by supplying the necessary links."[112] As Jeffrey Lang points out, "we know from *rijal* and other Hadith related literature that besides *matn* fabrication, *isnad* theft, invention, and tampering had also occurred on an enormous scale, so that the focal point of Hadith evaluation had also suffered from extensive corruption. Yet if the main evidence of Hadith criticism had often been manipulated, then we have every right to wonder how well suited was *isnad* criticism to detecting corrupted chains of transmission."[113] Lang further notes, "Another weak point of classical *isnad* appraisal is that systematic *rijal* criticism upon which it depends did not commence until around 130 AH/747 CE, nearly a century after the origins of the *isnad* system. Hence we find ourselves in a serious predicament: the assessment of the reliability of Hadith reports is based on information that is in nature less reliable than the material we are supposed to judge. This is all the more disconcerting since we have every reason to believe that *tadlis* (*isnad* tampering) occurred on as massive a scale as *matn* fabrication."[114]

And how could one be fully certain that the narrator fully

remembered what he had heard from another narrator, that any of the narrators involved in the chain had not made even the slightest mistake in communication, and that there was absolutely no communication gap between the narrator who narrated a certain story and the narrator who heard the story? There was almost always the possibility for human error, even assuming that the narrators had all the good qualifications and good intentions? As we know from the experience of extensive scientific experimentation carried out in the field of modern information science, it is a proven fact that we find most people not able to exactly reproduce statements made by others – sayings change swiftly from one set of ears to another set. We also know that the compilers had biases in their choice of narrators and both the compilers and the narrators had biases in their choice of Hadith texts, motivated by political and theological grounds. One critic cites that a Hadith originating from Abdullah bin Umar was rejected by Bukhari, although the basically same Hadith narrated by Abu Huraira was accepted, and although many other Hadith texts from Abdullah bin Umar were accepted by Bukhari.[115] In a nutshell, there were too many unknowns and uncertainties as well as biases involved in the selection process of so-called authentic Hadith, which it could not be humanly possible to resolve fully satisfactorily by people like Bukhari. Kassim Ahmad notes:

> However accurate the methodology of the *isnad*, the scholars first started talking about it and started writing it down only about 150 - 200 years after the deaths of the very last *tabi'i tabi'in*. This means that when the research to establish the *isnad* got started, none of the Companions, the succeeding generation, or the generation coming after them [was] available to provide any kind of guidance, confirmation or rebuttal. Therefore, the authenticity of the statements cannot be vouched for at all.

It is not our intention to say that Bukhari, Muslim and others were fabricators. However, even students of elementary psychology or communication will testify that a simple message of, say, 15 words will get distorted after passing through only about five messengers. (Our readers are welcome to try out this experiment). Keep in mind that the Hadith contains thousands of detailed and complex narrations – everything from ablution to jurisprudence. These narrations passed through hundreds of narrators who were spread out over thousands of miles of desert, and spanned over two to three hundred years of history. All this at a time when news traveled at the speed of a camel gait, recorded on pieces of leather or bone or scrolls in a land that had neither paper nor the abundance of scribes to write anything down![116]

Kassim Ahmad continues, "It stands to reason that the Hadith writers depended on much story-telling to fill in the blanks. Many `authentic' narrators whom the Hadith writers allude to in their chains of *isnad* were wholly fabricated names."[117] It was "preposterous and impossible' for Bukhari to have meticulously considered over six hundred thousand Hadith texts to pick his authentic 7,275 Hadith texts in his lifetime in an age when the camel journey was the only available means to cover long desert distances.[118]

Some of the *matn* criteria that were used are flawed or weak on grounds as follows:

1. The criterion that a text should not be inconsistent with other texts of Hadith is weak, as even if a text is not inconsistent with other Hadith texts, all such texts could be simultaneously wrong. Also, this criterion is found

violated by Hadith texts included in the so-called *sahih* category that are either self-conflicting or conflicting with one another (See the next chapter for some examples).

2. Texts prescribing heavy punishments for minor sins or exceptionally large rewards for small virtues were rejected. But this involved the value judgments of the Hadith compilers about what constituted «too heavy» or «too large». There are serious instances of violation of this criterion – One glaring example is Hadith-prescribed punishment for apostasy by killing, though the Quran allows full religious freedom. (See the next chapter for more examples.)

3. Texts referring to actions that should have been commonly known and practiced by others but were not known and practiced were rejected. This criterion is flawed; it does not guarantee the veracity of the text about the Prophet.

4. Most importantly, the criterion such as that the Hadith texts should not be contrary to the Quran, reason, or logic has been flagrantly flouted in numerous cases. Many scholars have demonstrated that numerous Hadith texts do in fact contradict the Quran or do not stand to reason or logic or scientific truths. Illustrations of such inconsistencies are provided in the next chapter.

As Hadith critics have pointed out, the Hadith scholars were mostly concerned with the *isnad* criteria and in the process they neglected the *matn* criteria. Otherwise, how could they compile traditions that were clearly absurd or simply unacceptable from the point of view of the Quran? Khaled Abou El Fadl points out:

> [T]he methodologies of the field [of *'ilal al-matn*, i.e., the field within the science of Hadith related to the defects of Prophetic reports] were elusive, and the judgment reached was fairly subjective. Furthermore, most of the efforts of past scholars of Hadith were directed at authenticating the *isnad* of Hadith. *Matn* analysis remained undeveloped and under-utilized. Even more, the science of Hadith did not correlate the authenticity of Hadith with its theological and social ramifications. The scholars of Hadith did not demand a higher standard of authenticity for a Hadith that could have sweeping theological and social ramifications. Additionally, [...] Hadith scholars did not engage in historical evaluation of Hadith or examine its logical coherence or social impact. Consequently, Hadith scholars often accepted the authenticity of Hadith with problematic theological and social implications.[119]

Thus the so-called criteria used to authenticate Hadiths are inherently flawed and simply inadequate to the massive task. They rather mask or camouflage the real character of the Hadith and thus mislead unsuspecting Muslims.

Annex to Chapter X

Criteria Used For Hadith Evaluation

Cannons for the Evaluation of AHadith[1]

A *Hadith* consists of two parts: its text, called matn, and its chain of narrators, called *isnad*. Comprehensive and strict criteria were separately developed for the evaluation of *matn* and *isnad*. The former is regarded as the internal test of *aHadith*, and the latter is considered the external test. A *Hadith* was accepted as authentic and recorded into text only when it met both of these criteria independently.

Criteria for the Evaluation of *Isnad*

The unblemished and undisputed character of the narrator, called *rawi*, was the most important consideration for the acceptance of a *Hadith*. As stated earlier, a new branch of *'ilm al-Hadith* known as *asma' ar-rijal* was developed to evaluate the credibility of narrators. The following are a few of the criteria utilized for this purpose:

1. The name, nickname, title, parentage and occupation of the narrator should be known.

2. The original narrator should have stated that he heard the *Hadith* directly from the Prophet.

3. If a narrator referred his *Hadith* to another narrator, the

---

[1] Kazi, *op. cit.*, pp. 12-14. All information in this annex has been taken from Kazi's work and shows the orthodox Muslim view of the criteria used to 'authenticate' Hadith. Also cited in, Anonymous author, *Hadith Authenticity: A Survey of Perspectives*, at website: http://www.rim.org/muslim/Hadith.htm, or at http://www.rim.org/muslim/islam.htm, pp. 9-10.

two should have lived in the same period and have had the possibility of meeting each other.

4. At the time of hearing and transmitting the *Hadith*, the narrator should have been physically and mentally capable of understanding and remembering it.

5. The narrator should have been known as a pious and virtuous person.

6. The narrator should not have been accused of having lied, given false evidence or committed a crime.

7. The narrator should not have spoken against other reliable people.

8. The narrator's religious beliefs and practices should have been known to be correct.

9. The narrator should not have carried out and practiced peculiar religious beliefs of his own.

Criteria for the Evaluation of *Matn*

1. The text should have been stated in plain and simple language.

2. A text in non-Arabic or couched in indecent language was rejected.

3. A text prescribing heavy punishment for minor sins or exceptionally large reward for small virtues was rejected.

4. A text which referred to actions that should have been commonly known and practiced by others but were not known and practiced was rejected.

5. A text contrary to the basic teachings of the Qur'an was rejected.

6. A text contrary to other *aHadith* was rejected.
7. A text contrary to basic reason, logic and the known principles of human society was rejected.
8. A text inconsistent with historical facts was rejected.
9. Extreme care was taken to ensure the text was the original narration of the Prophet and not the sense of what the narrator heard. The meaning of the *Hadith* was accepted only when the narrator was well known for his piety and integrity of character.
10. A text derogatory to the Prophet, members of his family or his companions was rejected.
11. A text by an obscure narrator, which was not known during the age of *sahabah* [the Prophet's companions] or the *tabi'een* [those who inherited the knowledge of the *sahabah*], was rejected.

Along with these generally accepted criteria, each scholar then developed and practiced his own set of specific criteria to further ensure the authenticity of each *Hadith*. For instance, Imam al-Bukhari would not accept a *Hadith* unless it clearly stated that narrator A had heard it from narrator B. He would not accept the general statement that A narrated through B. On this basis he did not accept a single *Hadith* narrated through 'Uthman, even though Hasan al-Basri always stayed very close to 'Ali. Additionally, it is stated that Imam Ahmad bin Hanbal practiced each *Hadith* before recording it in his *Musnad* [book or collection of *Hadith*].

XI. The Hadith is Unreliable
The Objective Test

And among men are those who purchase idle tales (Hadith) without knowledge to mislead (human beings) from the Path of God, and make a mockery of it (God's Path). For them there awaiteth a humiliating punishment. – The Quran, 31:6

Introduction

Scrutiny of the content of the Hadith from the point of view of its consistency with the Quran, reason, or facts, which is the *matn* or objective criterion, is the litmus test of the reliability of the Hadith as a source of religious guidance and law. Indeed, numerous Hadith texts, which are passed as sound on the *isnad* test, are found to fail the *matn* test. The main purpose here will be to demonstrate that the Hadith is a major distraction from the Quranic message and that instead of complementing and explaining the Quranic message, it contradicts or confounds this message. The content of the Hadith is open to question on various counts:

- Inconsistency with the basic message of the Quran;
- Inconsistency with basic reason or scientific or historical truth;
- Internal incongruities; and
- Inclusion of fragmentary, evanescent, and insubstantial details, or idle tales, which have little or no religious or spiritual significance.

What the Hadith does to Islam can be summarized as follows:

1. It muddles the very conception of God and encourages

fatalism;

2. It presents a misleading image of the Prophet Muhammad and his wives;
3. It explicitly negates parts of the Quran and claims omission of certain verses in the Quran in addition to being anti-Quran in an overall way;
4. It misguides on religious practices;
5. It denigrates women's status;
6. It encourages intolerance, violence, and terror and misleads on *jihad*;
7. It encourages cruel punishments;
8. It misguides on marriage;
9. It justifies slavery and slavery-like practices; and
10. It is against progress and modernity and conflicts with scientific truth and reason

Some notes are presented below on these points.

The Hadith Muddles The Very Conception of God and Encourages Fatalism

Contrary to what the Quran says about human freedom of choice and accountability for actions, as discussed before, some Hadith texts promote the idea of divine predestination by asserting that man's actions in life, his nature, longevity, and livelihood are all decided in the mother's womb (*Sahih Bukhari*, Vol. 8, Book 77, #595; Vol. 8, Book 77, #59).[1] The Hadith thus misconceives God and encourages fatalism.

There are many Hadith texts that give the believer the impression that he can get forgiveness for all of his past sins regardless of the kind and degree of sins committed if he just utters certain words of belief or recites certain verses of the Quran or does some religious rituals! For example, one Hadith says, "Allah has forbidden the (Hell) fire for those who say, 'None has the right to be worshipped but Allah' for Allah's sake only" (*ibid*, Vol. 1, Book 8, #417). Another Hadith narrated by Abu Huraira says: Allah's Apostle said: Whoever says, *'Subhan Allah wa bihamdihi*,' (God is Magnificent and all praise is His) one hundred times a day, all his sins will be forgiven if they were as much as the foam of the sea (*ibid*, Vol. 8, Book 75, #414). Likewise, the Hadith is replete with sayings that performance of certain rituals such as prayer at certain special times, e.g., during the nights of the Ramadan (*ibid*, Vol. 1, Book 2, #36) and in the night of the *qadar* (*ibid*, Vol. 1, Book 2, #34; Vol. 3, Book 31, #125), observance of fasts during the Ramadan (*ibid*, Vol. 1, Book 2, #37; Vol. 3, Book 31, #125), and utterances of certain words a certain number of times (*ibid*, Vol. 4, Book 54, #514), etc., will entitle one to complete remission of all past sins. Such examples are legion. Clearly, such Hadith texts not only exaggerate the virtues of beliefs, sayings, or rituals but also by so doing also give a perverted conception of God. The Quran emphasizes righteous deeds along with rituals.

The Hadith Presents a Misleading Image of the Prophet Muhammad and His Wives

The Hadith has greatly distorted the image of the Prophet Muhammad first, by tarnishing his character and second, by eulogizing him beyond all bounds. It makes a fanfare of his multiple marriages and maligns and insults him with outrageous stories about his and his wives' private lives – an awful read in *Bukhari* and *Muslim* Hadiths (See Vol. 1, Books 5 and 6 and other parts of *Sahih Bukhari* and Book 007, #2698-2700 of *Sahih Muslim*). These Hadiths have razed the Prophet Muhammad's image to the ground, in sharp contrast to what the Quran says about him (33:21; 68:4-6). One may wonder how a good believer can believe that the Prophet's companions would go beyond the generally accepted norms of propriety to ask the Prophet's wives, who were like their mothers (33:6), about their private lives. And is it believable that some of the Prophet's wives would come forward to talk about such things? Such stuff undeniably projects a view of ideology, which is far removed from, and fundamentally opposed to, the central spiritual message of the Quran and the ideal image of the Prophet Muhammad that we have been urged to emulate.

The Quran depicts the Prophet Muhammad as of a very gentle nature (3:159). On the other hand, the Hadith, in some places, depicts him as a cruel person. For example, the Hadith says that he pronounced a very harsh judgment just for the offence of killing of livestock and stealing – cutting off hands and feet without cauterization and branding of the eyes with red-hot iron (*Sahih Bukhari*, Vol. 8, Book 82, #794-797; Vol. 1, Book 4, #234; Book 52, #261). Another Hadith text reports that the Prophet burned the garden of date palms of Bani an-Nadir (*ibid*, Vol. 4, Book 52, #263). Still another Hadith states that the Prophet sent a group of people to kill Abu-Raffi in his house (*ibid*, Vol. 4, Book 52, #264). There are even reports that the Prophet did not forgive the Jewish tribe Bani al-Qurayza, whose necks were struck, whose children were made slaves, and whose members estimated between 400 and 900 were killed.[2]

The Hadith idolizes the Prophet Muhammad at the same time by upholding his alleged claim that he was given five things that were not given to earlier prophets. Among these, one is that he is sent for all humankind, while earlier prophets were sent to their own nations. Another is that he has the exclusive privilege of intercession with God for all people (*ibid*, Vol. 1, Book 7, #331). But the Quran does not support all this. It is inconceivable that the Prophet Muhammad could ever make such a boastful claim about his own position *vis-à-vis* that of the earlier Prophets, who have been presented in the Quran as beautiful examples for all humanity. The Quran warns us against a Day when there would be no bargaining nor friendship nor intercession (2:254); and it says that none can intercede with God except with His permission (2:255).

The Hadith Explicitly Negates Parts of The Quran and Claims Omission of Certain Verses in The Quran

A Hadith narrated by Nafi, who heard it from Ibn Umar at (*Sahih Bukhari*, Vol. 6, Book 60, # 33) abrogates the Quranic verse (2:184) that states that one who cannot fast should feed a poor man by way of expiation. Another Hadith at (*ibid*, Vol. 6, Book 60, #32) narrated by Ata who heard it from Ibn Umar implies that this verse is abrogated for persons other than old men and women. Still another Hadith, which ostensibly clarifies it further, is as follows:

> Narrated Salama: When the Divine Revelation: "For those who can fast, they have a choice either to fast, or feed a poor person for every day," (2.184) was revealed, it was permissible for one to give a ransom and give up fasting, till the verse succeeding it was revealed and abrogated it. (*Sahih Bukhari*, Vol. 6, Book 60, #34)

But this sort of abrogation of a verse or part of a verse by the Hadith is not tenable, as god cautions against disbelief in parts of the Quran (2:85). The verse (2:184) states that one should fast a certain number of days, and if he is sick or on a journey, he can fast other days, or those who find it difficult to fast and can afford it, they should pay a ransom in feeding poor persons. The verse at (2:185) advises believers to fast during the Ramadan and repeats the statement that if one is sick or on a journey, he or she can fast other days. This verse does not repeat the earlier statement that one could pay a ransom in the event that he or she cannot fast. This does not mean that the earlier verse message about the ransom has been abrogated. The Hadith misinterprets the Quran.

Another Hadith narrated by Ibn Abbas at (*ibid*, vol. 6, book 60, #68, 69) states that the verse "whether you show what is in your minds or conceal it" (2:284) is abrogated by the following verse (the following verse is not mentioned). The full verse at (2:284) gives a very important message that whether we make known what is in our minds or conceal it, we will have to account for it to God. The Hadith negates this very important message of God, which is not only anti-Quran but it also does not stand to reason. Still another Hadith narrated by Al-Qasim bin Abi Bazza who asked Said bin Jubair at (*ibid*, Vol. 6, Book 60, #285) states that the verse revealed in Mecca: "Nor kill such life as God has forbidden except for a just cause" in (6:151) was abrogated by another verse revealed later in Medina, which is at (4:93) that says that whoever intentionally kills a believer is destined for Hell. Both verses convey important, complementary messages. God never changes His Words (10:64).

Contemporary Muslim scholar Jeffrey Lang notes that some Hadiths claim that some verses were revealed to the Prophet but were omitted from the Quran. These include the Hadith prescribing stoning to death of married adulterers, which is in *Muwatta* of Imam Malik and a shorter version in *Sahih Bukhari* (Vol. 8, Book 82, #816-817). In another Hadith, Anas reports that they used to recite regarding the martyrs in the battle of Bir Mauna a Quranic verse "Inform our people that we have met our Lord. He is pleased with us and He has made us pleased", but this verse was retracted later on (*Bukhari*, Volume 4, Book 52, Number 69; also *Muslim*). "This and the stoning verse tradition indicate that at least two verses of the Qu'ran have been eliminated from the text. Other sound traditions indicate that much larger sections were withdrawn."[3] These Hadiths suggest that the present Quran is not complete, a contention that is hardly tenable in light of the verse (15:9) that clearly assures protection of the Quran from any corruption. Such an assertion of the Hadith can easily turn out to be a Pandora's box.

The Hadith Misleads on Religious Practices

The distortion of the institution of *salat* or prayer by the Hadith has already been covered in Chapter IV.

The Hadith misleads on fasting in several ways. One way is already mentioned above in relation to the abrogation of Quranic verses. While the Quran allows one to feed a poor person as expiation for not being able to fast, the Hadith denies it except for old people. This is a flagrant distortion of the Quranic message. In addition, the Hadith exaggerates the virtues of fasting by claiming that the Ramadan fast washes away all of one's past sins (*Sahih Bukhari*, Vol. 1, Book 2, #37), and that during the Ramadan the gates of Heaven are open and those of Hell are closed and the devils are chained (*ibid*, Vol. 3, Book 31, #120, 123), and by making similar more claims. Prayer and fasting are striving for self-purification and self-development. Unless the striving is successful, and unless one is righteous in all respects, such rituals may not erase one's past sins, regardless of the level of sins.

The Hadith prescribes very harsh to very light atonement for breaking fast, engaging in sexual activity, in a day during the Ramadan: freeing of a slave, or fasting for two successive months, or feeding sixty poor people, and failing that, charity to a poor person with a basket of dates brought before him, and failing that feeding his family with that basket (*ibid*, Vol. 3, Book 31, #S 157-158; similar text also in *Sahih Muslim*). It is inconceivable that the Prophet would ever engage in religious discourse in such a light manner, without reminding him of the straightforward Quranic admonition for repentance and atonement.

There are two Hadith texts reportedly narrated by Aisha or Ibn Abbas, which suggest that one can fast on another's behalf who is dead to fill the dead person's missed days of fasting (*ibid*, Vol. 3, Book 31, #173-174). What a fabrication! The Quran clearly says: one's efforts count for one's own self, not for another self (29:6).

Note also that even the conception and date of the night of power (*shab al qadar*) given by the Hadith has a dubious basis. Various texts indicate different dates (See *ibid*, Vol. 3, Book 32, #232; Vol. 3, Book 32, #233-239). Another Hadith, which suggests that this night should be searched on the odd nights – 25th to 29th – of the last five nights of the Ramadan, is worth citation as a classic example of fabrication:

> Narrated 'Ubada bin As-Samit: The Prophet came out to inform us about the Night of Qadr but two Muslims were quarreling with each other. So, the Prophet said: I came out to inform you about the Night of Qadr but such-and-such persons were quarreling, so the news (knowledge) about it had been taken away; yet that might be for your own good, so search for it on the 29th, 27th and 25th (of Ramadan) (*Sahih Bukhari*, Vol. 3, Book 32, # 240).

Is it conceivable that the Prophet's knowledge about this night was snatched away because of the quarrelling of two Muslims? Note also, some of the Hadith texts referred to above also state that the Prophet was informed of the date, but he forgot it. All these texts sound ludicrous and are inconsistent with one another. It is inconceivable that the Prophet would speak about a night with such a level of uncertainty. The Hadith is a well of conjecture. The Quran cautions us against conjecture (6:116, 148; 10:36; 53: 28; etc.). The glorious night that the Quran talks about was a night when the Quran was revealed. If it was a definite date, it could be celebrated. Such a date could not be based on a conjecture.

Some distortions of the Pilgrimage to Mecca (*hajj*) institution have already been mentioned in Chapter II. A major distortion is giving the impression that performing the *hajj* erases one's life's sins, regardless of the level of sins (*Bukhari*, Vol. 3, Book 28, #45 and 46).

The Hadith Denigrates Women's Status

While the Quran has brought about a revolutionary social egalitarianism by lifting women's status relative to men in a situation when they were treated little better than slaves, the Hadith has, on the other hand, relegated their position to one that is far degrading and disgraceful. One Hadith says that the Prophet stood at the gate of Hell and found that the majority there were women (*ibid*, Volume 7, Book 62, #124). Another Hadith says that the Prophet remarked that he has left no affliction more harmful to men than women (*ibid*, volume 7, book 62, #33). Still another brackets women with the house and the horse as a bad omen (*Bukhhari*, volume 7, book 62, #31). Similar texts are also in *Muslim, Tirmidhi* and *Nasa'i*. There are, of course, some Hadith texts that display respect for women. However, these are overwhelmingly overshadowed by the negative texts against them. Yet another virulent Hadith against women narrated by Abu Said al-Khudri depicts women as deficient in intelligence and religion (*Bukhari*, Vol. 1, Book 6, #301). In regard to this Hadith, Reza Aslan remarks that many have considered Abu Said al-Khudri's memory as "unchallenged, despite the fact that Muhammad's biographers present him as repeatedly asking for and following the advice of his wives, even in military matters."[4] Still another Bukhari Hadith speaks of women as ungrateful to their husbands (*ibid*, Vol. 7, Book 62, #125; Vol. 1, Book 2, #28). One wonders how a man of the stature of a prophet could speak so ill of women and, most importantly, against the very spirit of the message of the Quran.

Referring to a number of Hadiths reported in *Tirmidhi, Abu Dawud, Ibn Majah, Nasai, Musnad* of Ahmad Ibn Hanbal, *Ibn Hibban*, Khaled Abou El Fadl comments that these traditions make wives virtually slaves to their husbands, which are unreliable and problematic, since they ignore the overall moral teachings of Islam.[5] He further observes:

> The difficulty with this genre of traditions is that they promote a formalistic obligation of obedience to husbands while ignoring all competing moral values in Islam. [...] It makes God's pleasure contingent on the husband's pleasure. [...] Furthermore, these traditions are not consistent with the Qur'anic conception of the marital relationship. [...] the Qur'anic conception of marriage is not based on servitude but on compassion and cooperation, and the Qur'anic conception of virtue is not conditioned on the pleasure of another human being, but on piety and obedience to God.[6]

Abou El Fadl rightly points out that these Hadiths have terrible theological and social implications. Obviously, all such Hadith texts, apart from conflicting with the Quranic conception of the marital relationship, also cast aspersions on the chivalrous and good-natured character of the Prophet.

The Hadith Encourages Intolerance, Violence, and Terror, and Misleads On *Jihad*

One way the Hadith promotes intolerance and violence is by showing Muhammad as an intolerant person. We have already discussed this point above. There are numerous other Hadith reports that show Paradise as being under the shades of swords (*Sahih Bukhari*, Vol. 4, Book 52, #73, 210, 266I), that preach

particularly anti-Semitic sentiment, where Muslims are urged
to fight and kill the Jews wherever they are found (*ibid*, Vol. 4,
Book 52, #176, 177), and that urge Muslims to kill young people
with foolish thoughts and ideas who appear in the last days of the
world (*ibid*, Vol. 6, Book 61, #577; repeated at Vol. 9, Book 84,
#64). The Hadith promotes aggressive *jihad* against other
communities until they accept that none except God is to be
worshipped (*ibid*, Vol. 4, Book 52, #196), until they accept that
Muhammad is His Messenger, and until they pray and offer *zakat*
(*ibid*, Vol. 1, Book 2, #24). This approach of the Hadith on *jihad* or
fighting is fundamentally opposed to that proclaimed by the Quran,
which never endorses any aggressive *jihad*. Not surprisingly, it is
from such Hadith texts that the extremist groups among Muslims
get their inspiration for committing intolerant, violent, and terrorist
acts against civilians and other communities in various parts of the
world.

The Hadith Encourages Cruel Punishments

The cruel punishments attributed to the Prophet
Muhammad as discussed above are an encouragement to such
punishments. The Hadith is the source from where the *shariah*
(*hudud*) punishments are largely drawn, which include stoning the
adulterer and adulteress to death, death for apostasy, and limb
cutting for theft. The first two punishments are not mentioned in
the Quran. As discussed in Chapter VI, some modern progressive
Islamic scholars question whether the concerned verse in the
Quran regarding punishment for theft should really mean limb
cutting. According to them, it should be limb marking. As argued
before, since the Quranic law is flexible between two extremes –
between a maximum punishment and an outright forgiveness, it
should be applied judiciously from lighter to harder punishments
depending on what turns out to be effective as a deterrent
punishment. The Quran states that God first sends lighter

punishments; should these prove insufficient, He sends heavier punishments afterwards (32:21).

Since the Quran allows full religious freedom, no punishment for apostasy (which is meant as converting to another religion from Islam) is justified, let alone death. As noted by some Hadith critics, the Hadith prescribes a much more brutal punishment – *rajam* or stoning to death – for adultery than what the Quran prescribes – a maximum of hundred lashes. The Quran prescribes punishment for adultery in the following ways:

> 24:2-3 If a married wife is found and confirmed guilty of such a criminal offence, which requires to be confirmed by four witnesses, she should be punished with confinement to a house until death or until a way (of exit) is found for her (4:15). The way of exit from confinement to a house until death for a woman of this character would be flogging by a hundred lashes and, if she wishes, being married to a man of similar character, or to an idolater. (See also 24:26.)
>
> 4:15 The adulterer and the adulteress should be both punished after confirmation. The confirmation should be by four witnesses. The maximum punishment prescribed is one hundred lashes for each (24:2). But if they repent and mend their conduct, then they could be left alone without such punishment.

The Quranic punishment for adultery is thus a choice or variation between a maximum of hundred lashes for the adulterer and the adulteress, confinement to house for the wife guilty of adultery, or outright forgiveness for both. Society needs to decide which punishment would serve as a sufficient or effective deterrent to such a crime. It is not right to maintain, as the *ulama* would have us believe, that the verse (24:2) abrogates the verse (4:15). It is the Hadith that erroneously misleads believers by saying that some verses are abrogated or replaced by others in the Quran.

The Hadith Misguides On Marriage

As explained in Chapter VII, the Quran allows polygamy to respond to extra-ordinary circumstances, subject to certain restrictions, but it does not encourage polygamy. But the Hadith brazenly encourages polygamy. Look at the following Hadith:

> Narrated Said bin Jubair: Ibn 'Abbas asked me: Are you married? I replied: No. He said: Marry, for the best person of this (Muslim) nation (i.e., Muhammad) of all other Muslims, had the largest number of wives. (*Sahih Bukhari*, Vol. 7, Book 62, # 7)

A slanderous Hadith on the Prophet Solomon states that one night he said that he would have sexual intercourse with one hundred (or ninety-nine women) (*ibid*, Vol. 4, Book 52, #74I). This as well as the earlier cited Hadith are an indirect incitement to polygamy and sexual activity. The Prophet could never say such an outrageous thing about the Prophet Solomon, who has been presented as a much honoured and spiritually advanced Messenger of God in the Quran.

One Hadith narrated by Abu Huraira, which also undermines the status of women, and indirectly encourages polygamy, is that the Prophet allegedly said that it is not lawful for a woman (at the time of wedding) to ask for the divorce of her sister (i.e. the other wife of her would-be husband) in order to have everything for herself, for she will take only what has been written for her (*ibid*, Vol. 7, Book 62, #82). This Hadith denies a woman's legitimate right to ask a would-be husband, who asks her to marry him, to divorce her other wife, if the former does not wish to marry a man who wants to retain his existing wife. Note that this Hadith directly conflicts with another, which states that the Prophet has disapproved of the idea that Ali should be allowed to take another wife without divorcing his current wife Fatima who was the Prophet's daughter (*ibid*, Vol. 7, Book 62, #157).

There are two Hadith texts in *Bukhari*, which say that the Prophet permitted *muta* marriage, i.e., marriage with a temporary contract (*ibid*, Vol. 7, Book 62, #130 and 51). One self-conflicting Hadith says both that *muta* marriage is permissible, and also not permissible (*ibid*, Vol. 7, Book 62, #52). There is another Hadith narrated by Ali that says that the Prophet forbade such marriage during the battle of Khaibar (*ibid*, Vol. 7, Book 62, #50). However, it is unthinkable that the Prophet could ever permit *muta* marriage, which is clearly adultery (*zina*) and simple prostitution according to the Quran.

Should the silence of a bride be always taken to mean consent for marriage with a bridegroom? Probably No. Girls can best vouch on this. There are occasions when a bride may not actually like to marry the particular bridegroom, but remains silent under duress. But *Bukhari* (Vol. 7, Book 62, #67 and 68) passes off silence as indicating consent for marriage.

Bukhari (Vol. 7, Book 63, #186, 187, 190, 238) and also *Ibn Majah* do not legitimate divorce of a wife from a current husband without consummation of marriage, which is in direct conflict with the Quran (2:236). Another Hadith states that a divorced wife cannot go back to, or remarry, her husband until she marries another person, and until that person divorces her (*ibid*, Vol. 7, Book 63, #249). The Hadith is then the source of the notorious *halala* or *hilla* system, which misinterprets the Quranic advice, as discussed in Chapter VII. There is another Hadith, which upheld the Quranic advice by allowing a divorced wife to remarry her husband without requiring her to marry another person (*ibid*, Vol. 7, Book 63, #248), but this Hadith is, for some reason, ignored by the *ulama*.

The Hadith Justifies Slavery and Slavery-Like Practices

The Hadith is ambiguous on slavery and slavery-like practices. While there are texts that extol the virtues of freeing slaves, these are undermined by other texts that justify continuing these practices. Indirect but strong justification of slavery by the Hadith is embodied in texts that strongly encourage slaves to be loyal to their masters. One such text is as follows:

> Narrated 'Abdullah: The Prophet said, "If a slave serves his Saiyid (i.e., master) sincerely and worships his Lord (Allah) perfectly, he will get a double reward" (*ibid*, Vol. 3, Book 46, #726, similar texts also at #727 and 722).

The Hadith has texts that sanctify keeping female captives as concubines, but such texts nullify its other advice that slaves should be freed. As mentioned in Chapter VII, the Quran has clear, categorical directions against forcing slaves to serve as concubines and for freeing them or marrying them.

The Hadith is against Progress and Modernity and Conflicts with Scientific Truth and Reason

As noted above the Hadith encourages fatalism and, by so doing, it stunts the very spirit of striving and enterprise, which the Quran so forcefully extols and presents to humankind. Quite sensibly, the Quran stresses spiritual piety in preference to material prosperity. At the same time the Quranic conception of the *sirat al-mustaqim* (the straight path of God's *niamat* or abundance) does not rule out material prosperity alongside spiritual progress. Indeed, Goc has made available and subjected everything on earth and in the heavens to the disposal and service of humankind (31:20; 45:13; 16:12-14).

Against the backdrop of this Quranic perspective, the Hadith erroneously propagates the idea that impoverishment is better than affluence and, by so doing, it has contributed to the holding back of Muslims' progress on earth. Several *Bukhari* texts show the poor as better people – better qualified to go to Heaven – than the rich (Vol. 7, Book 62, #28, #124, #126). There is a Hadith text that says that one of the signs of the last days before the last hour of the world is an increase in material abundance and construction of high-rise buildings (ibid, Vol. 9, Book 88, # 237). Another Hadith suggests that men owning sheep are better than those who have horses and camels (*ibid*, Vol. 4, Book 54, # 520). Still another Hadith suggests that a time will come when the best property of Muslims will be some sheep (*ibid*, Vol. 1, Book 2, # 18). Is there any logical connection between poverty and virtue? Are those who beg better than others? The Hadith suggests that they are, but the Quran says that it is the devil that makes one fear and experience poverty, while God promises one bounty (2:268). God also says that He gives sustenance to whomever he likes without measure or beyond one's expectation (3:27). How can He at the same time condemn them to hell? One may rightly wonder whether it is the Hadith that has influenced Muslims to remain relatively backward and poverty-stricken on earth.

A Hadith states that the Prophet said that a person in debt tells lies whenever he speaks and breaks promises whenever he makes (them) (*ibid*, Vol. 1, Book 12, #795). While one could legitimately wish to remain debt-free, it is unthinkable that the Prophet could ever make such an irresponsible statement that a person in debt tells lies and breaks promises. If lending is good and could be *qarz-hasana* (beautiful loan) according to the Quran, why is being in debt so bad? A modern economy could not thrive, or even survive, without having lending and borrowing operations in place.

The Hadith makes absurd statements on scientific

subjects. A text suggests that the sun travels and then prostrates under the Throne, then rises and moves again with permission, but a time will come when it will be ordered to return whence it has come and so it will rise in the west (*ibid*, Vol. 4, Book 54, # 421), which is shown as an interpretation of the Quranic verse (36:38). We know from science that no heavenly bodies, including the earth, are stationary, but move in space. The relevant verses of the Quran read as follows:

> 36:38-40 The sun runneth (in its course or orbit) for an appointed term. Such is the design of the Mighty, the All-Knowing. And as for the moon, We have ordained it to appear in stages until it reverteth to an old thin palm leaf. It is not for the sun to overtake the moon, nor doth the night outstrip the day. Each floateth in its own orbit.

Note that many translators have interpreted the first verse as the sun running to a fixed resting place on the basis of the Hadith, thus compounding the confusion.

Another Hadith text says that if a housefly falls in the drink of anyone, he should dip it (in the drink), for one of its wings has a disease and the other has the cure for the disease (*ibid*, Vol. 4, Book 54, #537). One should ask a microbiologist whether it is safe to have such a drink.

Still another text reads as follows:

> The (Hell) Fire complained to its Lord saying, 'O my Lord! My different parts eat up each other.' So, He allowed it to take two breaths, one in the winter and the other in summer, and this is the reason for the severe heat and the bitter cold you find (in weather) (*ibid*, Vol. 4, Book 54, #482).

Severe heat or bitter cold are due to some scientific reasons such as relative distance from the sun, the condition of the ozone layer (the upper atmospheric layer) through which the sun rays pass, variation in atmospheric pressure, formation of clouds, winds, storms, etc. The Hadith provides an imaginary reason.

The Hadith discourages any inquisitive thought about God (*ibid*, Vol. 6, Book 61, #496). The Quran advises us not to doubt God and His revelations (2:186; 2:147; 3:60; 10:94-95), but does not discourage thinking about who is really God, as evidenced by the inquisitive search of God by the Prophet Abraham (6:75-79).

Conclusion

Examples of such fabricated Hadiths could be multiplied. The Hadith is a major source of religious misguidance in Islam. I have considered texts mostly from *Bukhari*, which is generally held to be the most authentic. If one can find serious problems with texts in *Bukhari*, it is more likely that problems are even more serious with the other compilations such as *Muslim, Abu Dawud, Tirmidhi, Ibn Majah*, etc. Other Hadith critics have cited other Hadith texts that they consider as inauthentic.[7] The whole Hadith is full of absurd, mutually contradictory, and confusing messages, which have given us an entirely misleading and distorted view of Islam. The tenor of the Hadith is essentially anti-Quran, anti-modernity, anti-progress, anti-women, anti-peace, and anti-tolerance. The roots of religious fanaticism, religious intolerance, and terrorism are found right in such literature. It should not, therefore, be surprising if the enemies of Islam use such Hadith texts to defame the Prophet Muhammad and ridicule Islam. The Hadith must be rejected as a reliable, authentic source of religious law and guidance in Islam.

XII. Epilogue: The Rise of Religious Fanaticism and The Direction for True Islamic Revival

Now verily We have caused the Word to reach them, that they might take heed. — *The Quran*, 28:51

Introduction

Like Bernard Lewis, author of *What Went Wrong? Western Impact and Middle Eastern Response*, Muslims should wonder what has gone wrong with them. Once the torchbearer of human progress and civilization, Muslims have reduced themselves to a global underclass. Name any area of progressive human activity; it is not difficult to pinpoint their failure or stark underperformance in that area as a community. In recent years, months, and days, Muslim fundamentalists or extremists excel in one thing – terrorism and violence. The recent spate of terrorist attacks and sectarian violence and atrocities has probably no parallel in modern history. Hardly a day passes by when we do not hear of a bomb blast or some form of violence taking place in some corner of the globe –Pakistan, Afghanistan, Iraq, India, or some part of the developed world – with a toll of human life and immense human suffering. It is lamentable, yet undeniable, that Muslim extremists are orchestrating much of this violence. No doubt, by doing so they are tarnishing the image of Islam and making Muslims in general despicable in the eyes of other communities.

Indeed it may not be an exaggeration to say that the biggest threat to peace and security facing the world today is not "the clash of civilizations", but the clash of ideas that has led to a rise of religious fanaticism and extremism among some people who claim to be Muslims. Civilization should not be classed into different categories such as the Western Christendom, the Muslim World, the Hindu Civilization, the Sinic Civilization, etc., as Samuel

Huntington has done.[1] Civilization in proper sense of the term has essentially the same pattern with a convergence of some core characteristic features. So-called Western civilization is built upon the bedrock of some core human values that are the values of religion – Islam, Christianity, Judaism or any earlier religion – values of truthfulness and honesty, fairness and justice and the rule of law, and respect for human dignity, freedom and human rights. It is a civilization where human decency and social harmony are the norms, and peaceful and prosperous living conditions prevail, and where all men and women can uninterruptedly pursue their spiritual, social, cultural, intellectual, political, and economic goals for all round human progress and development. It is precisely because of this that modern Muslim thinker Muhammad Abduh of Egypt lamented that there was Islam in the Western society though he could not find Muslims there, but he could not find Islam in his own country though there were "Muslims" there.[2] Religion in a proper sense embraces all elements of modernity that make things better, more fair and just for all people with proper checks against the bad elements. Many of such elements of modernity have been embraced by the Western civilization. Other religious groups like Muslims have lagged behind because of their obsession with wrong traditions. Once Muslims also become modernized with adoption of all the progressive ideas, the current divide between the so-called Western civilization and the Islamic civilization will wither away.

Many scholars have characterized religious extremism among some Muslims as "Islamic fundamentalism or radicalization," or "Islamic militancy," or simply, "Islamism". Though the self-proclaimed Muslims perpetrating acts of intolerance and violence and fostering a climate of militancy are giving a negative image of Islam itself, it will be wrong to equate their activities with having anything to do with Islam. As explained in this book, Islam as professed by the Holy Quran is far above their professed ideology of intolerance and violence. Hence, and since "fundamentalism" has come to be used in a derogatory way, "Islamic fundamentalism," or "Islamic militancy," or, for that matter, "Islamism" is, in a way, an inappropriate term to use, or a contradiction in terms. As Aḥmad Mansour notes, "A religion should be judged by the teachings of its holy book, not by the actions and the opinions of its followers. [...] If, for example, we were to judge Christianity as presented by the opinion of Christian scholars in the medieval era of Europe, or by the actions of Christian people throughout the ages, we must conclude that Christianity is a terrible religion. Yet we know that Jesus was a peace-loving person who preached peace and love."[3]

The Rise of Muslim Fanaticism

As noted scholar of comparative religion Karen Armstrong points out, the militant form of religiosity known as "fundamentalism" is not unique to the Muslim faith. It "is a global fact and has surfaced in every major faith in response to the problems of our modernity. [... And it] exists in a symbiotic relationship with a coercive secularism."[4] "But the desperation and fear that fuel fundamentalists', she further notes, "also tend to distort the religious tradition, and accentuate its more aggressive aspects at the expense of those that teach tolerance and reconciliation."[5] As examples of the exponents of Muslim fundamentalism, Armstrong cites the names of twentieth-century Islamic writers and political activists Abul Ala Mawdudi, the founder of the Jamaat-i Islami in Pakistan, and one of his ardent followers Sayyid Qutb of Egypt, who at one time joined the Muslim Brotherhood of Egypt. Mawdudi encouraged religious fanaticism and extremism by advocating the punishment of renegades or apostates by death and by declaring Ahmadiyas renegades from Islam, even though the Quran nowhere speaks of punishing renegades or apostates in such a manner, and even though the

Quran gives man the freedom of choice in matters of religion (18:29). Mawdudi also disregarded the clear directions of the Quran for tolerance and no coercion in religion (2:256; 10:99; 109:1-6). Mawdudi's writings provided the inspiration for the passage of the highly problematic "blasphemy" and "hudud" (or rigid *shariah*) laws that have led to many human rights violations committed against religious minorities, especially the Ahmadiyas of Pakistan, and women. In 1953, because of writing a seditious pamphlet against Ahmadiyas, which led to rioting, he was sentenced to death by the martial law authorities, who then held sway in Pakistan, but under public pressure, this sentence was first commuted to life imprisonment and then totally withdrawn. About Qutb, Armstrong notes:

> The violent secularism of al-Nasser had led Qutb to espouse a form of Islam that distorted both the message of the Quran and the Prophet's life. Qutb told Muslims to model themselves on Muhammad: to separate themselves from mainstream society (as Muhammad had made the hijrah from Mecca to Medina), and then engage in a violent jihad. But Muhammad had in fact finally achieved victory by an ingenious policy of non-violence; the Quran adamantly opposed force and coercion in religious matters; and its vision - far from preaching exclusion and separation – was tolerant and inclusive. Qutb insisted that the Quranic injunction to toleration could occur only after the political victory of Islam and the establishment of a true Muslim state. The new intransigence sprang from the profound fear that is at the core of fundamentalist religion. [...] Every subsequent] Sunni fundamentalist movement has been influenced by Qutb.[6]

Though Armstrong did not see the existence of "a militant, fanatic strain" of fundamentalism in Islam and though Muslims who represent mainstream and moderate Islam are admittedly peace-loving and law-abiding, an evidently fanatic and militant version of "Islam" called Wahhabism surfaced in the Middle East during the eighteenth century and spread throughout the world over the years. Mawdudi and Qutb basically followed and espoused this Wahhabism. This is "a radically ultraconservative and puritanical ideology", based on a strictly literal interpretation of the Quran and the Hadith, which was aggressively promoted by Muhammad ibn Abd al-Wahhab and his followers and vigorously championed by the Saudi Kingdom after it had been founded in 1932. Armstrong notes, "Because the Ottoman Sultans did not conform to his true vision of Islam, Abd al-Wahhab declared that they were apostates and worthy of death."[7] Reza Aslan notes that King Ibn Saud and Abd al-Wahhab entered into an unholy alliance. They, in addition to "destroying the tombs of the Prophet and his Companions, including those pilgrimage sites that marked the birthplace of Muhammad and his family", were guilty of killing any Muslim "who did not accept their uncompromisingly puritanical version of Islam." And Abd al-Wahhab was guilty of publicly stoning a woman to death in a village, wherefrom he was expelled by the stunned, shocked villagers. Among other things, the Wahhabis also "sacked the treasury of the Prophet's Mosque in Medina and set fire to every book they could find, save the Quran. They banned music and flowers from the sacred cities and outlawed the smoking of tobacco and the drinking of coffee. Under the penalty of death, they forced the men to grow beards and the women to be veiled and secluded [even though the veiling and secluding of women had not been the case in the Prophet's time]." The Wahhabis – the most fanatic of Sunni Muslims – were also guilty of massacring two thousand Shiite worshippers when they were celebrating Muharram in Karbala.[8] Even in modern times, the Wahhabi-inspired fundamentalists were responsible for the slaughter of tens of thousands of Algerians. In Egypt, modern

Muslim thinkers have been subjected to Wahhabi-instigated and often government-supported killing, torture, and harassment, including banning of their works. Recent notable examples are the stabbing and maiming of Nobel Laureate Naguib Mahfouz, the assassination of human rights defender Farag Foda, the arrest and incarceration of the Ibn Khaldun Center's head Saad Eddin Ibrahim, and of many of his colleagues, and the court ruling of apostasy on the Cairo University Professor Nasr Abu Zayd which called for divorcing of his Muslim wife, a ruling that led the couple to seek exile in a foreign country. Al-Azhar University Professor Dr. Ahmad Mansour and his followers who follow only the Quran and reject the traditions also became victims of harassment, persecution, and tortures at the hands of the Wahhabi followers in Egypt.

In the tradition of Ibn Taymiyyah[9], the Wahhabis call for rigid adherence to *shariah* as literally found in the Quran and the Hadith. But they encourage only outward piety; they discourage and suppress Muslims' inner search to know and experience God and their quest and endeavor for spiritual development and real wisdom. Muslim Sufis and saints have been the targets of their persecution and torture. In their zeal to enforce puritanical Islam, they have flagrantly flouted the finer and more fundamental human values enshrined in the Quran and they committed horrendous crimes against humanity. They blocked human thinking urging blind imitation of past traditions (*taqlid*), discouraged studies of science, fine arts, and culture, and created hurdles in the way of human progress and modernization. In his recent book, Khaled Abou El Fadl provides a detailed critique of the narrowly defined, archaic, inherently incoherent, and essentially extreme, intolerant and militant, and fundamentally perverted nature of this ideology's interpretation of Islamic teachings.[10] This Wahhabi version is still followed today in Saudi Arabia and is being preached as an official version of Islam, even though the Quran does not support their archaic extreme and militant positions. Following the Wahhabi dictates, the Saudi Government enforces rigid adherence to archaic *shariah* punishments, such as the mutilation of thieves. Note also that the Quran does not support monarchical or authoritarian rule, which is a major violation of the Quranic principles by the Saudi regime. The Saudi monarchs are also guilty of having ostentatious living styles in contravention of fundamental Islamic values. Over the years, with newfound oil wealth, the Saudi government has distributed lavish funds throughout the world to build mosques and *madrasahs*, and even to finance religious teachers and preachers to preach and spread their version of Islam in all Muslim countries as well as in developed countries like the United States and Europe. Osama bin Laden's Al-Qaeda group and other terrorist organizations have also benefited from the Saudi dole-outs. An enquiry instituted by the National Security Council of the United States government in late 1998 revealed that "Over the past 25 years, the desert kingdom has been the single greatest force in spreading Islamic fundamentalism, while its huge, unregulated charities funneled hundreds of millions of dollars to *jihad* groups and al Qaeda cells around the world."[11] A contemporary Muslim writer and journalist Stephen Suleyman Schwartz argues in a book, "Wahhabism, vigorously exported with the help of Saudi oil money, is what incites Palestinian suicide bombers, Osama bin Laden, and other Islamic terrorists throughout the world."[12] A recent Newsweek article suggests, "at least 50 percent of American mosques may receive some funding from foreign governments or institutions, mostly Saudi Arabia. [...] Whatever its source, fundamentalist Islamic ideology is readily available on the Internet as well as in U.S. mosques."[13]

Thus what some historians and scholars of comparative religions have termed as contemporary Islamic revival or resurgence in the world is in large part a Wahhabi phenomenon fueled by Saudi patronization. As a result of this resurgence, as John Esposito notes, "In recent years, tensions and clashes between Muslim and non-Muslim communities have [rather] increased"; the minority religious groups such as "the Copts in Egypt, Bahai and Jews in Iran, Chinese in Malaysia, and Christians in the Sudan, Pakistan, and Nigeria" have become targets of attacks by Muslims. "The creation of more Islamically oriented societies, especially the introduction of Islamic laws, has resulted in varying degrees of tension, conflict, violence, and killing in the name of religion. [...] The Bahai of Iran and the Ahmadiya of Pakistan, on the other hand, are regarded as apostates or heretics."[14]

What has become a more ominous trend currently is that some fundamentalists among Muslims are continuing to increasingly use the aggressive techniques of Wahhabism, and are systematically conducting terrorist attacks in various countries. Abdel Rahman al-Rashed, a Saudi journalist in London, appropriately comments: "It is a certain fact that not all Muslims are terrorists, but it is equally certain, and exceptionally painful, that almost all terrorists are Muslims. [...] We cannot clear our names unless we own up to the shameful fact that terrorism has become an Islamic enterprise; an almost exclusive monopoly, implemented by Muslim men and women."[15] Amir Taheri, an Iranian-born journalist, points out, "the Muslim world today is full of bigotry, fanaticism, hypocrisy and plain ignorance – all of which create a breeding ground for criminals like bin Laden."[16] Bassam Tibi, a Syrian Professor of International Relations at the University of Göttingen, Germany forcefully argues in his book written prior to the September 11 attacks, "Islamic fundamentalism [or, Islamism in contrast to Islam] ... poses a grave challenge to world politics, security, and stability."[17] Indeed, starting with the September 11, terrorist attacks perpetrated by Muslim extremists have proliferated in recent years, months and days. Recent episodes of post-September Eleven ghastly suicide car or other bomb attacks in Indonesia, Saudi Arabia, Turkey, Morocco, Spain, the United Kingdom, Egypt, Jordan, Iraq, India, Pakistan, and Bangladesh – and more frequently in more recent time in Iraq, Afghanistan, and Pakistan – highlight trends of dangers worldwide that have to be effectively confronted to strive for enduring peace in the world.

Muslims still dote on their glorious past. In the peak of their civilizational role, Europe was in the Dark Ages, and dependent on Muslims for their enlightenment. What is the reason for Muslims' decay and degeneration? Today all Muslims need to dispassionately ponder what has gone wrong with them. Bernard Lewis observed, "For many centuries the world of Islam was in the forefront of human civilization and achievement. [...] In most of the arts and sciences of civilization, medieval Europe was a pupil and in a sense a dependent of the Islamic world, relying on Arabic versions even for many otherwise unknown Greek versions."[18] Then he pondered about the decline and degeneration in Muslim civilization, and legitimately asked the question: What went wrong with them? Certainly this question is more pertinent today after the September Eleven and subsequent tragic events. Observing the stark differences between the West and the Middle East in economics, politics, reforms in various fields such as education and law, and modernization, Lewis appropriately thought that the underlying reasons were not so much the differences in the visible sources of power and prosperity – military, economic and political as the "more profound, yet somehow for long overlooked [...] crucial differences in approach, in attitude, and in perception between two neighboring civilizations" with regard to topics covering women, science and music (or arts), and slavery.[19] Attitudinal differences between Muslims living in Muslim countries and non-Muslims of the West, especially after the Renaissance and the Enlightenment, make considerable difference in explaining the backwardness of Muslims. Also, as emphasized by Hassan

Hanafi, an Egyptian Professor of Philosophy at Cairo University, what Muslims lack most is "thinking". Their first duty should be thinking, "Because to say "There is no God but Allah" you have to think. You have to know what that means. It's an act of consciousness. It's thinking. This is our Cartesianism. I think therefore I am."[20] The "most urgent problem facing us, the Muslims, is neither political nor economical, but a crisis of our own thinking and learning process in relation to ourselves, Islam, Muslims and humanity at large," wrote Leith Kubba, an Iraqi-born Islamist thinker. "Without an objective, relative and rational Islamic discourse, our relationship to Islam will remain as that of a sentiment to the past or a mere slogan at present but it will not become an alternative towards a better future."[21]

The Direction for True Islamic Revival

Islam's real revival is yet to take place. And this can take place only when Muslims start to seriously think about their own predicament. They need to do a lot of their own soul searching. It is as early as fourteen centuries ago that the Quran laid so much emphasis on thinking: "Do they not then think in their own minds? ..." (30:8) "Do they not then ponder the Quran? Or is it that there are locks upon their hearts (or minds)?" (47:24). While the vast majority of Muslims have stopped thinking, some thinking has no doubt already begun among some modern educated Muslims, despite the deplorable fact that such thinking is brutally suppressed and repressed in many Muslim countries. Richard Bullet, writing in 1994, observed, "We are currently living through one of the greatest periods of intellectual and religious creativity in Islamic – and human – history."[22] This is even truer after the September 11 events: "[...] more Muslims than ever before are reexamining their faith in light of the political, economic, and intellectual challenges of contemporary life. They are reshaping Islam for the next millennium."[23]

In recent years and contemporary times, many Muslims have been engaging in *ijtihad* (rethinking and reinterpretation) of Islam, the doors of which were closed by the tenth century. Evidently, the absence of *ijtihad* for many centuries has had a lot to do with the backwardness of Muslims in terms of civil norms – respect for human dignity, freedom, human rights, pluralism and tolerance, and reason and justice, as well as in scientific, technological, and economic developments. Muqtedar Khan, a contemporary staunch exponent of *ijtihad*, aptly notes, "If Muslims wish to unite and revive the great spirit of Islam and its civilizing ethos, then we must learn to be more tolerant and more open minded in our approach to contending arguments. Strength, legitimacy and vitality come from openness, tolerance of difference and from the willingness to create rather than to burn bridges. [...] The present rigid and inflexible approach to Islamic legal opinions of the past must be discarded and replaced with a more open and compassionate understanding of Islam."[24] "The practice of hero-worship of past scholars," Muqtedar Khan further notes, "determines which interpretation is accepted. I believe that this traditionalist approach is counter-productive. It merely recycles past opinions without actually making Islam relevant to specific times and circumstances."[25] He also observes:

> The biggest disservice that Muslims do to Islam and Muhammad is their uncritical approach to Islamic sources. [...] It is time Muslims revisited their sources with a critical perspective and discarded what is false, improbable and inconsistent with the values of mercy, tolerance and justice. [...] By adhering to *irrational, anachronistic — and often meaningless — traditions*, they obscure the power and beauty of Islam and deprive themselves and the rest of the world from its message.[26]

These observations beautifully capture the gist of one of the main points this book has tried to expound: we Muslims do need to rethink and reevaluate the so-called Prophetic traditions, which are "irrational and anachronistic – and often meaningless" and misleading. However, the proponents of *ijtihad* have come only half way to discard the Hadith. They need to come the full way to embrace the idea that the so-called Hadith, which contains anti-Quran, anti-Muhammad, anti-women, anti-reason, anti-progress, anti-peace, and anti-tolerance ideas, cannot be claimed as authentic prophetic discourse, and hence must be discarded as part of Islam. Contrary to the view of some scholars, *ijtihad* is not the exclusive domain of the Muslim *ulama*. They have in fact proved to be ill equipped and incapable of doing *ijtihad*. Because of the wrong and anachronistic teachings in traditional religious schools – *madrasahs*, their knowledge, and consequently their vision, has become limited and bigoted, and their minds closed. The leadership for *ijtihad* has mostly come from Muslim intellectuals who have received modern education, and it is they who should carry forward this *ijtihad*. As a Pakistan-born professor of an American university legitimately points out, Islam's interpretation should "no longer be left to the most regressive segment[s] of Muslim society. Muslims who believe that their faith is compatible with progressive humanist ideals must express themselves – not as apologists of Islam to the West but as proponents of new possibilities for Muslims."[27]

Madrasahs, where only traditional religious instruction is imparted and no modern subjects in science and arts are taught, instead of becoming real learning centers of Islam, have rather become breeding grounds of religious fanatics. Fourteen centuries ago, the Prophet Muhammad came with the Quran to civilize and purify mankind and make them wise (62:2; 36:2). It is ironic that *madrasahs* have failed to produce wise people, and their alumni, being deprived of education and training in modern subjects, have failed to become men of any real practical utility to themselves and to their families in particular, and to humankind in general. With fanatically oriented education, it should not be surprising to see that some of these alumni would turn into extremists to embrace militant techniques.[28]

One of the most important first steps to revive and revitalize Islam would, therefore, be to thoroughly remodel these *madrasahs* on the pattern of modern schools, which should include religious education as well; but such education should be purged of the teaching of traditional material (such as the Hadith) as sacred religious sources. Also, religion should be a special subject in general education at the university level. At the same time, a vigorous campaign for genuine reform within Islam needs to be launched and continued – the kind of campaign that one scholar has termed "the Fourth Jihad" " – one that requires a relentless fight against meaningless dogmas the Muslim society is possessed with.[29]

As always, the clash of ideas will always be there. In the book, I have made reference to what I interpreted as the Quranic (or, basically any religious) idea of the clash of good elements (or ideas) with bad elements (or ideas) and that the good will ultimately prevail over the bad (8:7-8; 9:48; 20:68-70; 26:45-48; 21:18). Today, as Neier has put it, the real clash is between fundamentalism and modernity.[30] Fundamentalism does not belong to Islam. Religion and modernity are not necessarily antithetical. Islam properly understood does embrace the elements of modernity that define the western economic system.

This book has tried to explain what it means to be a true and devout Muslim in light of the Quran. The Light the Quran brought fourteen centuries ago is as luminous and bright today as when it came (5:15). To learn how to become a good Muslim, one does not need another book. The Quran provides right and complete guidance (2:2; 17:9; 10:57; 16:89). For long, Muslims have neglected the Quran, and followed spurious messages from the Hadith and misguided teachings from sectarian teachers. It is time they returned to their only Holy Book – the Quran – and understand and follow its message. The return to the Quran will mark Islam's true revival.[31] None should think that reciting the verses of this Holy Book without understanding the meaning is any virtue. This is utter misguidance to keep Muslims ignorant of the true message of Islam. Both Muslims and non-Muslims should read this Holy Book to get Islam's true message, which remains as true, civilizing and relevant to our time as before. Mere observance of some rituals does not make one a good Muslim. To become a good Muslim, one needs first to be a good human being, and a thoroughly moral, and ethical person. A fifteenth century Bengali poet-priest Chandidas wrote this strikingly modern word of wisdom: Above all is Man – respect for humanity or human values; nothing is above it (*Shobar upor manush shotto; tahar upore nai*). The Quran has laid a lot of emphasis on our becoming just and kind to fellow human beings. We need to serve humanity, just as God serves humanity. Unfortunately, the human aspect of Islam has been overshadowed by spurious religious teachings, which amply explain our deplorable plight.

Works Cited

Books and Articles

Abdelkader, Engy, "Muslims Redefining Community," *Huffington Post*, 04/01/2013; available at http://www.huffingtonpost.com/engy-abdelkader/muslims-redefining-community_b_2992801.html.

Ahmad, Aksaruddin, *Musings of the Heart in Lyrics* (Bengali manuscript *Gaan-e Praaner Kotha*, undated).

--------------------------, *The Holy Quran: Bengali Translation and Word Rendering* (*Pabitra Quran: Banganubad o Shabdartha*, the first of the thirty parts of the Quran, undated).

--------------------------, *Whither Muslims are Today* (Bengali manuscript *Mussalman Aj Kon Path-e*? undated).

Ahmad, Kassim, *Hadith: A Re-Evaluation*, Translated from his original book in Malay *Hadis — Satu Penilaian* first published in 1986; web link: www.barry-baker.com/Articles/documents/HADITH.pdf.

Ahmad, Panaullah, *Creator and Creation*, Islamic Foundation, Bangladesh, 1986.

Ahmed, Akbar S., *Islam under Siege: Living Dangerously in a Post-Honor World*, Polity Press in association with Blackwell Publishing Ltd., Cambridge, UK and Malden, MA, USA, 2003.

Akyol, Mustafa, *Islam without Extremes: A Muslim Case for Liberty*, W.W. Norton & Company, 2011

................., "Islamocapitalism: Islam and Free Market" in Edip Yuksel, et. al. (ed.), *Critical Thinkers for Islamic Reform*, Brainbow Press, United States of America, 2009.

Al-Shibli, *Sirat al-Numan*, Lahore, n. d. Trans. Muhammad Tayyab Bakhsh Badauni as *Method of Sifting Prophetic Tradition*, Karachi, 1966.

An-Naim, Abdullahi, *Islam and the Secular State: Negotiating the Future of Shari`a*, Harvard University Press, 2010

Anonymous author, "Hadith Authenticity: A Survey Of Perspectives", website link: http://www.rim.org/muslim/Hadith.htm.

Armstrong, Karen, *A History of God: The 4000-Year Quest of Judaism, Christianity and Islam*, Gramercy Books, New York, 1993.

--------------------------, *Islam – A Short History*, Random House Inc., New York, Modern Library Paperback Edition, 2002, 164-66.

Asad, Muhammad (trans.) *Sahih al-Bukhari: the Early Years of Islam*, Dar al-Andalus, 1981.

Aslan, Reza, *No god but God: The Origins, Evolution and Future of Islam*, Random House, New York, 2005.

Azami, M. A., *Studies in Hadith Methodology and Literature*, Islamic Book Trust, Kuala Lumpur, cited in Akbarally Meherally, undated.

Barq, Ghulam Jilani, "Hadith ke bare men mera mawqaf," Chatan, Lahore, January 9, 1956.

------------------------, *Do Islam (Two Islams)*, 1950.

Berk, Jan Marc, "Book Review" (Review of two books by A.L.M. Abdul Gafoor: *Interest-Free Commercial Banking*, Apptech Publications, Groningen, 1995, and *Participatory Financing through Investment Banks and Commercial Banks*, Apptech Publications, Groningen, 1996), De Economist (Quarterly Review of the Royal Netherlands Economic Association), Vol. 146, No. 1, April 1998.

Brown, Daniel W., *Rethinking Tradition in Modern Islamic Thought*, Cambridge University Press, 1996 (Paperback 1999).

Buccaille, Maurice, *The Bible, the Qur'an and Science*, Seghers Publishers, Paris, 1977. Also published as The Bible, the Quran and Science – the Holy Scriptures Examined in the Light of Modern Knowledge, Translated from French by Alastair D. Pannell and the Author, the American Trust Publications, 1979.

Bullet, Richard W., *Islam, the View from the Edge*, New York, Columbia University Press, 1994.

Einstein, Albert, *The Human Side*: (New Glimpses from his Archives), Selected and edited by Helen Dukas and Banesh Hoffmann, published by Princeton University Press, Princeton, New Jersey, 1979.

Esposito, John L., Islam- *The Straight Path*, New York, Oxford University Press, 1991.

--------------------, *What Everyone Needs to Know About Islam*, Oxford University Press, 2002.

--------------------, "Ten Things Everyone Needs to Know about Islam," web link: http://teachmideast.org/essays/35-religion/58-ten-things-to-know-about-islam.

...................., "Rising Tide of Islamophobia," in *Middle East Online*, July 28, 2011; web link: http://www.middle-east-online.com/english/?id=47385.

Fadl, Khaled Abou El, *Conference of the Books: The Search for Beauty in Islam*, University Press of America, Inc., Lanham, (New York, Oxford,) 2001

........................., *And God Knows the Soldiers: The Authoritative and the Authoritarian in Islamic Discourses*, University Press of America, Inc., Lanham and Oxford, 2001.

--------------------, *Speaking in God's Name: Islamic Law, Authority and Women*, Oneworld Publications, Oxford, 2001

--------------------, *The Great Theft: Wrestling Islam from the Extremists*, HarperSan Francisco, A Division of Harper Collins Publishers, New York, 2005.

--------------------, et. al, *The Place of Tolerance in Islam*, Beacon Press, Boston, 2002.

-----------------------------, "The Ugly Modern and the Modern Ugly: Reclaiming the Beautiful in Islam", in Omid Safi (ed.), *Progressive Muslims: On Justice, Gender, and Pluralism*, Oneworld Publications, Oxford, 2003.

Farooq, Dr. Muhammad Umar, "Dr. Farooq's Study Resource Page" in website: http://globalwebpost.com/farooqm/study_res/islam/Hadith/akramkhan_Hadith.html.

Ghouse, Mike, Section on pluralism at *The Ghouse Diary*, available at http://foundationforpluralism.com/ Goldziher, Ignaz, *Muhammedanische Studien*,. 2 vols., Leiden, 1896. Trans. by S.M. Stern as MUSLIM STUDIES, 2 VOLS., London, 1967.

Grof, Stanislav, Toward a New Paradigm of the Unconscious, a video presentation in the website: http://www.thinking-allowed.com/2sgrof.html.

Guillaume, Alfred, *The Traditions of Islam*, Pakistan 1977.

Huntington, Samuel, "The Clash of Civilizations," *Foreign Affairs*, 1993, expanded into a book *The Clash of Civilizations and the Remaking of World Order*, Simon and Schuster, New York, 1996.

Iqbal, Muhammad, *The Reconstruction of Religious Thought in Islam*, edited by M. Saeed Sheikh, Acam Publishers and Distributors, Delhi, 1997; also published earlier (in 1934) by the Oxford University Press.

Jayrajpuri, Muhammad Aslam, *Ilm-i-Hadith* (*Knowledge of Hadith*), Lahore, not dated.

Juynboll, G.H.A., *Muslim Tradition - Studies In Chronology, Provenance And Authorship Of Early Hadith* (New York: Cambridge University Press, 1983.

Kazi, Mazhar U., *A Treasury Of Ahadith*, Jeddah, Saudi Arabia, Abul-Qasim Publishing House, 1992.

Khalifa, Rashad, *Quran, Hadith and Islam*, available on the link: http://www.masjidtucson.org/publications/books/qhi/contents.html; also published by Universal Unity, 2000.

Khan, Aasma, "How Muslims can Combat Terror and Violence" in Michael Wolfe & Beliefnet (ed.), *Taking Back Islam: American Muslims Reclaim Their Faith*, Rodale Inc and Beliefnet Inc, 2002.

Khan, Sayyid Ahmad, *Maqalat*, as cited in Daniel W. Brown, 1996 (paperback 1999).

............................, *Tafsir al-Qur'an*, Aligarh, 1297 AH.

Khan, Haroon A., "The Clash of Civilization Thesis and Bangladesh: A Case Study", *Asian Profile*, Vol. 32, No. 2, April 2004.

Khan, M.A. Muqtedar, *American Muslims: Bridging Faith and Freedom*, Amana Publications, 2002.

Khan, M. Muhsin (trans.), *Sahih Bukhari*, available on the website: http://www.searchtruth.com/Hadith_books.php#bukhari.

Lang, *Losing My Religion: A Call for Help*, Amana Publishers, Beltsville (Maryland), 2004.

Lewis, Bernard, *What Went Wrong? Western Impact and Middle Eastern Response*, Oxford University Press, New York, 2002.

MacDonald, Duncan B., *Development of Muslim Theology Jurisprudence and Constitutional Theory* (George Routledge and Sons), London, 1903.

Majid, Raja F. M., *Ghulam Jilani Barq: A Study in Muslim 'Rationalism,'* M.A. thesis, McGill University, Institute of Islamic Studies, 1962.

Malek, M.A., *A Study of the Qur'an: The Universal Guidance for Mankind*, 1997, third edition 2000, Sutton, Surrey, UK.

Manji, Irshad, , *The Trouble with Islam: A Muslim's Call for Reform in Her Faith*, St. Martin's Press, New York, 2003.

Mansour, Ahmed Subhy, *Penalty of Apostasy: A Historical and Fundamental Study*, English translation by Mostafa Sabet, Original title in Arabic: *Haddur Riddah: Dirasah Usooliyya Tareekhiyya*.

Mashriqi, Inayat Allah Khan, *Tadhkira*, Amritsar, 1924.

Mauro, Paolo, "The Persistence of Corruption and Slow Economic Growth", 2002 International Monetary Fund Staff Working Paper (IMF WP 02/213).

Meherally, Akbarally, *Myths and Realities of Hadith – A Critical Study*, (published by Mostmerciful.com Publishers), Burnaby, BC, Canada, available in the web link: http://www.mostmerciful.com/Hadithbook-sectionone.htm.

Miller, Lisa, "Islam in America: A Special Report", *Newsweek*, July 30, 2007.

Minai, Ali, "A Time for Renewal" in Michael Wolfe (ed.), *Taking Back Islam: American Muslims Reclaim Their Faith*, Rodale Inc. and Beliefnet Inc., 2002, 10. Reprinted from www.chowk.com.

Muir, William, *The Life of Mahomet and the History of Islam to the Era of Hegira*, 4 vols., London, 1861; repr. Osnabruck, 1988.

Murphy, Caryle, *Passion for Islam: Shaping the Modern Middle East: The Egyptian Experience*, Simon & Schuster, New York, 2002.

Musa, Aisha Y., *Hadith As Scripture: Discussions On The Authority Of Prophetic Traditions In Islam,* Palgrave Macmillan, 2008.

Neier, Aryeh, "The Real Clash is Fundamentalists vs. Modernity," *International Herald Tribune*, October 10, 2001.

Parwez, Ghulam Ahmed, *Muquaam-e-Hadith* (in Urdu - The True Status of the Hadith), 2nd edn., Karachi, 1965.

---------------------------------, *Salim ke nam khutut*, Karachi, 1953.

Pipes, Daniel, "Identifying Moderate Muslims," *New York Sun*, November 23, 2004; website: http://www.danielpipes.org/article/2226.

-----------------, "Calling Islamism the Enemy" Weblog, June 13, 2002, website: http://www.danielpipes.org/blog/300.

Rab, Abdur, *Exploring Islam in a New Light*, Brainbow Press, 2010 and IUniverse, 2008.

........., "Fifteen Great Reasons We Should Embrace and Follow the Quran-only Islam" in *OpEd News*, December 4th, 2008. Web Link: http://www.opednews.com/articles/Fifteen-Great-Reasons-We-S-by-Abdur-Rab-081202-982.html.

........., "Divine Will and Human Freedom," *Aslan Media*, July 29, 2012; available at http://www.aslanmedia.com/arts-culture/mideast-culture/9352-divine-will-and-human-freedom

........., "Divine Will and Human Freedom: Part 1. Divine Predestination: How Far Real?" *OpEd News*, January 8, 2010. Web link: http://www.opednews.com/articles/Divine-Will-and-Human-Free-by-Abdur-Rab-100102-748.html.

........., "How God Exists: What Can We Glean from the Quran?" Available at *Aslan Media*, March 3, 2013; available at http://aslanmedia.com/component/content/article/11-faith/islam/21173-how-god-exists-what-can-we-glean-from-the-quran.

............, "Reform in Finance: Riba vs. Interest in the Modern Economy," 42nd Naaims Conference Paper presented at Princeton University, September 28, 2013; available at http://naaims.org/uploads/Abdur_Rab_-_42FP.pdf **or at** https://www.academia.edu/4822162/Reform_in_Finance_Riba_vs._Interest_in_the_Modern_Economy.

Rahman, Fazlur, *Islam & Modernity: Transformation of an Intellectual Tradition*, University of Chicago Press, Chicago, London, Paperback Edition, 1984 (Original 1982)

...................., "Major Themes of the Qur'an," *Bibliotheca Islamica*, Minneapolis, Chicago, 1980.

...................., "Riba and Interest," *Islamic Studies* (Karachi), 3(1), March 1964, pp. 1-43 (the original article titled "Tahqiq-i Riba" is published in Urdu in the journal *Fikr-o Nazar*, i/5, 1963, translation by Mazheruddin Siddiqi) available at http://www.globalwebpost.com/farooqm/study_res/i_econ_fin/frahman_riba.pdf.

Rauf, Imam Feisal Abdul, *What's Right with Islam: A New Vision for Muslims and the West*, HarperCollins Publishers Inc., New York, 2004.

Rippin, Andrew, *Muslims: Their Religious Beliefs And Practices* vol. 1 (New York: Routledge, 1990.

Rauch, Jonathan, "Inequality and its Perils," *National Journal*, September 27, 2012.

Sachedina, Abdulaziz, *Islam & the Challenge of Human Rights*, Oxford University Press, 2009

Safi, Omid (ed.), *Progressive Muslims: On Justice, Gender, and Pluralism*, Oneworld Publications, Oxford, 2003.

Schacht, Joseph, *Muhammadan Jurisprudence*. Oxford University Press, Oxford, 1950.

Schwartz, Stephen, *The Two Faces of Islam: Saudi Fundamentalism and its Role in Terrorism*, Knopf Publishing Group, paperback published by Anchor, 2003, cited in Website: http://www.islamicpluralism.org/books.htm.

Scriven, Michael, Explanations of the Supernatural (1998 Thinking Allowed Productions), discussion in the website: http://www.intuition.org/txt/scriven3.htm.

Siddiqui, Abdul Hamid (trans.), *Sahih Muslim*, available on the web link: http://www.iium.edu.my/deed/Hadith/muslim/index.html.

Sidqi, Muhammad Tawfiq, "al-Islam huwa al-Qur'an wahdahu," *al-Manar* 9, 1906.

Spencer, Robert, *Islam Unveiled: Disturbing Questions about the World's Fastest-Growing Faith*, Encounter Books, San Francisco, 2002.

Sprenger, Alois, "On the Origin of Writing Down Historical Records among the Musulmans', *Journal of the Asiatic Society of Bengal 25*, 1856.

Soroush, Abdolkarim, *Reason, Freedom, and Democracy in Islam*, Oxford University Press, Oxford-New York, 2000.

Taheri, Amir, *Spirit of Allah: Khomeini and the Islamic Revolution*, Adler and Adler, 1986.

Taher, Amiri, "Islam can't Escape Blame for Sept. 11," *Wall Street Journal*, 24 October 2001.

The American Center for Progress, Report of August 2011: *Fear, Inc., The Roots of the Islamophobia Network in America* by Wajahat Ali et. al.

Tibi, Bassam, *The Challenge of Fundamentalism: Political Islam and the New World Disorder*, Berkeley University Press, 1998, updated edition 2002.

United Nations (United Nations Office for the High Commissioner for Human Rights (OHCHR)), *Report of the World Conference against Racism, Racial Discrimination, Xenophobia and Related Intolerance*, held in Durban during 31 August - 8 September 2001, January 25, 2002.

------------------, (UNAIDS), *AIDS in Africa*, March 4, 2005.

von Grunebaum, G.E., *Classical Islam: A History 600-1258*, (Translation by Katherine Watson), Barnes and Noble Books, 1996, originally published in 1970 by Aldine Publishing Company.

Wadud, Amina, *Qur'an and Woman: Reading the Sacred Text from a Woman's Perspective*, Oxford University Press, New York, 1999.

Wolfe, Michael & Beliefnet (ed.), *Taking Back Islam: American Muslims Reclaim Their Faith*, Rodale Inc and Beliefnet Inc, 2002.

World Bank, Poverty, Growth, and Inequality (based on a survey done by Lopez in 2004); available at
http://web.worldbank.org/WBSITE/EXTERNAL/TOPICS/EXTPOVERTY/EXTPGI/0,,contentMDK:20263370~menuPK:524064~pagePK:148956~piPK:216618~theSitePK:342771,00.html.

Yuksel, Edip, *Manifesto for Islamic Reform*, 2nd revised and enlarged edition, Brainbow Press, U.S.A., 2009.

................, *Peacemaker's Guide to War Mongers: Exposing Robert Spencer, Osama bin Laden, David Horowitz and Other Enemies of Peace*, Brainbow Press, U.S.A., 2010.

................, Layth Saleh al-Shaiban and Martha Schulte-Nafeh, *Quran: A Reformist Translation*, Brainbow Press, 2007.

Other Publications

Middle East Quarterly, March 2000.
The Concise Columbia Encyclopedia, Columbia University Press, 1995.

The Economist, March 6th-12th, 2010 issue.

The New International Pocket Quotation Dictionary of the English Language, Trident Press International, 2000.

Time magazine, December 3, 2005.

Notes

Chapter I

[1] The abbreviation stands for "Peace be upon him," an expression of reverence and well wishing used by Muslims for the Prophet Muhammad. Muslims use this expression also in the case of other prophets.

[2] Muhammad lost his father while he was still in the mother's womb, and his mother died when he was only six years old.

[3] Ahmad, Panaullah, *Creator and Creation*, Islamic Foundation, Bangladesh, 1986, 29. For this Quranic idea, see (41:34).

[4] Lang, Jeffrey, *Losing My Religion: A Call for Help*, Amana Publishers, Beltsville (Maryland), 2004, 72.

[5] Lang, *ibid*, 73.

[6] *Ibid*, 71.

[7] The term has been used and elaborately discussed by Muhammad Iqbal in his monumental work *The Reconstruction of Religious Thought in Islam*; see end note below.

[8] Iqbal, Muhammad, *The Reconstruction of Religious Thought in Islam*, Adam Publishers and Distributors, Delhi, 1997, 13 (also published earlier (in 1934) by the Oxford University Press).

[9] Buccaille, Maurice, The Bible, the Qur'an and Science, Seghers Publishers, Paris, 1977. Also published as The Bible, the Quran and Science – the Holy Scriptures Examined in the Light of Modern Knowledge, Translated from French by Alastair D. Pannell and the Author, the American Trust Publications, 1979.

[10] For a full description of the thesis, see Edip Yuksel, *NINETEEN: God's Signature in Nature and Scripture*, Brainbow Press, 2011.

[11] This is an issue precisely because it is at odds with the Quranic claim that it is divinely protected from

possible corruption and change. Also, the verses in question look quite consistent with the worldview of the Quran.

[12] It seems that "Nineteen" could instead well be interpreted to denote a possible number of the stages of a human being's progress in knowledge and power, based on a similar approach to human progress made by Panaullah Ahmed in his book, *Creator and Creation*, op. cit., 1986. In line with his thinking, eighteen stages can be derived as follows:

The Quran states that we are of three kinds (56:7). Following this clue we can say that existence/creation is in three kinds, and that our progress/evolution or knowledge goes through three stages:

Act on another particular or other particulars;

Act on the universal, i.e., on God Who represents the universal; and

Allow the universal to act on the particular.

When one person works with some object or comes into contact with another person, the result is always some new experience or knowledge. This is the first stage of knowledge. The second stage is signified by the worker working selflessly or on behalf of or for the universal, i.e., acting on the universal. The third stage is when his knowledge is strengthened or fortified by gaining insight from the universal.

Another three stages are for application of such knowledge to others: acting on particulars, acting on the universal, and allowing the universal to act on the particulars.

These six stages confirm or complete one's knowledge.

The application of this knowledge thereafter requires another six stages, twelve in all, to get real power.

Power needs application, which means another six stages in each act. This gives creation in eighteen stages. Ahmad did not indicate still another stage, which would give us nineteen stages in all, which can enable us to decisively overcome hell fire.

[13] Esposito, John L., Islam - *The Straight Path*, New York, Oxford University Press, 1991, 30-31.

Notes

[14] Rahman, Fazlur, *Islam & Modernity: Transformation of an Intellectual Tradition*, University of Chicago Press, Chicago, London, Paperback Edition, 1984 (Original 1982), 14, 19.

[15] von Grunebaum, *Classical Islam: A History 600-1258*, (Translation by Katherine Watson), Barnes and Noble Books, 1996, originally published in 1970 by Aldine Publishing Company, 39.

[16] This confusion has been caused by the Hadith literature, as shown in Chapter 11.

[17] These comments of Dr. Nasr Hamid Abu Zayd are cited by Caryle Murphy, *Passion for Islam: Shaping the Modern Middle East: The Egyptian Experience*, Simon & Schuster, New York, 2002, 190.

[18] Taken from the web link: http://www.freerepublic.com/focus/news/792720/replies?c=2.

[19] Aslan, Reza, *No god but God: The Origins, Evolution and Future of Islam*, Random House, New York, 2005, Chapter 6, 140-170. In these pages, Aslan provides a good discussion of this contentious issue.

[20] Iqbal, *op. cit.*, 1997, 1.

[21] *Ibid*, 1-2.

[22] *Ibid*, 1997, 12.

[23] *Ibid*, 1997, 10.

[24] Lang, *op. cit.*, 64-70.

[25] Ahmad, Panaullah, *op cit.*, 113.

[26] Iqbal, *op. cit.*, 16.

[27] Lang, *op. cit.*, 137.

[28] Iqbal, *op, cit.*, 63.

[29] For more on this, see Chapter II (The section on "Turning to God and the Conception of God"). For further illumination, see the author's two articles: (1) "Divine Will and Human Freedom," Aslan Media, July 29, 2012 (Link: http://www.aslanmedia.com/arts-culture/mideast-culture/9352-divine-will-and-human-freedom) and (2) "Divine Will and Human Freedom – Part 1. Divine Predestination: How Far Real?" January 10, 2010 (Link:

http://www.opednews.com/articles/Divine-Will-and-Human-Free-by-Abdur-Rab-100102-748.html.

[30] Note that this view of the Quran is that of the Rationalists, which is at odds with that of the Traditionalists. The origins of the Rationalists' argument are most clearly traceable first to the Qadarites group who lived during the Umayyad rule and later to the Mutazilite group during the time of Shafi'i (d. 820). The Traditionalists' position is dominated by the Asharite group who accepts the notions of predestination, and t*aqlid* (blind acceptance of juridical precedent).

[31] Lang, *op. cit.*, 64.

[32] *Ibid.*, 65.

[33] *Ibid,* 66.

[34] For documentation of this point as well as for that of the overall distortion of the Quranic message by the Hadith, see Chapter 11.

[35] Rahman, Fazlur, *op. cit.*, 1984, 19.

[36] Iqbal, 1997, *op. cit.*, 134; also cited in John L. Esposito, 1991, *op. cit.*, 138.

[37] Esposito, John L., *op. cit.*, 1991, 138.

[38] Khan, Sayyid Ahmad, *Tafsir al-Qur'an*, Aligarh, 1297 AH, I, 31-34; cited in Daniel W. Brown, *Rethinking Tradition in Modern Islamic Thought*, Cambridge University Press, 1996 (Paperback 1999), 44.

[39] Khan, Sayyid Ahmad, *Muqalat*, II, 197-258; cited in Brown, *op. cit.*, 44.

[40] Esposito, *op. cit.*, 1991, 21.

[41] Iqbal, 1997, *op. cit.*, 7.

Chapter II

[1] The conception of God as the Creator has an inherent problem. Both Intelligent Design and cosmological (First Cause) arguments for God"s existence involve, or assume away, an infinite regress. The ontological argument – simplified by the Cartesian expression "I think, therefore I am" –

Notes

involves a fallacy of *petitio principii* – one that assumes the conclusion in the very premise. Recent scientific discovery of multiple universes leads scientists to conclude that the birth of the universes as well as life's origin are products of the same evolutionary process.

[2] See author's article "How God Exists: What Can We Glean from the Quran?" Available at http://www.academia.edu/2902541/How_God_Exists_What_Can_We_Glean_from_the_Quran.

[3] See author's article "Divine Will and Human Freedom," *Aslan Media*, July 29, 2012 referred to at end note 29 of Chapter I.

[4] Cited in Paul Davies, *The Mind of God*, p. 183.

[5] Lang, *op. cit.*, 97.

[6] Ahmad, Panaullah, *op. cit.*, 68.

[7] Ahmad, Panaullah, *op. cit.*, 97.

[8] Lang, *op. cit.*, 112-113, 117.

[9] Ahmad, Panaullah, *op. cit.*, 235-236.

[10] Ahmad, Panaullah, *op. cit.*, 107.

[11] Lang, *op. cit.*, 141.

[12] For more illumination on this topic, see author's two articles referred to at end note 29 of Chapter I.

[13] For further discussion, see Chapter X.

[14] Ahmad, Panaullah, *op. cit.*, 9.

[15] *Ibid*, 1986, 15.

[16] *Ibid*, *op. cit.*, 12.

[17] *Ibid*, 59, 436.

[18] Scriven, Michael, *Explanations of the Supernatural*, an interesting television transcript of conversation between Michael Scriven and Jeffrey Mishlove on the former's *Explanations of the Supernatural* (1998 Thinking Allowed Productions); available at http://www.thinkingallowed.com/2mscriven.html

[19] Grof, Stanislav, *A New Paradigm of the Unconscious*; available at http://www.thinking-allowed.com/2sgrof.html.

[20] Some details of what makes us righteous are provided in Chapters VII.

[21] Soroush, Abdolkarim, *Reason, Freedom, and Democracy in Islam*, Oxford University Press, Oxford-New York, 2000, 96-97.

Chapter III

[1] This theory is, according to our knowledge, originally attributable to a little known Eastern sage Shah Aksaruddin Ahmad, who verbally explained its broad outlines to some of his students, and some description of it was found scribbled in some of his unpublished manuscripts. Later in the work of his student Panaullah Ahmad, *op. cit.*, 249, 370-378), we find some sketchy outlines of this theory.
[2] Ahmad, Panaullah, *op. cit.*, 249.
[3] Iqbal, *op. cit.*, 82.
[4] Ahmad, Panaullah, *op. cit.*, vii.
[5] *Ibid,* 50.
[6] *Ibid,* 34.
[7] *Ibid,* 8.

Chapter IV

[1] Ahmad, Aksaruddin, "*Musings of the Heart in Songs*" (Bengali Manuscript *Gaan-e Praaner Kotha*, undated), translation by the author.
[2] Ahmad, Panaullah, *op. cit.*, 9.
[3] *Ibid*, 435, 439.
[4] von Grunebaum, *op. cit*, 47. According to Karen Armstrong, the Prophet first enjoined two times and later three times *salat* (prayer). See her *A History of God: The 4000-Year Quest of Judaism, Christianity and Islam*, Gramercy Books, New York, 1993, 142, 153.
[5] Fadl, Khaled Abou El, *The Great Theft: Wrestling Islam from the Extremists*, HarperSan Francisco, A Division of Harper Collins Publishers, New York, 2005, 117.
[6] Ahmad, Panaullah, *op. cit.*, 324.

Notes

[7] It is always preferable however, though not essential, that one's spiritual pursuit is carried forward under the guidance of an adept spiritual teacher, and monitored by him. But one should be very careful to choose a spiritual guide.

[8] Ahmad, Aksaruddin, "*Musings of the Heart in Lyrics*" (Bengali Manuscript undated), translation by the author.

Chapter V

[1] World Bank, *Poverty, Growth, and Inequality* (based on a survey done by Lopez in 2004); available at http://web.worldbank.org/WBSITE/EXTERNAL/TOPICS/EXTPOVERTY/EXTPGI/0,,contentMDK:20263370~menuPK:524064~pagePK:148956~piPK:216618~theSitePK:342771,00.html.

[2] Rauch, Jonathan, "Inequality and its Perils," *National Journal*, September 27, 2012.

[3] I am grateful to Layth Al-Shaiban, who manages the Internet website http://free-minds.org and is also a co-author of *Quran—A Reformist Translation*, for a comment on an earlier interpretation of mine, which has helped to rephrase the interpretation into the present one.

Chapter VI

[1] Esposito, John L., "Rising Tide of Islamophobia," in *Middle East Online*, July 28, 2011; web link: http://www.middle-east-online.com/english/?id=47385. See also Nathan Lean's book *The Islamophobia Industry: How the Right Manufactures Fear of Muslims*, Pluto Press, 2012 that illuminates on a systematic tirade against Islam and Muslims by some American groups. Also see the American Center for Progress report of August 2011: *Fear, Inc., The Roots of the Islamophobia Network in America* by Wajahat Ali et. al.

[2] Soroush, 97.

[3] Fadl, Khaled Abou El, *op. cit.,* 2005, 209.

[4] Esposito, John L., *op. cit.,* 2002, 70-71.

[5] "Many of the Nazis who slaughtered millions of civilians during World War II were Christians (in that they were of the Christian religion); many of the Crusaders who massacred unarmed Muslim men, women, and children in the name of God were devoted Christians; the Spanish inquisitors who tortured and murdered non-Christians were committed Christians; the white soldiers who brought about the genocide of native American peoples in North and South America – often accompanied by missionaries – were Christians; and so were the armies of Charlemagn who eagerly slaughtered tens of thousands of pagan Anglo Saxons." (Lang, *op. cit,* 302, Footnote 206.)

[6] Akyol, Mustafa, *Islam without Extremes: A Muslim Case for Liberty*, W.W. Norton & Company, 2011, 74.

[7] Lewis, Bernard, *The Crisis of Islam: Holy War and Unholy Terror*, Weidenfeld & Nicholson, 2003, 30; cited in Akyol, *ibid.* 73.

[8] Only a handful of people were executed due to breach of law. A few rich men were persuaded to make a contribution to compensate the poorer followers who were deprived of the booty. See von Grunebaum, *op. cit.*, 44.

[9] Available at http://www.bbc.co.uk/news/world-middle-east-24893808.

[10] Fadl, Khaled Abou El et. al, *The Place of Tolerance in Islam*, Beacon Press, Boston, 2002, 21-22.

[11] Yuksel, Edip, *Peacemaker's Guide to Warmongers: Exposing Robert Spencer, Osama bin Laden, David Horowitz, Mullah Omar, Bill Warner, Ali Sina and Other Enemies of Peace*, Brainbow Press, USA, 2010, 41.

[12] Khan, Aasma, "How Muslims can Combat Terror and Violence" in Michael Wolfe & Beliefnet (ed.), *Taking Back Islam: American Muslims Reclaim Their Faith*, Rodale Inc and Beliefnet Inc, 2002, 51.

Notes 289

[13] Armstrong, *Islam – A Short History*, Random House Inc., New York, Modern Library Paperback Edition, 2002, 155-156.

[14] For reference to the relevant Hadith texts, see Chapter 11.

[15] Ghouse, Mike, Section on pluralism at *The Ghouse Diary*, available at http://foundationforpluralism.com/.

[16] Meanings of pluralism on the Pluralism Project at Harvard University; available at http://pluralism.org/pages/pluralism/meanings.

[17] Abdekader, Engy, "Muslims Redefining Community," *Huffington Post*, 04/01/2013, available at http://www.huffingtonpost.com/engy-abdelkader/muslims-redefining-community_b_2992801.html.

[18] United Nations (United Nations Office for the High Commissioner for Human Rights (OHCHR)), *Report of the World Conference against Racism, Racial Discrimination, Xenophobia and Related Intolerance*, (held in Durban, during 31 August - 8 September 2001), January 25, 2002.

[19] The UN report cited in the preceding endnote.

[20] Sachedina, Abdulaziz, *Islam & the Challenge of Human Rights*, Oxford University Press, 2009, (in Foreword by David Little, Harvard Divinity School), x.

[21] *Ibid*, ix.

[22] An-Naim, Abdullahi, Islam and the Secular State: Negotiating the Future of Shari`a, Harvard University Press, 2010.

[23] The Quran makes a distinction between men and women in two cases: inheritance laws and giving witness in financial matters. But these are context-specific. If context changes, the rules should change, too. See Chapter VIII for a discussion on this.

Chapter VII

[1] Einstein, Albert, *The Human Side: (New Glimpses from his Archives),* Selected and edited by Helen

Dukas and Banesh Hoffmann, published by Princeton University Press, Princeton, New Jersey, 1979, p. 95.

[2] Einstein, A., *ibid*, 1979, 70-71. It looks a little odd that Einstein omits the Prophet Muhammad's name along with Jesus and Moses, especially since Muhammad preached the same religion as Moses and Jesus did.

[3] For example, the Hadith encourages fatalism, which blunts individual initiative and enterprise. For details, see Chapter XI.

[4] Ahmad, Panaullah, *op. cit.*, 1986, 219.

[5] Quoted in Abd al-Ghafir al-Khatib, *Ghazali*, trans. MacCarthy, 15-17, 75; also cited in Imam Feisal Abdul Rauf, *What's Right with Islam: A New Vision for Muslims and the West*, HarperCollins Publishers Inc., New York, 2004, 73.

[6] *The New International Pocket Quotation Dictionary of the English Language*, Trident Press International, 2000, 121.

[7] *Ibid*, 122.

[8] *Ibid*, 26.

[9] HIV stands for Human Immuno-Deficiency Virus.

[10] AIDS stands for Acquired Immune Deficiency Syndrome.

[11] Yuksel, Edip, Layth Saleh al-Shaiban and Martha Schulte-Nafeh, *Quran: A Reformist Translation*, Brainbow Press, 2007.

[12] Iqbal, Muhammad, *op, cit.*, 1997 (Oxford University Press, 1934), 136-137. Also cited in Daniel W. Brown, *Rethinking Tradition in Modern Islamic Thought*, Cambridge University Press, 1996 (Paperback 1999), 25.

[13] Fadl, Khaled Abou El, *op. cit.*, 2005, 131.

[14] Esposito, John L., *op. cit.*, 2002, 149.

[15] Fadl, Khaled Abou El, *op. cit.*, 2001, 111.

[16] Ahmad, Panaullah, *op. cit.*, 246.

[17] Ahmad, Aksaruddin, "*The Musings of the Heart in Lyrics*" (Bengali manuscript *Gaan-e Praan-er Kotha* undated), translation by the author.

Chapter VIII

[1] "Gendercide" and other articles, *The Economist*, March 6th-12th, 2010 issue, 13, 77-80 and 104-105. The seriousness of the gender imbalance in China is illustrated by a statistic: there are almost as many unmarried young men in China as the total number of (both married and unmarried) young men in the United states – *ibid*, 13.

[2] Lewis, Bernard, *What Went Wrong? Western Impact and Middle Eastern Response*, Oxford University Press, New York, 2002, 71.

[3] It is unfortunate that the Hadith literature gives such a horrible impression about the Prophet.

[4] One, of course, does benefit from a good religious teacher or guide. But one should be wary of wrong teachers, gurus, or *pirs* who mislead people. Another point to note is that good religious teachers, priests, gurus, or *pirs* can only inspire us to be religious and give us guidance and knowledge, but they cannot themselves give us salvation or make us evolve spiritually (72:21). That can happen only when we ourselves put in required efforts.

[5] As reported in Amir Taheri, *Spirit of Allah: Khomeini and the Islamic Revolution*, Adler and Adler, 1986,51; cited in Spencer, Robert, *Islam Unveiled: Disturbing Questions about the World's Fastest-Growing Faith*, Encounter Books, San Francisco, 2002, 87.

[6] In recent years, notable reforms have been carried out in the Muslim marriage and divorce laws in a number of countries such as limitation of polygamy rights, expansion of rights for women seeking divorce, including the right to financial compensation, expansion of rights for women to participate in contracting their marriage and to stipulate conditions favorable to them in the marriage contract, the requirement that the husband provide housing for his divorced wife and children as long as the wife holds custody over the children, raising of the minimum age for marriage for both spouses, prohibition of child

marriage, and expansion of the rights of women to have custody over their older children. Cf., Esposito, *op. cit.*, 2002, 93.

[7] For more on this, check out this link: http://www.aslanmedia.com/news-politics/world-news/16142-everything-you-need-to-know-about-islam-and-divorce.

[8] Armstrong, *op. cit.* 2002, 157-158.

[9] Esposito, *op. cit.*, 2002, 90-91.

[10] Fadl, Abou El, *op. cit.*, 2005, 268.

[11] For some illumination on this point, see Irshad Manji, *The Trouble with Islam: A Muslim's Call for Reform in Her Faith*, St. Martin's Press, New York, 2003, 160-167.

[12] Aslan, *op. cit.*, 69-70.

[13] Yuksel et.al., *op. cit.*, 2007, 93, verse 4:34.

[14] Lang, *op. cit.*, 430.

[15] It is also extended to beings and things other than humans (2:116; 30:27).

[16] Wadud, Amina, *Qur'an and Woman: Reading the Sacred Text from a Woman's Perspective*, Oxford University Press, New York, 1999, 74.

[17] Wadud, *ibid*, 69-74.

[18] Wadud, *ibid*, 95-99.

[19] Fadl, Abou El, *Conference of the Books: The Search for Beauty in Islam*, University Press of America, Inc., Lanham, (New York, Oxford,) 2001, 14.

[20] Fadl, Abou El, *op. cit.*, 2005, 263-264.

[21] Esposito, *op. cit.*, 2002, 92.

[22] Lewis, Bernard, *What Went Wrong? Western Impact and Middle Eastern Response*, Oxford University Press, 2002, 71.

[23] Esposito, *op. cit.*, 1991, 144.

[24] Aslan, *op. cit.*, 73-74.

[25] Aslan, *op. cit.*, 74.

[26] Esposito, *op. cit.*, 2002, 93-94.

[27] Esposito, *op. cit.*, 2002, 96.

[28] Esposito, *op. cit.*, 2002, 95.

[29] See the relevant section in Chapter 10.

[30] Fadl, Khaled Abou El, "The Ugly Modern and the Modern Ugly: Reclaiming the Beautiful in Islam", in

Omid Safi (ed.), *Progressive Muslims: On Justice, Gender, and Pluralism*, Oneworld Publications, Oxford, 2003,44. For a systematic analysis of the deprecating treatment of women, see Khaled Abou El Fadl, *Speaking in God's Name: Islamic Law, Authority and Women*, Oneworld Publications, Oxford, 2001, 170-249.

[31] Lewis, *op. cit.*, 73.
[32] Lewis, *op. cit.*, 64-75.
[33] Rahman, Fazlur, *op. cit.*, 1984, 19.
[34] Esposito, *op. cit.*, 2002, 148.
[35] Toledano, Ehud R., *Slavery and Abolition in the Ottoman Middle East*, University of Washington Press, 1998, 118; cited in Mustafa Akyol, *op. cit.*, 2011, 169.
[36] Source: *The Concise Columbia Encyclopedia, 1995* by Columbia University Press from MS Bookshelf, as cited and compiled by Eddie Becker on the Internet.
[37] Lewis, *op. cit.*, 69.
[38] Manji, *op. cit.*, 2003, 37.

Chapter IX

[1] This is an economic argument. It states that tinkering with taxes and subsidies that may affect production itself or prices (of goods, services or factors of production) would distort the appropriate allocation and efficiency of productive resources, resulting in less than optimal production and growth in the economy. Hence public assistance programs should be devised in such a way that they do not distort production and prices in the economy.

[2] Akyol, Mustafa, "Islamocapitalism: Islam and Free Market" in Edip Yuksel, et. al. (ed.), *Critical Thinkers for Islamic Reform*, Brainbow Press, United States of America, 2009.

[3] Rab, Abdur, *Exploring Islam in a New Light: A View from the Quranic Perspective*, 2010.

[4] Rab, Abdur, "Reform in Finance: *Riba* vs. Interest in the Modern Economy," 42nd NAAIMS Conference

Paper presented at Princeton University, September 28, 2012; available at http://naaims.org/uploads/Abdur_Rab_-_42FP.pdf or at https://www.academia.edu/4822162/Reform_in_Finance_Riba_vs._Interest_in_the_Modern_Economy.

[5] Rahman, Fazlur, "Riba and Interest," *Islamic Studies* (Karachi), 3(1), March 1964, pp. 1-43 (the original article titled "Tahqiq-i Riba" is published in Urdu in the journal *Fikr-o Nazar*, i/5, 1963, translation by Mazheruddin Siddiqi) available at http://www.globalwebpost.com/farooqm/study_res/i_econ_fin/frahman_riba.pdf. Cited in Abdur Rab, 2012, *ibid*.

[6] Cited in Mustafa Akyol, "Islamocapitalism: Islam and the Free Market," *Critical Thinkers for Islamic Reform: A Collection of Articles from Contemporary Thinkers on Islam*, Brainbow Press, 2009.

[7] Ali, A. Yusuf, *The Holy Qur'an: Text, Translation and Commentary*, Lahore, 1975, p.111, n.324; cited in Ahmad, Abu Umar Faruq and M. Kabir Hassan, "Riba and Islamic Banking," at *Journal of Islamic Economics, Banking and Finance*, available at http://ibtra.com/pdf/journal/v3_n1_article1.pdf.

[8] Rauf, Imam Feisal Abdul, *What is Right with Islam: A New Vision for Muslims and the West*, HarperCollins Publishers, Inc., New York, 2004, 3-4.

[9] Akyol, Mustafa, *op. cit*.

[10] Al-Muharrami, Saeed and Daniel C. Hardy, "Co-operative and Islamic Banks: What Can They Learn from Each Other?" *IMF Working Paper*, 2013, WP/13/184, pp. 14-15. (Available at http://www.imf.org/external/pubs/ft/wp/2013/wp13184.pdf).

[11] Ali, Salman Syed, "Islamic Banking in the MENA Region," WP# 1433-01, Islamic Research and Training Institute, 2012, pp. 14-15, 35.

[12] For more details, see the author's two articles on links: https://www.academia.edu/4822162/Reform_in_Finance_Riba_vs._Interest_in_the_Modern_Economy or

Notes 295

https://www.academia.edu/2711594/Is_Interest_Really_Banned_in_Islam.

[13] Al-Muharami and Hardy 2013, *IMF Working Paper*, op. cit., p. 14.

[13] Foster, John (Former editor, Islamic Business & Finance magazine), "How Sharia-compliant is Islamic banking?" *BBC News*, Friday, 11 December 2009, Available at http://news.bbc.co.uk/2/hi/business/8401421.stm.

[14] Cited in William Barnes, "Islamic finance sits awkwardly in a modern business school," *Financial Times*, July 21, 2013, available at http://www.ft.com/intl/cms/s/2/ee2a2b36-9de5-11e2-9ccc-00144feabdc0.html#axzz2fGNtt2Rv.

Chapter X

[1] *Hadith* – sing. (pl. *aHadith*), lit., a report, account or statement In generally used Islamic law and discourse, it refers to traditions attributed to the Prophet Muhammad.

[2] *sunnah* – lit., the way, course or conduct of life. In general Muslim belief, it refers to the way of the Prophet Muhammad.

[3] Other alleged sources of Islam are the *Qiyas* and the *Ijma*. *Qiyas* refers to comparative or analogical deduction in a particular case derived from the analogy of similar cases. *Qiyas* is used to provide parallels between similar situations or principles when no clear text is found in the Quran or *Sunnah*. *Ijma*, regarded as the fourth source of law, originated from Muhammad's reported saying, "My community will never agree on an error." This came to mean that a consensus among religious scholars could determine permissibility of an action. The *Fiqh* literature is an anthology of Islamic law or jurisprudence derived from the Hadith sources. However, as this work has argued, the Quran is the only authoritative book by which Islam should be understood, as Islam came

with the Quran and was perfected with the Quran (5:3).

[4] Note, however, that Sunnis who form the majority of Muslims believe in one set of Hadith compilations such as *Bukhari, Muslim*, etc., while the Shiites believe in another set.

[5] This is what modern Muslim and non-Muslim scholars generally have attempted to do, as reflected in many of their works. See in particular the cover page introduction to the book Michael Wolfe and the Producers of Beliefnet (ed.), *Taking Back Islam: American Muslims Reclaim Their Faith*, Rodale Inc. and Beliefnet Inc., 2002.

[6] Musa, Aisha Y., *Hadith as Scripture: Discussions on the Authority of Prophetic Traditions in Islam*, Palgrave Macmillan, New York, 2008.

[7] Al-Shafii is known as the founder of one of the four known Sunni divisions (*madhhabs*) and was an ardent champion of the Hadith (*sunnah*), holding it as divinely inspired.

[8] Josef van Ess, *Zwischen Hadith and Theologie* (Berlin, Walter de Gruyter, 1975), 56; cited in Musa, *ibid*, 17.

[9] Michael Cook, *Muslim Dogma*, (Cambridge, Cambridge University Press, 1981), 9; cited in Musa, *ibid*, 38.

[10] Musa, *ibid*, 36-37.

[11] *Ibid*, 41, 56.

[12] *Ibid*, 44.

[13] *Ibid*, 21.

[14] *Ibid*, 1, 3.

[15] Brown, Daniel W., *Rethinking Tradition in Modern Islamic Thought*, Cambridge University Press, 1996 (Paperback 1999), 15-16.

[16] Musa, *op. cit.*, 18.

[17] Brown, *op. cit*, 15.

[18] Azami, M. A., *Studies in Hadith Methodology and Literature*, Islamic Book Trust, Kuala Lumpur, 92; cited in Akbarally Meherally, *Myths and Realities of Hadith – A Critical Study*, (published by Mostmerciful.com Publishers), Burnaby, BC, Canada,

6; available in the website http://www.mostmerciful.com/Hadithbook-sectionone.htm.

[19] Azami, *ibid*, 92, cited in Akbarally Meherally, *ibid*.

[20] Esposito, *Islam – The Straight Path*, Oxford University Press, 1991, 134.

[21] Cited in Brown, *op. cit*, 88.

[22] Khan, Sayyid Ahmad, *Maqalat*, I, 27-28; cited in Brown, *op. cit.*, 97.

[23] Musa, *op. cit.*, 6.

[24] Sidqi, Muhammad Tawfiq, "al-Islam huwa al-Qur'an wahdahu," *al-Manar* 9 (1906), 515; cited in Brown, Daniel, 1996, *op. cit.*, 88-89.

[25] Brown, *op. cit.*, 47, 40-41.

[26] Sidqi, *op. cit.*, 515. Also see Ghulam Ahmed Parwez, Maqam-i-Hadith, 2nd edn., Karachi, 1965, 350. Cited in Brown, Daniel, 1996, *op. cit.*, 54.

[27] Cited in Kassim Ahmad, *Hadith: A Re-Evaluation*, Translated from his original book in Malay by Syed Akbar Ali, 1997; web link: www.barry-baker.com/Articles/documents/HADITH.pdf.

[28] Brown, *op. cit.*, 89.

[29] Brown, *op. cit.*, 38.

[30] Brown, *op. cit.*, 38-39.

[31] He was the founder of a Bengali Daily "*The Azad*" and writer of a biography of Prophet Muhammad "*Mustafa Charit*" in Bengali.

[32] Cited in Dr. Muhammad Omar Farooq, "Dr. Farooq's Study Resource Page" in website: http://globalwebpost.com/farooqm/study_res/islam/Hadith/akramkhan_Hadith.html.

[33] He wrote many books in Urdu covering the Quranic teachings. He is also the author of *Islam – A Challenge to Religion* in English. His position on the Hadith is detailed in his Urdu work "Muquuam-e-Hadith" (The True Status of the Hadith). His books are available on the website "Bazm-e-Tolu-e-Islam"; link: http://www.tolueislam.com/.

[34] Rippin, Andrew, *Muslims: Their Religious Beliefs And Practices* vol. 1 (New York: Routledge, 1990), 74;

cited in *Hadith Authenticity: A Survey Of Perspectives (By Anonymous Author)*, at website: http://www.rim.org/muslim/Hadith.htm.

[35] Parwez, Ghulam Ahmed, *Salim ke nam khutut*, Karachi, 1953, Vol. 1, 43; cited in Brown, Daniel, 1996, *op. cit.*, 54.

[36] Rippin, Andrew, *op. cit.*, 74, 78.

[37] Parwez was an admirer of, and took inspiration from, the great Muslim thinker and philosopher Muhammad Iqbal. At his request, he published and founded in 1938 the *Tolu-e- Islam* in Urdu, a monthly magazine.

[38] Author of *Do Islam* (Two Islams), 1950 and other works.

[39] Barq, Ghulam Jilani, "Hadith ke bare men mera mawqaf," Chatan, Lahore, January 9, 1956; cited by Raja F. M. Majid, "Ghulam Jilani Barq: A Study in Muslim 'Rationalism,'" M.A. thesis, McGill University, Institute of Islamic Studies, 1962, 80; cited in Daniel W. Brown, *op. cit.*, 1996 (Paperback 1999), 128.

[40] Khalifa, Rashad, *Quran, Hadith and Islam;* available on the web link: http://www.masjidtucson.org/publications/books/qhi/contents.html. He has a good and easy to understand English translation of the Quran.

[41] In addition, I found the "index" provided at the end of his translation as the most detailed and useful for Quranic reference purposes.

[42] Ahmad, Kassim, *op. cit.*

[43] Rippin, *op. cit.*, 78; cited in "Hadith Authenticity: A Survey Of Perspectives," *op.cit.*

[44] Cited in Rippin, *op. cit.*,, 78-79.

[45] It was rather unusual but encouraging seeing that the Bangladesh Islamic Foundation, which is found generally to represent the traditional view, published his book *Creator and Creation* in 1986.

[46] Ahmad, Panaullah, *op. cit.*, 1986, 138-140, 295, 328-330, 347-348.

[47] Two editions of this author's first book *Exploring Islam in a New Light* published respectively in 2008

and 2009 and this book are also aimed at making some contribution to this ongoing movement.

[48] For some description and evaluation of their contribution to Islamic reforms, see Esposito, *op. cit.*,1991, 126-147.

[49] Author of *The Life of Mahomet and the History of Islam to the Era of Hegira*, 4 vols., London, 1861; repr. Osnabruck, 1988. First serialized in Calcutta *Review* 19, (January- June 1853): 1-8. Also cited in Brown, *op cit.*

[50] Sprenger, Alois, "On the Origin of Writing Down Historical Records among the Musulmans', *Journal of the Asiatic Society of Bengal 25*.(1856), 303-329, 375-381; Cited in Brown, *op. cit.*

[51] Author of *Muhammedanische Studien,*. 2 vols., Leiden, 1896. Trans. by S.M. Stern as MUSLIM STUDIES, 2 VOLS., London, 1967. Also cited in Daniel Brown, 1996, *op. cit.*

[52] Author of *Muhammadan Jurisprudence*. Oxford University Press, Oxford, 1950, especially pages 138-76; cited in Esposito, *op.cit.*, 1991.

[53] Author of *Muslim Tradition - Studies In Chronology, Provenance And Authorship Of Early Hadith* (New York: Cambridge University Press, 1983. Also cited in Brown, *op. cit.*

[54] Brown, *op. cit.*, 21.

[55] Muir, William, *The Life of Mahomet and the History of Islam to the Era of Hegira*, 4 vols., London, 1861; repr. Osnabruck, 1988, I, xxvii; cited in Brown, *op. cit.*, 35.

[56] Brown, *op. cit.*, 35.

[57] Cited by Aslan, *op. cit*, 68.

[58] Esposito, 1991, *op. cit.*, 82.

[59] Juynbcll, G.H.A, *Muslim Tradition - Studies In Chronology, Provenance And Authorship Of Early Hadith*, 1983, 71. Also cited in "Hadith Authenticity: A Survey Of Perspectives," *op. cit.*

[60] Juynbcll, *ibid*, 1983, 15-17, 45, 52-55, 60, 70, 89; cited in Lang, *op. cit*, 2004,226-228.

[61] Ahmad, Kassim, *op. cit.*, 1997.

[62] Musa, Aisha, op. cit., 80.
[63] Brown, *op. cit.*, 54-55.
[64] Mashriqi, Inayat Allah Khan, *Tadhkira*, Amritsar, 1924, 91; quoted in Majid, "Ghulam Jilani Barq," 3; cited in Brown, *op. cit.*, 45.
[65] See Khalifa, *op. cit*, 1982, and Kassim Ahmad, *op. cit*.
[66] Ahmad, Kassim, *op. cit.*, 1997.
[67] Kazi, Mazhar U., *A Treasury Of Ahadith*, Jeddah, Saudi Arabia, (Abul-Qasim Publishing House), 1992.
[68] Musa, *op. cit.*, 29.
[69] Meherally, Akbarally, *Myths and Realities of Hadith – A Critical Study*, available on the web site www.mostmerciful.com/Hadithbook.
[70] Musa, *op. cit.*, 75-76.
[71] *Ibid*, 76.
[72] *Ibid*, 29, 76.
[73] Rahim, M. Abdur, *The History of Hadith Compilation* (in Bengali), 290.
[74] Jayrajpuri, Muhammad Aslam, Ilm-i-Hadith, Lahore, n. d., 2; cited in Brown, Daniel W., 1996 (paperback 1999), *op. cit.*, 86.
[75] Musa, op. cit., 22-9, 74-9.
[76] Brown, *op. cit.*, 96.
[77] Ahmad, Kassim, *op. cit.*
[78] Iqbal, 137.
[79] Al-Shibli, *Sirat al-Numan*, Lahore, n. d. Trans. Muhammad Tayyab Bakhsh Badauni as *Method of Sifting Prophetic Tradition*, Karachi, 1966. 179; cited in Brown, *op. cit.*, 114.
[80] Early books of Hadith writing are the *Muwatta* of Malik ibn Anas (d. 179 AH) that related to legal matters and the *Musnad* of Ahmad ibn Hanbal (d. 241 AH).
[81] MacDonald, Duncan B., *Development of Muslim Theology Jurisprudence and Constitutional Theory* (George Routledge and Sons), London, 1903, 76.
[82] MacDonald, Duncan B., 1903, *ibid*, 76-77.
[83] Ahmad, Kassim, 1997.
[84] Brown, *op. cit.*, 96.

Notes

[85] Jayrajpuri, *Ilm-i-Hadith*, 16, cited in Brown, *op. cit.*, 96.

[86] First Muslim ruling dynasty after the *Khulafai Rashidun*; it ruled during 41 AH/661 CE-132 AH/750 CE

[87] The second ruling dynasty of the Muslim empire after the Umayyads, who ruled during 132 AH/750 CE-923 AH/1517 CE

[88] Brown, *op. cit.*, 96.

[89] Juynboll, *op. cit.*, 145.

[90] Brown, *op. cit.*, 86.

[91] *Ibid*, 86.

[92] *Ibid*, 86.

[93] Mustafa, Ibrahim, *Hadith and the Corruption of the Great Religion of Islam*, undated, 9-10.

[94] Ibn Sa'd, *Tabaqat*, II, ii, 135; cited in Azami, *Studies in Early Hadith Literature*, Beirut, 1968; repr. Indianapolis, 1978, 285; cited in Brown, *op. cit.*, 92.

[95] MacDonald, *op. cit.*, 77-78.

[96] Malik b. Anas (716-794 CE) is recognized as the founder of one of the four juristic divisions of Sunni Muslims. He was a major collector of Hadith.

[97] Goldziher, Ignaz, *op. cit.*, 45; cited in Also cited in *Hadith Authenticity: A Survey Of Perspectives*, *op.cit.*

[98] Lang, *op. cit*, 251-252.

[99] Asad, Muhammad (trans.) *Sahih al-Bukhari: the Early Years of Islam*, Dar al-Andalus (1981), 47-48; cited in Lang, *op. cit*, 251-252.

[100] Lang, *op. cit*, 2004, 253.

[101] Lang, *op. cit*, 2004, 255.

[102] Lang, *op. cit*, 2004, 263.

[103] Aslan, *op. cit.*, 68.

[104] Aslan, *op. cit.*, 68.

[105] Brown, *op. cit.*, 95.

[106] Cited in *Hadith Authenticity: A Survey Of Perspectives*, *op. cit.*

[107] Jayrajpuri, *Ilm-i-Hadith*, 22-23; cited in Brown, *op. cit.*, 98.

[108] Lang, *op. cit.*, 214-215.

[109] Jayrajpuri, *op. cit*, 26; cited in Brown, *op. cit.*, 98.

[110] Juynboll, *op. cit.*, 1983, 179-180; cited in Lang, *op. cit*, 2004, 218.
[111] Lang, *op. cit*, 2004, 218.
[112] Lang, *op. cit*, 2004, 222.
[113] Lang, *op. cit*, 2004, 215.
[114] Lang, *op. cit*, 2004, 246. To be fair to the author, note that though he displays a critical outlook to the Hadith, he is not totally disposed toward dismissing all Hadith as unacceptable. He accepts those "authenticated legal traditions that do not seem to conflict with the Qur'an." He also thinks "it necessary to take into consideration the historical contexts of the Prophet's acts. [He thinks] it important to derive general ethical and spiritual lessons from them, rather than attempt to replicate the cultural and historical specifics they describe or to mimic tangential aspects of the Prophet's example." And he admits that his position on the Hadith is an evolving one. (Lang, *op. cit*, 265) He is "more wary of non-legal traditions ... [and] especially cautious with regard to the theological traditions". These points are also repeated on pages 270-271 of the same reference.
[115] Hadith Authenticity: A Survey Of Perspectives, *op. cit.*, 3-4.
[116] Ahmad, Kassim, *op. cit.*
[117] *Ibid.*
[118] *Ibid.*
[119] Fadl, Abou El, *And God Knows the Soldiers: The Authoritative and the Authoritarian in Islamic Discourses*, University Press of America, Inc., Lanham and Oxford, 2001, 70-71.

Chapter XI

[1] We, however, grant that destiny plays some role in human life as discussed in Chapters 1 and 2.
[2] Yuksel, et. al., *op. cit.*, 2007, 447.
[3] Lang, *op. cit.*, 255.
[4] Aslan, *op. cit.*, 69.

[5] Fadl, Abou El, "*Speaking in God's Name: Islamic Law, Authority and Women*," Oneworld Publications, Oxford, 2001, 62-82.
[6] Fadl, Khaled Abou El, *ibid*, 2001, 72-76.
[7] For a good collection of absurd, weird Hadith ideas and those of Muslim sectarian clerics, see Edip Yuksel, *Manifesto for Islamic Reform*, Brainbow Press; 2nd revised & enlarged edition, 2009; an earlier version is at Appendix 5 of their *Quran: A Reformist Translation*, *op. cit.*, 2007.

Chapter XII

[1] Huntington, Samuel, "The Clash of Civilizations", *Foreign Affairs*, 1993, expanded into a book *The Clash of Civilizations and the Remaking of World Order*, Simon and Schuster, New York, 1996. Huntington's central thesis is that "post-Cold War conflict would occur most frequently and violently along cultural (often civilizational, e.g., Western, Islamic, Sinic, Hindu, etc.) instead of ideological lines, as under the Cold War."
[2] Cited by Karen Armstrong in a Foreword she wrote for Imam Feisal Abdul Rauf, *What is Right with Islam: A New Vision for Muslims and the West*, HarperCollins Publishers, Inc., New York, 2004.
[3] Mansour, Ahmed Subhy, *Penalty of Apostasy: A Historical and Fundamental Study*, English translation by Mostafa Sabet, Original title in Arabic: *Haddur Riddah: Dirasah Usooliyya Tareekhiyya*.
[4] See Armstrong, *op.cit.*, 2002, 164-66.
[5] *Ibid*, 167.
[6] *Ibid*, 169-170.
[7] *Ibid*, 135.
[8] Aslan, *op. cit.*, 243-244.
[9] A late thirteenth-early fourteenth century Muslim preacher who declared the Mongols who converted to Islam as infidels and apostates, and who attacked as inauthentic such Islamic developments as Shiism,

Sufism and Falsafah. Cf., Armstrong, *op. cit.*, 2002, 104.

[10] See his book, *op, cit.*, 2005, especially Chapters 3 and 4, 45-110. For a succinct critical review of Wahhabism, see Abou El Fadl (ed.), *The Place of Tolerance in Islam*, Beacon Press, Boston, 2002, the first article by Abou El Fadl, especially the sections on Wahhabism and Modern Islam, and The Theology of Intolerance. Also another presentation on the same topic is available in his article "The Ugly Modern and the Modern Ugly: Reclaiming the Beautiful in Islam", in Omid Safi (ed.), *Progressive Muslims: On Justice, Gender and Pluralism*, Oneworld, Oxford, 2003, especially the section on Wahhabis, Salafis and Salafabis.

[11] "The Saudi Connection: How billions in oil money spawned a global terror network," US News and World Report in *USNews.com* dated December 15, 2003, Report by David Kaplan, website: http://www.usnews.com/usnews/news/articles/031215/15terror.htm.

[12] Schwartz, Stephen, *The Two Faces of Islam: Saudi Fundamentalism and its Role in Terrorism*, Knopf Publishing Group, paperback published by Anchor, 2003.

[13] Miller, Lisa, "Islam in America: A Special Report", *Newsweek*, July 30, 2007.

[14] Esposito, *op. cit.*, 1991, 192.

[15] Pipes, Daniel, "Identifying Moderate Muslims", *New York Sun*, November 23, 2004. See his Website: http://www.danielpipes.org/article/2226.

[16] Taher, Amiri, "Islam can't Escape Blame for Sept. 11," Wall Street Journal, 24 October 2001; cited in Robert Spencer, *Islam Unveiled: Disturbing Questions about the World's Fastest-Growing Faith*, Encounter Books, San Francisco, 2002, 37.

[17] Tibi, Bassam, *The Challenge of Fundamentalism: Political Islam and the New World Disorder*, Berkeley University Press, 1998 (updated edition 2002), xxv. Cited in a review by Daniel Pipes in *Middle East Quarterly*, March 2000.

[18] Lewis, op. cit., 3 and 7.
[19] Ibid, 46-53, 64-69.
[20] Murphy, Caryle , Passion for Islam: Shaping the Modern Middle East: the Egyptian Experience, Simon and Schuster Inc., New York, 2002, 189-190.
[21] Ibid, 192.
[22] Bullet, Richard W., Islam, the View from the Edge, New York, Columbia University Press, 1994, 207; cited in Murphy, op. cit., 316.
[23] Murphy, op. cit., 191.
[24] Khan, M. A. Muqtedar, American Muslims: Bridging Faith and Freedom, Amana Publications, 2002, 86.
[25] Ibid, 316.
[26] Taken from some of Muqtedar Khan's articles on his website: www.ijtihad.org. Emphasis is mine.
[27] Minai, Ali, "A Time for Renewal" in Michael Wolfe (ed.), Taking Back Islam: American Muslims Reclaim Their Faith, Rodale Inc. and Beliefnet Inc., 2002, 10. Reprinted from www.chowk.com.
[28] A recent (2007) glaring example is the Red Mosque and madrasah complex in Islamabad, which housed dozens of well-armed Muslim militants led by a hard-line Muslim cleric who sought to impose a Taliban-style Islamic rule in Pakistan. The Pakistan government army's eight-day siege of, and final assault on, this complex left more than 100 dead.
[29] Voss, Richard S., "The Fourth Jihad" in Yuksel et. al. (ed.), Critical Thinkers for Islamic Reform, Brainbow Press, USA, 2009.
[30] Neier, Aryeh, "The Real Clash is Fundamentalists vs. Modernity," International Herald Tribune, October 10, 2001. Cited in Haroon A. Khan, "The Clash of Civilization Thesis and Bangladesh: A Case Study," Asian Profile, Vol. 32, No. 2, April 2004.

[31] For a brief recount of fundamental reasons why Muslims and non-Muslims should understand Islam through the lens of the Quran alone, see my article "Fifteen Great Reasons We Should Embrace and Follow the Quran-only Islam" in OpEd News, December 4th, 2008; web link:
http://www.opednews.com/articles/Fifteen-Great-Reasons-We-S-by-Abdur-Rab-081202-982.html.

- not speak louder
- not walk ahead
- not enter rooms
- Put things in writing
- Greetings

Made in the USA
Lexington, KY
11 December 2017